BEST EVER BUDGET RECIPES
200 FABULOUS LOW-COST DISHES FOR THE THRIFTY COOK

BEST EVER BUDGET RECIPES
200 FABULOUS LOW-COST DISHES FOR THE THRIFTY COOK

MORE THAN 200 DELICIOUS STEP-BY-STEP RECIPES SHOWN IN 800 PHOTOGRAPHS,
INCLUDING HANDY TIPS, HINTS AND GUIDELINES FOR SAVING MONEY IN THE KITCHEN

LUCY DONCASTER

southwater

This edition is published by Southwater
an imprint of Anness Publishing Ltd
Hermes House, 88–89 Blackfriars Road, London SE1 8HA
tel. 020 7401 2077; fax 020 7633 9499
www.southwaterbooks.com; www.annesspublishing.com

If you like the images in this book and would like to investigate using them for publishing, promotions or advertising, please visit our website www.practicalpictures.com for more information.

UK agent: The Manning Partnership Ltd; tel. 01225 478444; fax 01225 478440;
sales@manning-partnership.co.uk
UK distributor: Book Trade Services; tel. 0116 2759086; fax 0116 2759090;
uksales@booktradeservices.com; exportsales@booktradeservices.com
North American agent/distributor: National Book Network; tel. 301 459 3366; fax 301 429 5746;
www.nbnbooks.com
Australian agent/distributor: Pan Macmillan Australia; tel. 1300 135 113; fax 1300 135 103;
customer.service@macmillan.com.au
New Zealand agent/distributor: David Bateman Ltd; tel. (09) 415 7664; fax (09) 415 8892

Publisher: Joanna Lorenz
Project Editor: Lucy Doncaster
Design: Paul Oakley Associates
Production Controller: Wendy Lawson

ETHICAL TRADING POLICY

NOTES

Bracketed terms are intended for American readers.
For all recipes, quantities are given in both metric and imperial measures and, where appropriate, in standard cups and spoons. Follow one set, but not a mixture, because they are not interchangeable. Standard spoon and cup measures are level. 1 tsp = 5ml, 1 tbsp = 15ml, 1 cup = 250ml/8fl oz.
Australian standard tablespoons are 20ml. Australian readers should use 3 tsp in place of 1 tbsp for measuring small quantities of gelatine, flour, salt, etc.
American pints are 16fl oz/2 cups. American readers should use 20fl oz/2.5 cups in place of 1 pint when measuring liquids.
Electric oven temperatures in this book are for conventional ovens. When using a fan oven, the temperature will probably need to be reduced by about 10–20°C/20–40°F. Since ovens vary, you should check with your manufacturer's instruction book for guidance.
The nutritional analysis given for each recipe is calculated per portion (i.e. serving or item), unless otherwise stated. If the recipe gives a range, such as Serves 4–6, then the nutritional analysis will be for the smaller portion size, i.e. 6 servings. Measurements for sodium do not include salt added to taste. Medium (US large) eggs are used unless otherwise stated.

Main front cover image shows Courgette and Potato Bake – for recipe, see page 165.

PUBLISHER'S NOTE

Contents

What is Clever Cooking?

Clever cooking is the notion of buying and using ingredients that will enable you to create a fabulous feast for less than it would cost to buy an ordinary sandwich from a store. Whatever your skill level or culinary preferences, with just a little common sense and planning you can produce a healthy, hearty and tasty two-course meal, complete with side dishes and accompaniments, for any occasion – from simple family suppers to dinner parties, barbecues and buffets.

About this book

Feeding a hungry family can be an expensive business, and with today's hectic lifestyle it is all too easy to disregard the importance of fresh, healthy home-made food. Lack of planning can result in huge amounts of food being thrown away, wasting both money and resources. However, with just a little bit of thought, some simple shopping tips and a wealth of inspiring recipes, you can create delicious meals without breaking the bank.

This book contains everything you need to know about what, when and where to buy the best value, best quality ingredients, and how to turn them into a wide range of healthy and delicious home-cooked meals. Detailed guidance on planning and preparation is given, covering everything from drawing up a weekly menu and managing a budget to shopping tips and buying in bulk. Techniques for storing and freezing raw ingredients, as well as inspiring ideas for converting left-overs into delicious dishes, make ingredients stretch further and will enable you to enjoy seasonal ingredients all year round.

Expert advice about growing your own herbs and foraging for free food, such as berries, nuts and mushrooms, is provided, as well as tips and techniques for easy ways to introduce flavour and texture to dishes using a range of herbs, spices and aromatics.

There then follows a comprehensive section outlining which foods are the best value for money, ranging from fresh fruit and vegetables to dairy, fish and meat, as well as pasta, beans, peas and grains. This invaluable directory provides essential information about when and where to buy ingredients so you get the most for your money.

Storecupboard staples – ranging from baking basics such as flour and sugar to stock (bouillon) cubes, oils and aromatics –are also listed in a separate directory, and arm the clever cook with the power to convert simple ingredients into stunning meals. Seasonality charts and sample menus make planning meals easy, although with over 200 mouth-watering recipes to choose from, you may well find that you are spoiled for choice!

Above: *A well-stocked storecupboard can save you time and money when cooking, and will encourage you to try your hand at more home baking.*

How recipes are costed

The cost of each recipe is based on average prices of ingredients at large supermarkets, and assumes the use of goods that are middle of the range rather than at either end of the price scale. Unless otherwise specified, all fruit, vegetables, dairy, fish and meat are fresh rather than canned or frozen, and all eggs are free-range. Fresh ingredients are priced when they are in season, and it is important that you bear in mind that the price of these foods may rise, and their availability may be limited, when they are out of season.

Many items may be cheaper to buy at wholesalers, markets or independent stores – such as butchers, fishmongers and greengrocers – and special offers and bulk-buying will also bring the cost of ingredients down: shopping around is vital.

Items that appear under the "From the storecupboard" heading in the ingredients list are not included in the final cost, since they should be part of the clever cook's storecupboard. Wherever possible, the use of home-made stocks, sauces, condiments, flavoured oils and pastries is encouraged, and there are recipes for a range of basics at the back of the book. Not only are home-made versions much cheaper, but they also taste better and contain no additives or preservatives.

How to use the key

Each recipe has been placed into one of three categories, depending on the overall cost of the dish per person. These categories are clearly illustrated by the symbols that appear beside each recipe name.

Below: *Choosing fresh, seasonal, good-quality ingredients will help you to create delicious dishes with the minimum effort and cost, as well as contributing to a healthy diet.*

The categories are:

❋	Bargain
❋ ❋	Very economical
❋ ❋ ❋	Economical

These price bands are a guide to the relative cost of each recipe, and they are invaluable when planning a menu for any occasion and any budget. All you have to do is work out how much you want to spend, which courses you want to serve, and then simply combine recipes to create your perfect meal. Suggestions for side dishes and accompaniments for each recipe are provided, as well as cook's tips and variations to allow you greater flexibility. Alternatively, you could use one of the menu plans provided – the possibilities are endless!

How to be a Clever Cook

BEING A CLEVER COOK INVOLVES THE APPLICATION
OF SEVERAL BASIC, COMMONSENSE PRINCIPLES,
INCLUDING: PLANNING AHEAD; SHOPPING AROUND;
BUYING GOOD QUALITY FOODS WHEN THEY ARE IN
SEASON; MAKING THE MOST OF BARGAINS AND
SPECIAL OFFERS; HAVING A STORECUPBOARD THAT IS
WELL STOCKED WITH BASIC ESSENTIALS; KNOWING
HOW TO STORE AND FREEZE FRESH FOODS; AND, OF
COURSE, BEING EQUIPPED WITH THE NECESSARY
KNOWLEDGE TO TRANSFORM SIMPLE INGREDIENTS
INTO A FEAST FOR EVERY OCCASION.

Preparation and Planning

Proper prior planning helps to ensure that you eat a wide variety of foods and make the most of seasonal produce. If you know that you are going to be short of time in the evenings, then you should consider preparing make-ahead meals and stocking up the freezer, so that you avoid the temptation to buy an expensive store-bought meal or unhealthy fast foods.

Weekly planning

For many people, the thought of planning an evening meal simply never crosses their minds until dinner-time arrives. This lack of forethought often results in people eating out or buying ready meals, both of which can be very costly if indulged in on a regular basis. A little bit of planning not only saves money, but it also ensures greater variety in the diet and can save time at the end of a busy day.

Nutritional guidelines indicate that the main meal each day should include a balance of protein, carbohydrates and several portions of vegetables, which help us on our way to the recommended 5-a-day target. Planning a weekly menu ensures that this balance of food groups is covered every day, makes shopping easier, and gives us greater control over the variety of foods eaten. It also helps to prevent waste, as you can plan how and when to use fresh ingredients, ensuring that if necessary they are either eaten shortly after they are bought, or that they are incorporated into dishes that are then frozen.

The easiest way to plan a weekly menu is to fill in a simple chart that you create yourself at home. This shows at a glance which courses and dishes are going to be served, and makes sticking to a budget much easier. All the family can be involved in this planning process, making everyone feel that their food preferences are being acknowledged and that they are taking an active role in deciding what they eat. Below is a sample weekly menu planner with some ideas for different combinations of courses and dishes:

Left: *Although fast food is great for an occasional treat, it is relatively expensive compared to home-made food, and it is liable to be high in salt and fat.*

Day of the week	Appetizer	Main dish	Accompaniment	Dessert
Monday	Lentil Soup	Mexican Spicy Beef Tortilla	Steamed Seasonal Vegetables	
Tuesday		Barley Risotto With Roasted Squash and Leeks		Apple Pie
Wednesday	Mushrooms With Garlic and Chilli Sauce	Dublin Coddle	Champ Braised Red Cabbage	
Thursday		Tofu and Green Bean Thai Red Curry	Boiled Rice	Lemon Sorbet
Friday		Hake with Lemon Sauce	Boiled Potatoes Carrot and Parsnip Purée	Treacle Tart
Saturday	Summer Minestrone	Lamb and Carrot Casserole	Mashed Potatoes	Nut and Chocolate Chip Brownies
Sunday	Leek and Potato Soup	Roasted Duckling with Potatoes	Steamed Seasonal Green Vegetables	

Above: *Strip the tender roasted flesh from the carcass of a roast chicken and use the meat to make a casserole, pie or curry and the bones to make chicken stock.*

How to make the most of left-overs

Left-over food accounts for a large proportion of the food that is wasted every day. But this senseless waste is completely unnecessary, as left-over food can easily be transformed into a wide range of delicious new dishes. As part of the planning process you should take left-overs into account, and even make more than you need for one meal so that the left-overs can be converted into something else. Here are some budget-friendly ideas for ways in which you can make the most of the food you buy:

- A surprising amount of flesh can be stripped from a carcass after a roast meal, and this delicious cooked meat can be converted into a wide range of pies, curries, soups or even simply fried with onions to create a tasty and very quick supper. The stripped carcass can then be converted into home-made stock for use in any number of recipes. Left-over vegetables can be combined with the stock and flesh, if you like, to create a tasty soup, or fried up to make a variation on Bubble and Squeak.
- Cold roast beef, pork, chicken and turkey make excellent sandwich fillers, or can be served with a baked potato and salad for an easy supper dish.
- It is a good idea to make more Bolognese sauce than you actually need, as it freezes very well and forms the basis of many dishes, such as lasagne, moussaka, cottage pie and chilli con carne.
- The same applies for meat stews, which are easily made into pies with the addition of a potato or pastry topping.
- With the addition of a few ingredients, most left-over fish can be made into pies, tarts, salads or sandwich fillings, and the bones can be used to make fish stock.
- Boiled or steamed potatoes are extremely versatile. Try slicing them and transforming them into a Spanish omelette, or cubing them and combining with corned beef, onions and home-made tomato sauce for a warming winter meal.
- Other boiled or steamed vegetables make an almost instant ragu or curry when combined with a can of chopped tomatoes and a few storecupboard flavourings.
- Left-over pasta and rice is often thrown away because it is cheap. This is a waste, as it can be used to create a cold pasta salad, or to bulk out omelettes and soups.
- Cooked beans, peas and lentils can be readily incorporated into many meat and vegetable dishes, adding protein, texture and flavour as well as making more expensive ingredients stretch further.
- Cooked chickpeas can be puréed to make home-made hummus, and black beans are delicious when combined with chopped tomatoes, avocado, spring onions (scallions), coriander (cilantro) and lemon juice.
- Cold beans make a nutritious salad when combined with a little olive oil, lemon juice and seasoning.
- Stale bread has many uses: it can also be brushed with oil and grilled (broiled) or fried to make home-made croûtons, added to soups, or dipped in egg and made into French toast. Some recipes such as Autumn Pudding or Bread and Butter Pudding with Whiskey Sauce actually specify that the bread should be several days old.
- Left-over stewed fruit makes a healthy and delicious topping for porridge (oatmeal), yogurt and ice cream, and can be added to fruit pies, cobblers and crumbles.
- You can use the hard rind from cheeses such as Parmesan or grano pedano to add flavour to soups and sauces. Simply add it to the pan at the start of cooking and remove before serving.
- Add left-over sauces and gravies to soups and pies, making sure that the flavours complement each other.

Above: *Making Autumn Pudding is an excellent way of converting a glut of fresh seasonal fruit and some stale bread into a truly stunning dessert.*

Clever Shopping

Before you go shopping, you should have a list of the items you want to buy. This list should be written when you are planning the weekly menu. Writing a list not only ensures that you don't forget anything, but it also helps to prevent you from impulse buying and going over budget.

Above: *Greengrocers and markets often offer a better range of locally grown seasonal produce than supermarkets, so shop around to get the best value, variety and quality.*

Shopping around

The cost of produce varies from store to store, as well as from season to season, and it is important that you shop around to get the best deal and the best quality. Many of us get into the habit of visiting the same supermarket every week and don't explore other retailers. This is a bad habit to get in to, because while supermarkets are convenient and usually offer a good range of products all year round, other outlets such as farmer's markets, butchers, greengrocers and other independent shops may be cheaper, or stock a wider range of fresh seasonal or speciality ingredients.

Many stores have multi-buy offers, as well as bargain bins and reduced-to-clear items, and it is a good idea to find out when stores do their stock turn-over, as this is the time when they are most like to drastically reduce the cost of items in order to clear the stock. By finding out this information, you can pick up great bargains on a weekly basis and drastically reduce your overall shopping bill. It is important to note, however, that you should look at the quality of the produce that has been reduced, and only buy it if it is on your list and you are going to use it immediately or freeze it.

The internet is a very convenient way of doing the weekly shopping, and it can save you money as well as time. By buying online you can avoid the temptation to impulse buy, and by comparing the prices at different stores, you can ensure that you get the best deal. The drawback with internet shopping, however, is that you can't check the quality of the fresh produce, and although multi-buy deals apply, you usually can't get reduced-to-clear items. Smaller, independent retailers often have their own websites, too, and it is important to check both the price and range of produce that they offer, as well as delivery costs.

Specialist wholesale stores represent extremely good value for money if you are bulk-buying for a party or have the space to store large quantities of food. Some outlets require membership, which may only be granted to businesses, so it is worth checking this before travelling to the store. You should also check that there is not a minimum purchase requirement, or you may end up spending more than you budgeted for.

Getting the best deal

Buying in bulk, in conjunction with shopping around, is often the best way to reduce the relative cost of foods. It is, however, important to take several factors into consideration. If you are buying fresh produce, you will need to either use it quickly, freeze it or preserve it as jams, pickles, chutneys or other long-lasting foodstuffs. If you are buying a large quantity of canned, bottled or packet goods, you will need space to store them, and you should be aware that they may have a limited shelf life.

Despite these factors, bulk-buying can save you money, as well as allowing you to stockpile seasonal produce so that it is available all year round. If you are short of space or have a small household, you could join forces with a friend or neighbour and split the cost and the produce. In this way you both benefit from the reduced cost but are not overwhelmed with more food than you can deal with.

Buying fresh produce when it is in season ensures that you get the best quality and value for your money. Almost all fresh food is most abundant at one particular time of the year, and it is a good idea to make the most of it when it is available. Eating seasonal meat, fish, fruit and vegetables also helps to ensure variety in your diet, and encourages experimentation in the kitchen.

Many supermarkets offer fresh produce all year round, whatever the season. It is worth considering that food that has been imported from abroad may have lost some of its taste and nutritional value, and may have been treated with preservatives. Imported food is also often more expensive than home-grown seasonal produce,

Picking your own fruit and vegetables, either from your own garden or from farms, is a fun way of gathering fresh produce. By taking children along to help, you will educate them about the food they eat as well as giving them a great day out in the fresh air. In rural areas you can often buy eggs directly from farms, which ensures that they are absolutely fresh, and they are often better value. Please note, you should always check that the eggs have both a use-by date and a mark to show that they have been produced to the highest standards of food safety. If in doubt, do not buy them.

Above: *Take children along to pick-your-own farms or to harvest home-grown produce from the garden – it is fun, and it will help them to understand how food is produced.*

Below: *Buying fresh produce to cook at home is not only cheaper than using ready-made meals, but it is also likely to be much healthier and taste better.*

Free Food

As our lives have become busier and our gardens have grown smaller, we have for the most part forgotten the art of growing and gathering our own food. Yet nature's bounty knows no bounds, and the pleasure that can be derived from planting, tending and harvesting home-grown fruit and vegetables should not be underestimated. Open spaces and hedgerows are a rich source of fresh, free food – from blackberries, sloes and elderflowers to nettles, dandelions and mushrooms – and with a little know-how and patience you can gather all the ingredients required to create a feast.

Grow your own

Sowing, growing and harvesting your own food is not only much cheaper than buying it, but the produce is inevitably fresher. It is usually healthier, too, as you have total control over the amount of fertilizers and pesticides you use, and it often tastes better than store-bought goods. But despite the obvious benefits, growing your own food is neither possible nor desirable for everyone. To grow fruit and vegetables, you need access to a garden or an allotment, and for the large number of people who live in apartments in cities, this is simply not an option. Many people also simply do not have the necessary time that growing and cultivating fruit and vegetables requires.

Home-grown herbs, however, require very little attention or horticultural know-how, and they can usually be grown in pots, either outdoors or on a window ledge. Everyday culinary herbs, such as basil, rosemary, mint, thyme and sage can be bought in pots from gardening centres or at many supermarkets, and provide you with a ready supply of fresh herbs.

Below: *Growing herbs indoors is easy, and will fill your kitchen with their distinctive aroma.*

Growing leafy herbs in containers

Most herbs grow well in containers, and there is a wide variety to choose from. A collection of containers of different shapes makes an attractive display on the patio. Do not choose anything too large if you want to be able to move pots around, for example, when you want to bring them into a sheltered position during the winter.

For convenience, several different herbs can be grown in one container, but bear in mind that they are not all compatible. Mint and parsley do not grow well together and fennel does not mix with caraway, dill or coriander (cilantro). Mint, tarragon and chives are best grown in separate containers as they will stifle any other herbs they are mixed with. Some herbs, such as rosemary, thyme, marjoram and sage like a sunny spot, while mint, chervil and chives prefer more filtered light.

During the spring and summer months all container-grown herbs need daily watering, as they can dry out in a matter of hours. However, do not be tempted to overwater any herbs. The soil should never become waterlogged.

Whatever type of pot you choose, make sure there is a hole in the base for drainage. Fill the base with a layer of broken terracotta or stones and then a layer of grit or sand before filling with potting compost (soil mix). Once the herbs have been planted and watered, raise the container off the ground using wooden battens or clay pot supports to free the drainage holes and prevent clogging.

Growing herbs indoors

Most culinary herbs will thrive indoors provided they are sited in a light and sunny position and enjoy a fairly humid environment, away from central heating and severe temperature extremes. Indoor herbs benefit from being grown collectively because of the massed humidity. Basil is one of the most successful herbs to grow indoors as it is protected from garden pests which often decimate it outside. Care must be taken not to overuse indoor herbs, otherwise the plant will die from loss of foliage.

Nature's bounty

If you go for a walk in the countryside at the right time of the day and in the right season, you may be lucky enough to come across such treasures as a hedgerow groaning under the weight of plump, juicy blackberries, wild strawberries nestling in the long grass, or tender mushrooms that have sprung up, as if by magic, overnight. If you live on the coast, the sea is a particularly bountiful source of free food, ranging from tender mussels and nutritious seaweed to fabulous fish and shellfish. Knowing what foods are available in each season, as well as the sort of habitat in which they are likely to thrive is all the knowledge that is required to successfully find many of these and other wild foods, and there are many specialist books devoted to the subject.

Mushrooms are a particularly sought-after delicacy, but you should note that they require extremely careful identification, since many wild mushrooms are poisonous. The same applies to berries, and you should always carry detailed identification guides with you when out foraging. If in doubt, don't pick them. You should also always check that you are not trespassing, and you should ask the owner's permission before walking over land that is not clearly marked as being a public path.

Above: *The early morning is the best time to go foraging for nuts, berries and mushrooms.*

If you respect your surroundings and forage thoughtfully, you will discover a whole new world of possibility, with the added bonus that you know that the food is absolutely fresh as well as being free. By gathering your own food you will become more aware of the natural cycles of food, as well as how produce should really taste. Foraging is also fun and can make a great day out in the fresh air for all the family.

Below: *Wear suitable clothing, take a container to collect into and, above all, carry a guide book when collecting mushrooms.*

Storage and Freezing Techniques

Having spent time and money buying, growing or foraging for fresh produce, it is important that you do not allow it to go to waste. Correct storage and freezing techniques will help you to make the most of fresh ingredients as well as left-overs, and will provide you with a supply of food throughout the year.

Storing foods

All foods in the refrigerator or freezer, and particularly raw meat and poultry, should be well wrapped or stored in sealed containers. Perishable items, such as meat, poultry, fish and shellfish, eggs and dairy products must be kept refrigerated at a temperature of 1–5°C /35–40°F. For longer storage, many can also be frozen at –18°C/0°F. Cooked left-overs must be refrigerated or frozen.

Storing fresh fruits

Keep apricots, kiwi fruits, mangoes, nectarines, papayas (pawpaws), peaches, pears, pineapples and plums at room temperature until ripe, then refrigerate and eat in 2–3 days.

Apples can be kept at room temperature for a few days, dates for a few weeks, and grapefruit and oranges for up to a week; beyond that refrigerate them.

Unless you intend to eat them on the day of purchase, refrigerate fully ripe and perishable fruits such as berries, cherries, figs, grapes, lemons, melons, pomegranates and tangerines. They can be kept refrigerated for 2–3 days.

Storing fresh vegetables

Store garlic, onions, potatoes and sweet potatoes, swedes and pumpkins in a dark, cool place (about 10°C/50°F) with good ventilation. All can be kept for about 2 months.

Store tomatoes at room temperature until they are ripe. After that, refrigerate them. Other vegetables should be stored in the refrigerator.

Below: *Store potatoes in a dark place for up to 2 months.*

Above: *Medium, wide-necked jars with plastic coated screw-top lids are ideal for most preserves.*

Types of containers

It is useful to have a range of different types of receptacle – from small to large containers and from airtight- to freezer-proof types. Think about what type of food you are storing when choosing a container; it is no use storing crisp items in a container that is not airtight, and large containers with only a small amount of food in them are a waste of space.

Ice cream tubs make ideal freezer-proof containers for fruit and vegetables, such as blackcurrants, after they have been frozen in a single layer. Some take-away (take-out) containers are microwave-proof, making them ideal for reheating food, but always check this before heating.

Jars and bottles are ideal containers for home-made preserves, sauces and salad dressings. Pickles or preserves made from whole or large pieces of fruit or vegetables should be packed into medium or large jars or bottles with a wide neck. Pourable sauces or relishes can be stored in narrow-necked bottles, but thicker, spoonable preserves should be packed in jars.

Before potting, it is essential to sterilize jars and bottles to destroy any micro-organisms. Check for cracks or damage, then wash in hot, soapy water, rinse and turn upside down to drain. Stand the containers, spaced slightly apart, on a baking sheet lined with kitchen paper. Rest any lids on top. Place in a cold oven, then heat to 110°C/225°F/Gas $\frac{1}{4}$ and bake for 30 minutes.

Freezing techniques

Different foods can be frozen for different amounts of time and may require a variety of freezing methods. Below is a table of the freezer life of some of the most common foods that are suitable for freezing. Handling hints are included where applicable. Unless otherwise specified, items are raw prior to being frozen.

Freezing soft fruit

Place on a baking sheet in a single layer. Once frozen, transfer to a container.

Meat and poultry	Storage time	Handling hints
Bacon	1 month	
Burgers	2–3 months	Separate each burger with a layer of waxed paper before freezing
Casseroles and stews, cooked meat, fish and poultry	3 months	Allow a small space above the cooked food for expansion
Minced (ground) beef, lamb and veal	2–3 months	
Minced (ground) pork	1–2 months	
Joints: Beef	6–12 months	Check that the packaging has no holes in it before freezing the joint
Lamb, veal	6–9 months	
Pork	3–6 months	
Sausages	1–2 months	
Steaks and Chops: Beef	6–9 months	
Lamb, veal	3–4 months	
Pork	2–3 months	
Venison, game birds	8–12 months	
Chicken, cooked	3 months	
Chicken, whole or cut-up	10 months	
Chicken liver	3 months	
Duck, turkey	6 months	

Fish and shellfish	Storage time	Handling hints
Fillets and steaks from lean fish: Cod, flounder haddock, sole	6 months	Wrap fish in clear film (plastic wrap) and freeze as soon after purchase as possible
Fillets and steaks from oily fish: Trout, mackerel, salmon, sardines	2–3 months	Freeze small fish in one piece. Freeze larger fish in thick steaks or fillets
Breaded fish	3 months	
Clams	3 months	
Cooked fish or shellfish	3 months	
Crab	10 months	
Lobster tails	3 months	
Oysters	4 months	
Prawns (shrimp)	12 months	
Scallops	3 months	

Fruit, vegetables and herbs	Storage time	Handling hints
Soft fruits: Apricots, berries, cherries, peaches, pears, pineapples, plums, etc	12 months	Freeze in a single layer on a baking tray before transferring to a moisture-proof container once frozen
Citrus fruit and freshly-squeezed fruit juice	6 months	
Fruit juice concentrate	12 months	
Other fruits: Apples, bananas grapes, pears	Do not freeze	
Vegetables: All except celery, greens, salad leaves and tomatoes	10 months	Freeze quickly in small batches to prevent large ice crystals forming
Fresh herbs: Rosemary, thyme, oregano, sage		Freeze in bags, or chop, mix with water and freeze in ice cube trays

Baked goods	Storage time	Handling hints
Yeast bread and rolls, baked	3–6 months	Cool completely before freezing
Rolls, partially baked	2–3 months	
Cake, baked: Chiffon, sponge	2 months	Freeze cakes in rigid containers to prevent them from being damaged. Frosting made from egg white does not freeze well
Cheesecake	2–3 months	
Chocolate	4 months	
Fruit cake	12 months	
Iced (frosted)	8–12 months	
Pound cake	6 months	
Cookies, baked	8–12 months	
Pie, baked	1–2 months	

Dairy	Storage time	Handling hints
Butter	6–9 months	Store in moisture-proof wrap
Margarine	12 months	
Milk	1 month	Pour some out before freezing as it will expand
Buttermilk, sour cream and yogurt	Do not freeze	
Cheese	4 months	Defrost slowly in the refrigerator before use

Fuss-free Flavour

You don't need to spend a fortune on expensive ingredients to make delicious family food. A whole range of simple herbs, spices and aromatics can be used to complement and bring out the flavours of the main ingredient of the dish, without the need for lots of costly extra ingredients. Match the seasoning to the ingredient and try some of the simple techniques outlined below, which include stuffing, dry rubbing, marinating, glazing and infusing.

Flavours for fish

Classic aromatics used for flavouring fish and shellfish include lemon, lime, parsley, dill, fennel and bay leaves. These all have a fresh, intense quality that complements the delicate taste.

• To flavour whole fish, such as trout or mackerel, stuff a few lemon slices and some fresh parsley or basil into the body cavity before cooking. Season, then wrap the fish in foil or baking parchment, ensuring the packet is well sealed. Place the fish in an ovenproof dish or on a baking tray and bake until cooked through.

• To marinate chunky fillets of fish, such as cod or salmon, arrange the fish fillets in a dish in a single layer. Drizzle with olive oil, then sprinkle over crushed garlic and grated lime rind and squeeze over the lime juice. Cover and leave to marinate in the refrigerator for at least 30 minutes. Grill (broil) lightly until just cooked through.

• To make a delicious marinade for salmon, arrange the fillets in a single layer in an ovenproof dish. Drizzle with a little light olive oil and add a split vanilla pod. Cover and marinate for a couple of hours or overnight, if you have time. Remove the dish from the refrigerator, cover with foil and bake in the oven until cooked through. Remove the vanilla pod before serving.

Pepping up meat and poultry

Dry rubs, marinades and sticky glazes are all perfect ways to introduce flavour into meat and poultry. Marinating the tougher cuts of meat, such as stewing steak, also helps to tenderize it.

• To make a fragrant Cajun spice rub for pork chops, steaks and chicken, mix together 5ml/1 tsp each of dried thyme, dried oregano, finely crushed black peppercorns, salt, crushed cumin seeds and hot paprika. Rub the Cajun spice mix into the raw meat or poultry, then cook over a barbecue or bake until cooked through.

• To marinate red meat, such as beef, lamb or venison, prepare a mixture of two-thirds red wine to one-third olive oil in a shallow non-metallic dish. Stir in some chopped garlic and bruised fresh rosemary sprigs. Add the meat and turn to coat it in the marinade. Cover and chill for at least 2 hours or overnight before cooking.

• To make a mild-spiced sticky mustard glaze for chicken, pork or red meat, mix 45ml/3 tbsp each of Dijon mustard, clear honey and demerara (raw) sugar, 2.5ml/$\frac{1}{2}$ tsp chilli powder, 1.5ml/$\frac{1}{4}$ tsp ground cloves, and salt and ground black pepper. Cook over the barbecue or under the grill (broiler) and brush with the glaze about 10 minutes before the end of cooking time.

Vibrant vegetables

Most fresh vegetables have a subtle flavour that needs to be enhanced. When using delicate cooking methods such as steaming and stir-frying, go for light flavourings that will enhance the taste of the vegetables. When using more robust cooking methods, such as roasting, choose richer flavours such as garlic and spices.

• To add a rich flavour to stir-fried vegetables, add a splash of sesame oil just before the end of cooking time. (Do not use more than about 5ml/1 tsp, because it has a very strong flavour and can be overpowering.)

• To make fragrant, Asian-style steamed vegetables, bruise a couple of lemon grass stalks with a mortar and add to the steaming water, then cook vegetables such as pak choi (bok choy) over the water until just tender. Alternatively add a few kaffir lime leaves to the water. You could also place the aromatics in the steamer under the vegetables and steam as before until just tender.

• To enhance the taste of naturally sweet vegetables, such as parsnips and carrots, try glazing them with honey and mustard before roasting. Simply mix together 30ml/ 2 tbsp wholegrain mustard and 45ml/ 3 tbsp clear honey in a small bowl, and season with salt and ground black pepper to taste. Brush the glaze over the prepared vegetables to coat completely, then roast until they are sweet and tender. You could also use maple syrup and/or omit the mustard, if you prefer.

Fragrant rice and grains

Accompaniments to main course dishes, such as rice and couscous, can be enhanced by the addition of simple flavourings. Adding herbs, spices and aromatics can help to perk up the rice and grains' subtle flavour as well as adding a splash of colour. Choose flavourings that will complement the dish that the rice or grains will be served with.

• To make fragrant rice to serve with Asian-style stir-fries and braised dishes, add a whole star anise or a few cardamom pods to a pan of rice before cooking. The rice will absorb the flavour during cooking.

• To make zesty herb rice or couscous, heat a little chopped fresh tarragon and grated lemon rind in olive oil or melted butter until warm, then drizzle the flavoured oil and herbs over freshly cooked rice or couscous.

• To make simple herb rice or couscous, fork plenty of chopped fresh parsley and chives through the cooked grains and drizzle over a little oil just before serving.

Making a bouquet garni

This classic flavouring for stews, casseroles and soups is very easy to make. Using a piece of string, tie together a fresh bay leaf and a sprig each of parsley and thyme. Alternatively, tie the herbs in a square of muslin (cheesecloth). It can be added to dishes at the start of the cooking time, left to impart its flavour for the duration, and then removed before serving.

Fruit

Widely incorporated in both sweet and savoury dishes, fruit can be used either as a main ingredient or as a flavouring to complement the taste of other ingredients. Make the most of the different types of fruit when they are in season – they can be eaten on their own, in combination with other fruits, in pies, tarts and cakes, or made into delectable preserves that can be enjoyed throughout the year.

Orchard fruit

This family of fruit includes apples, pears and quinces, which, depending on the variety, are in season from early summer to late autumn. Choose firm, unblemished fruit and store in a cool dry place.

Apples There are two main categories of apple – eating and cooking, and although imported varieties are available all year, they are at their best in autumn. Eating apples have sweet flesh and taste good raw as a healthy snack or dessert. Many can also be used for making pies and open tarts. Cooking apples have a sour flavour and are too sharp to eat raw. They are ideal for baking, or for making into sauces and preserves.

Pears Most commercially available pears are dessert fruits, just as good for eating as for cooking. They can be pan-fried or used in tarts and pies. They are also excellent poached, especially in a wine syrup.

Quinces Related to the pear, quinces have hard, sour flesh. Cooking and sweetening brings out their delicious, scented flavour. They are worth buying when you find them, and are often used in jellies and sauces.

Below: *Crisp, fresh-tasting apples are great as an economical and healthy snack or dessert.*

Stone fruit

Peaches, nectarines, plums, apricots and cherries all belong to this family of fruit, and contain a stone (pit) in the middle. Most stone fruits are at their best through the summer months, but some, such as plums, are best through the autumn. Choose firm, smooth-skinned fruit without any blemishes and store in a cool, dry place.

Apricots With their slightly sweet-and-sour flavour, soft texture and downy skin, apricots are delicious eaten raw, or they can be poached, made into desserts or converted into delicious preserves. Pick those with the strongest colour.

Cherries These fruits are divided into two main groups: sweet cherries, which may be black (actually dark red) or white (usually yellow), and sour cherries. They only have a short season, so enjoy them while you can. Choose ones with green, flexible stems and that are firm and plump, but not hard. You need to remove the stone when eating them raw, and before adding them to pies, tarts and puddings or making into preserves.

Nectarines and peaches These fragrant, sweet fruits are the essence of the summer. They should be richly coloured, heavy for their size and have a strong aroma. They are at their best when eaten raw; cut around the middle of the fruit through the crease that runs from the stem to the tip, then twist the two halves in opposite directions to separate, and remove the stone with a knife.

Plums, damsons and greengages These stone fruits are in season in autumn, and are extremely versatile in cooking. Plums and greengages have a sweet, refreshing taste, while damsons are fairly sour.

Soft fruit

These delicate fruits, which include strawberries, raspberries, blackberries, blackcurrants, redcurrants and white currants, need careful handling and storing, and for the best price and quality only buy them when they are in season. Store in the refrigerator for up to 2 days.

Citrus fruit

Oranges, lemons, limes, grapefruit, mandarins and satsumas are popular citrus fruits; but there are also hybrids such as clementines. Citrus fruits are available all year round, with satsumas and clementines at their best in winter. Choose plump fruit that feels heavy. The skin should be bright and not shrivelled. Most citrus fruit is coated with wax to prevent moisture loss, so buy unwaxed fruit when using the rind in a recipe, or scrub the fruit well before use.

Exotic fruit

Once expensive and difficult to find, these wonderful fruits are now widely available in supermarkets throughout the year. Eat them fresh or use them in recipes.

Kiwi fruit The pale green flesh of kiwi fruit is good in various desserts and savoury cooking. Kiwi fruit are rich in vitamin C. Choose plump fruit with smooth skin and store in the refrigerator for up to 4 days.

Mangoes There are many varieties of this fleshy fruit available throughout the year. Choose strongly fragrant mangoes that give slightly when gently squeezed. Store in a cool place, but not the refrigerator, for up to a week.

Below: *Perfectly ripe pineapples have sweet, tangy flesh with a crisp bite and a fragrance that is quite irresistible.*

Above: *Watermelon has bright pink flesh and a light, delicate flavour that is sweet yet refreshing.*

Passion fruit This small round fruit has tough, wrinkled purple-brown skin. A passion fruit should feel heavy if it is nice and juicy. Store in the refrigerator.

Pineapple These sweet, tangy, juicy fruits are delicious in fruit salads and desserts. When choosing a pineapple, pull off one of the green leaves at the top – if it comes away easily, the pineapple should be ripe. Store in a cool place, but not the refrigerator, for up to a week.

Other fruit

There are a few fruits that are delicious and very versatile but that don't fit into any particular group. These include rhubarb, melons, figs and grapes.

Figs Available in summer, fresh figs require careful handling. Store in the refrigerator for up to 2 days. Fresh figs can be expensive, so buy them when they are on offer.

Grapes At their best in late summer, there are many varieties of grape. Handle with care.

Melons There are two types of melon – dessert melon and watermelon. Charentais, Ogen, cantaloupe, Galia and honeydew melon are all dessert melons, which are in season from summer to winter. Watermelons are in season from summer to autumn.

Rhubarb Rhubarb is available from early spring to mid-summer. Pale, finer-textured pink forced rhubarb is available in winter. It has a good colour and flavour, and is considered the best.

Vegetables

Used in salads and savoury dishes, vegetables are delicious served as the main ingredient in a vegetarian dish, as an accompaniment, or as a flavouring ingredient in a meat, poultry or fish dish. For maximum flavour, select healthy-looking specimens that are in season.

Root vegetables and potatoes

Grown underground, these vegetables include carrots, parsnips, beetroot (beets) and turnips and many varieties of potato. They are available throughout the year but are at their best in the winter months, when they are very good value for money. Choose firm specimens with unblemished skins. Store in a cool, dark place for up to 2 weeks.

Cabbages, broccoli and cauliflower

Members of the brassica family, these vegetables are packed with nutrients and good served in many ways.

Broccoli Packed with antioxidants and with a delicious flavour and crisp texture, broccoli and purple sprouting broccoli can be boiled, steamed and stir-fried. Choose specimens with bright heads and no sign of yellowing. Store in the refrigerator and use within 4–5 days.

Cabbage Regardless of variety, cabbage has a distinctive flavour and can be steamed, stir-fried or boiled. The white and red varieties are tight-leafed and ideal for shredding, and can be enjoyed raw in salads such as coleslaw. Green cabbage can be loose or close-leafed, smooth or crinkly and is best cooked. Buy fresh-looking specimens and store in the refrigerator for up to 10 days.

Cauliflower Good cut into florets and served raw with dips, cauliflower can also be boiled or steamed, and is delicious coated in cheese sauce. To ensure even cooking, remove the hard central core, or cut into florets. Choose densely packed heads, avoiding specimens with any black spots or marks, and store in the refrigerator for 5–10 days.

Above: *Plump, juicy tomatoes have a rich, sweet flavour and are tasty used in salads or cooked in stews and sauces.*

Left: *Choose cauliflowers with firm, clean white florets.*

Vegetable fruits

Tomatoes, aubergines, peppers and chillies are actually fruit, although they are generally used as vegetables. They all have a robust flavour and lovely texture, and although available all year, they are at their peak in the summer.

Aubergines/eggplants These can be fried, stewed, brushed with oil and grilled (broiled), or stuffed and baked. Choose firm, plump, smooth-skinned specimens and store in the refrigerator, where they will keep for 5–8 days.

Chillies There are many types of chilli, all with a different taste and heat. As a general rule, the bigger the chilli, the milder it is; green chillies tend to be hotter than red ones.

Peppers/bell peppers These may be red, yellow, orange or green, with the green specimens having a fresher, less sweet flavour. Peppers can be grilled, roasted, fried and stewed. Choose firm, unblemished specimens and store in the refrigerator for 5–8 days.

Tomatoes There are numerous varieties of tomato, including cherry, plum and beefsteak. They are eaten raw or cooked. Choose plump, bright-red specimens and store in the refrigerator for 5–8 days.

Leafy green vegetables

There is a wide selection of leafy greens available, which may be used raw in salads or cooked.

Salad leaves There are many different salad leaves, including various types of lettuce. They are delicate and need to be stored in the refrigerator, where most will keep for a few days. Avoid buying vacuum-packed ready-to-eat leaves as they will be costly and less nutritious.

Spinach Tender young spinach leaves are tasty raw. Mature spinach leaves can be fried, boiled or steamed until just wilted; they overcook very easily. Store spinach in the refrigerator for 2–3 days, and wash well before use.

Leafy Asian vegetables Asian vegetables, such as pak choi (bok choy), can be used raw in salads or cooked. Prepare in the same way as cabbage or spinach.

The onion family

This family includes onions, shallots, spring onions (scallions), leeks and garlic. Choose firm, unblemished specimens. Store onions in a cool, dry place for up to 2 weeks; store leeks and spring onions in the refrigerator for 2–3 days.

Corn, beans and peas

These are good boiled or steamed and served as a side dish, or used in braised dishes and stir-fries.

Corn Large corn cobs are good steamed and served with butter, while baby corn is better added to stir-fries. Buy only the freshest specimens when they are in season, because stale vegetables can be starchy.

Green beans Many varieties of green beans are available throughout the year. Choose firm, fresh-looking beans with a bright green colour. Store in the refrigerator for up to 5 days.

Below: *Corn cobs are delicious steamed and served with butter.*

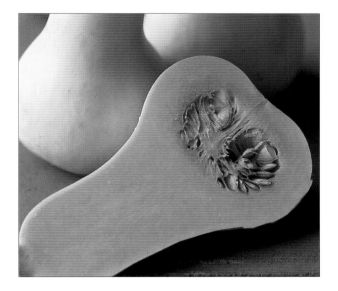

Above: *Butternut squash has orange flesh, a sweet taste and a smooth texture. Roasting brings out its flavour.*

Peas Fresh peas are generally only available in the summer and can be expensive. Frozen peas are often better than fresh ones because they are frozen within a short time of picking and retain all their natural sweetness. They are also much cheaper.

Squashes

These vegetables come in many different shapes and sizes and include courgettes (zucchini), and butternut, acorn and spaghetti squashes, and pumpkins and marrows (large zucchini). With the exception of courgettes, all need peeling and seeding before use. They can be cut up and boiled, or baked whole. Select smooth, unblemished vegetables with unbroken skin. Most squashes can be stored in a cool place for 1 week, although courgettes should be stored in the refrigerator for 4–5 days.

Mushrooms

Freshly picked mushrooms have a rich, earthy flavour, but are rarely available to most cooks. Brown cap (cremini) mushrooms are a good alternative; they have more flavour than cultivated mushrooms. Shiitake mushrooms are full-flavoured and delicious in Chinese- and Asian-style dishes.

There are many types of edible wild fungi or mushrooms of different flavours and textures. They tend to have a more intense taste than cultivated mushrooms and are also more expensive and more difficult to find. Wild mushrooms are seasonal and can generally be found in late summer, autumn and winter.

Dairy Produce and Eggs

Milk and milk products, such as yogurt, milk and cheese, are widely used in cooking and can add a delicious richness to many sweet and savoury dishes. Strong-tasting cheeses, such as Gorgonzola or Parmesan, not only contribute a wonderful texture, but also add real bite to many savoury dishes.

Milk, cream and yogurt
These products are widely used in both sweet and savoury cooked and uncooked dishes, adding a rich, creamy taste and texture. There are many varieties of each available in supermarkets, and most are reasonably priced, apart from double and clotted cream, which can be expensive.

Butter
There are two main types of butter – salted and unsalted (sweet). Unsalted is better for baking cakes and cookies.

Hard cheeses
These firm, tasty cheeses are good for cooking, and if you select stronger varieties you will not need to use as much to give a good flavour. Cheddar, Parmesan and Gruyère are the most popular, although grano pedano makes a very good economical alternative to Parmesan, which tends to be expensive. All should have a dry rind. Store wrapped in baking parchment in the refrigerator for up to 2 weeks.

Semi-hard cheeses
These vary in softness depending on the type. Choose cheeses that feel springy and have a firm rind. Wrap in waxed paper and store in the refrigerator for 1–2 weeks. Popular choices include fontina and halloumi.

Below: *It is worth paying a little extra to buy free-range or organic eggs; they will taste a lot better and even the most expensive varieties represent very good value for money.*

Above: *Stilton has a tangy flavour and creamy texture. It is good served on its own or used in salads and cooking.*

Blue cheese
These strong, often sharp, cheeses usually melt well and are good for cooking and flavouring sauces. Stilton is usually good value for money.

Soft and fresh cheeses
Store these unripened cheeses in a covered container in the refrigerator for up to 1 week. Mozzarella has a mild flavour and melts well. Feta is crumbly with a salty flavour and is good in salads. Marscapone is creamy and can be used in sweet or savoury dishes.

White rind cheeses
These creamy cheeses are delicious used fresh in salads or cooked. Brie is one of the best and its flavour ranges from mild to extremely strong. Goat's cheese has a distinctive flavour and can be used in a range of dishes.

Eggs
Widely used in sweet and savoury cooking, eggs are incredibly good value for money and are very versatile – they can be boiled, poached, fried, scrambled or baked. They are also widely used in baking. Buy the best you can afford – hens reared in better conditions produce better-tasting eggs.

Fish and Seafood

Always buy really fresh fish and seafood: look for bright-eyed fish with plump flesh and bright, undamaged skin; they should not smell "fishy" but should have a faint aroma of the sea. Store fish and shellfish, covered, towards the bottom of the refrigerator, and use within a day of purchase.

Above: *Mackerel are very good value for money, as well as being nutritious, tasty and versatile for cooking.*

Oily fish
The rich flesh of oily fish is tasty and rich in omega-3 fatty acids, which are an essential part of a healthy diet. Oily fish are also usually cheaper than other fish.

Mackerel These very economical fish have iridescent skin and quite firm, brownish flesh.

Salmon Wild varieties tend to be very expensive, so only eat them occasionally. If you buy farmed salmon, check that it is from a reputable supplier. Canned salmon can be used in pasta and rice dishes.

Sardines These small fish are delicious fresh, cooked over a barbecue with lime or lemon juice and herbs.

Whitebait These are the small fry of herring and sprats, and taste excellent fried and eaten whole.

Rich, meaty fish
This group of firm-fleshed fish has a meaty texture, and includes monkfish, red mullet, seabass, swordfish and tuna. They are often expensive, so look out for special offers in the supermarket or fishmongers. Canned tuna makes a good, cheap alternative to fresh tuna and can be used in omelettes, salads and pasta dishes.

White fish
These fish have firm yet delicate white flesh and are excellent cooked simply with subtle or piquant flavouring.

Cod Stocks of cod are diminishing due to overfishing, so check where the fish comes from before buying. Hoki or pollard are much cheaper and make good alternatives.

Haddock This flaky fish can also be used instead of cod. Smoked haddock is delicious but avoid the bright yellow dyed variety and go for the paler, undyed version.

Halibut This flat fish is very good value and tastes a bit like turbot. Do not overcook it, or the flesh will become dry.

Seafood
This group includes molluscs, such as mussels, crustaceans, such as crabs and prawns (shrimp), and squid. Store in the refrigerator and use within 1–2 days.

Crab This is available raw, ready-cooked or in a can. Fresh crab is relatively expensive, so use canned crab in baked pasta or rice dishes as a cheaper alternative.

Prawns/shrimp There are many types of prawns of different sizes, cooked or raw, in the shell, or peeled. Frozen prawns are usually very good value for money.

Squid This economical seafood is available all year. It needs to be cooked either very quickly or very slowly.

Below: *Buy fresh prawns when they are on special offer.*

Meat and Poultry

It is important to choose good quality meat as well as watching the price, so look out for special offers on organic and free-range meat and poultry, and avoid buying really cheap, bottom-of-the range packaged meat. Offal and other less well-used cuts of meat, such as beef shank, chuck or brisket represent very good value for money. Bulk out expensive cuts of meat with vegetables and beans.

Above: *Roast Loin of Pork with Stuffing makes a delicious, satisfying and healthy main meal.*

Pork

Comparatively inexpensive and available all year round, pork is a very versatile meat that can be roasted, grilled (broiled) or cooked on a barbecue. It is generally tender and has an excellent flavour that has a natural affinity with apples. Look for firm, pale pink flesh, which is moist but not damp or oily. The fat should be white, and the bones should be tinged with red.

Shoulder, leg and loin The shoulder or leg is the best cut of pork for roasting, and is cheaper than many other joints of meat. To make good crackling, ensure that the rind is completely dry and rub it generously with sea salt. Stuff boneless loin joints with herbs and onion before roasting. Loin or shoulder chops are suited to pan-frying or braising.

Bacon Available smoked or unsmoked, bacon comes in a variety of different forms, from rashers and steaks to joints. Dry-cured bacon rashers, although more expensive than some other types, have the best flavour and do not shrink when they are cooked, so you won't need to use as much. Streaky (fatty) bacon can be cooked to a crisp-fried texture and is excellent for placing on the breasts of chicken and turkey before roasting. Back bacon is normally more expensive than streaky bacon but has larger rashers (strips) and a good balance of lean to fatty areas.

Beef

Popular all over the world, beef provides a full-flavoured ingredient for stewing, succulent joints for roasting and tender steaks for grilling (broiling). It is available all year, and there are cuts suitable for all types of dish and for every budget. Ideally beef should be hung for several weeks before being eaten, and will be brown rather than red.

Fillet/beef tenderloin, forerib, topside and silverside/pot roast These reasonably expensive cuts taste best roasted. To make the most of the flavour of the beef, serve medium, not well-done, and to make the joint feed more people, serve with plenty of vegetables.

Shin or leg/shank, chuck and brisket These cuts are very good value for money. They can be quite tough and are best stewed slowly to tenderize them and bring out their excellent flavour.

Mince/ground meat This is a very versatile ingredient for a whole range of dishes. Avoid cheap, bought frozen mince as it is usually of inferior quality.

Lamb

Tender young lamb is delicious in roasts and superb grilled (broiled), pan-fried and stewed. It can be quite expensive, so buy it when it is in season in spring, and go for cheaper cuts. Look for firm, pink meat with a fine-grained, velvety texture. The fat should be creamy white, firm and waxy.

Chump chops and leg steaks These have a full flavour and can be either grilled (broiled) or pan-fried.

Scrag end, middle neck, and fillet These are inexpensive and ideal for stewing, braising and casseroling. Fillet is good for grilling.

Shank or knuckle An economical yet flavoursome cut, it can be tough so it needs long cooking, such as stewing, pot-roasting or braising.

Sausages and offal/variety meats

Offal refers to all offcuts from the carcass but in everyday use, this usually means liver and kidneys. Offal is very good value for money, tastes delicious and is packed with essential vitamins and minerals.

Sausages There are many types of fresh sausage from around the world. Depending on the variety, they may be fried, grilled (broiled) or baked. They are normally quick and easy to cook and a favourite with all the family.

Kidneys Lambs' kidneys are lighter in flavour than pigs'. They should be halved and the central core discarded before they are pan-fried or used in stews and pies.

Liver Pigs', lambs' or calves' liver has a strong flavour and tastes good pan-fried, with bacon and mashed potato.

Poultry

Many people prefer the lighter flavour of poultry to that of red meat, and it is incredibly versatile and easy to use. There is usually a range of options to choose from, and although organic birds taste better, they are normally considerably more expensive than intensively reared birds. It is often cheaper to buy a whole bird and joint it yourself at home than to buy ready-prepared joints.

Chicken Choose smooth-skinned, unblemished plump birds. You can use every part of the bird in cooking, including the carcass, which you can boil up to make stock. Chicken drumsticks, leg quarters, thighs and breast portions on the bone are usually better value than skinless chicken breast fillets. You can remove the skin yourself, if you wish, although the skin adds flavour and helps to keep the flesh moist.

Below (clockwise from top): *If you choose to buy ready-jointed chicken portions, then economical options include the leg quarter, drumsticks and thighs.*

Jointing a bird

1 Put the bird breast-side up on a chopping board. Use a sharp knife to remove the legs by cutting through the thigh joint.

2 Following the line of the breastbone and using poultry shears or kitchen scissors, cut the breast in half, making the cut as clean as possible.

3 Turn the bird over and cut out the backbone. Discard. Leave the wings attached to each breast half and turn over so the skin is uppermost.

4 Cut each breast in half crossways at the widest part. This will leave one portion attached to the wing. Cut off the wing tip at the first joint.

5 Using a sharp knife and firm pressure, cut each leg cleanly through the knee joint to separate the thigh and drumstick from each other.

Duck Traditionally, duck can be expensive and very fatty with a fairly small amount of meat on the carcass. An average duck will serve two or three people. Duck breasts and legs are a good choice for simple cooking. Buy when they are on offer and freeze until required.

Turkey This economical and versatile meat can be used in the same way as chicken and duck. When buying a whole bird, look for well-rounded breasts and legs, and soft and evenly coloured skin. Turkey mince (ground turkey) makes a good, cheap alternative to beef mince (ground beef).

Storecupboard Staples

A well-stocked storecupboard (pantry) is a must for the clever cook, and will help you to create delicious, economical dishes without the need for expensive ingredients or having to make a special trip to the supermarket. Staples range from flour, sugar, canned goods and oil to rice, pasta, dried herbs and stock (bouillon) cubes, and the following items have not been included when costing the recipes.

Above (clockwise from top): *Strong bread flour, self-raising flour, plain flour, and gluten-free flour.*

Flours

This is an essential ingredient in every kitchen. There are many different types, which serve many purposes in both sweet and savoury cooking – from baking cakes to thickening gravy and making cheese sauce.

Cornflour/cornstarch This very fine white flour is useful for thickening sauces and stabilizing egg mixtures, such as custard, to prevent them curdling.

Gluten-free flours For those with an allergy to gluten, which is found in wheat and other grains, gluten-free flour is an invaluable ingredient. It is widely available from most large supermarkets and health-food stores.

Wheat flours Plain (all-purpose) flour can be used in most recipes. Self-raising (self-rising) flour has a raising agent added and is useful for baking recipes. Wholemeal flour is available as plain (all-purpose) or self-raising (self-rising). Strong bread flour contains more gluten than plain flour, making it more suitable for making breads.

Raising agents You can add baking powder to plain flour to give a light texture to cakes and cookies. The powder reacts with liquids and heat during cooking and produces carbon-dioxide bubbles, which make the mixture rise.

Sugars

Refined and raw sugars can be used to sweeten and flavour many different types of dish, including cakes, bakes, pastries, cookies and desserts.

Brown sugars These dark, unrefined sugars have a rich, caramel flavour. There are several different types of brown sugar, including light and dark muscovado (brown) sugar and dark brown molasses sugar. As a general rule of thumb, the darker the sugar, the more intense its flavour. Always check that you are buying unrefined sugar, because "brown" sugars are often actually dyed white sugar.

Caster/superfine sugar This fine-grained white sugar is most frequently used in baking. Its fine texture is particularly well suited to making cakes and cookies.

Demerara/raw sugar This golden sugar consists of large crystals with a rich, slightly honeyish flavour. It is great for adding a crunchy texture to cookies.

Granulated sugar This refined white sugar has large crystals. It is used for sweetening drinks, and in everyday cooking; it can also be used as a crunchy cookie or cake topping, or stirred into crumble mixtures for extra texture.

Icing/confectioners' sugar The finest of all the refined sugars, this sugar has a powdery texture. It is used for making icing and sweetening flavoured creams. It is also excellent for dusting on cakes, desserts and cookies as a simple yet effective decoration.

Right: *Granulated sugar has larger crystals than caster sugar but both are good for making cakes and desserts.*

Pasta and noodles

These are invaluable storecupboard ingredients that can be used as the base of many hot and cold dishes.

Pasta Dried pasta keeps for months in an airtight container – check the packet for information on its keeping quality. There is a wide variety of pasta in all shapes and sizes. Egg pasta is enriched with egg yolks. It has a richer flavour than plain pasta and is often more expensive than dried varieties, which are very cheap. Generally, the choice depends on personal taste – use whichever type you have in the cupboard. Cook pasta at a rolling boil in plenty of water. Fresh pasta cooks very quickly and is available chilled. It can be stored in the refrigerator for several days, or in the freezer for several months.

Egg noodles Made from wheat flour and eggs, these may be thick, medium or thin. Use them for stir-fries or as a cheap accompaniment to Chinese and Asian dishes.

Rice noodles These transluscent white noodles are a good alternative to wheat noodles – particularly for those on a gluten-free diet. They are available as broad flat or thin noodles that can be added to stir-fries and soups as well as used cold as a base for salads. Rice noodles are easy to prepare, because they don't need to be cooked. Simply soak in boiling water for about 5 minutes, then stir-fry, add to soups or toss with salad ingredients.

Below: *Tiny soup pasta is available in hundreds of different shapes – buy whichever shape you prefer, and use to make substantial soups that can be eaten for lunch, or as a light meal when served with bread.*

Above: *Egg noodles have a nutty taste and are extremely good value for money, as well as being very versatile. They can be served hot in Asian-style stir-fries and soups, and cold in salads.*

Couscous and polenta

Like pasta and noodles, couscous and polenta are very cheap and can be served as an accompaniment or act as the base of many dishes. They have a mild flavour, and go particularly well with other, strongly flavoured ingredients, such as aromatics, herbs and spices.

Couscous Made from durum wheat, couscous is often regarded as a type of pasta. Traditional couscous needed long steaming before serving, but the majority of brands available in supermarkets today are "instant" and need only brief soaking in water. It is the classic accompaniment to Moroccan tagines, but also goes well with all kinds of meat, fish and vegetable stews. It makes an excellent base for salads and is very economical.

Polenta This is made from finely ground cornmeal. It is cooked with water and served either soft (rather like mashed potato) or left to set and then cut into pieces that can be grilled (broiled) or fried. Quick-cook and ready-made polenta are available in most supermarkets and can be made into simple, hearty dishes. It is best served with flavourful ingredients.

Above: *Canned beans are cheap and versatile and can be used in stews, healthy salads or tasty dips and pâtés.*

Rice

This great-value grain can be served as an accompaniment, or form the base of sweet and savoury dishes.

Basmati rice This long-grain rice is widely used in Indian cooking. It is aromatic and cooks to give separated, fluffy grains. Brown basmati rice is also available.

Long-grain rice The narrow grains of white rice cook to a light, fluffy texture and are generally served as an accompaniment to main dishes. They also make a perfect base for other dishes such as stir-fries and salads.

Risotto rice This rice has medium-length polished grains. The grains can absorb a great deal of liquid while still retaining their shape. There are several types of risotto rice, including the popular arborio and carnaroli. When cooking risotto rice, it is imperative to stir it regularly. Liquid or stock should be added periodically throughout cooking to prevent the rice sticking to the pan and burning, and spoiling the overall taste.

Short-grain rice There are several types of short, stubby, polished rice such as pudding rice and sushi rice. These usually have a high starch content and cook into tender grains that cling together and can be shaped easily.

Dried beans, lentils and peas

These staples are a fantastic resource for any cook and provide a very good low-fat source of protein. They are very good value, and can be used to help a meat dish go much further, thus reducing the overall cost.

Beans There are a wide variety of beans available in many stores, including red and white kidney beans, butter (lima) beans, haricot beans, flageolet beans and cannellini beans. To use, place the dried beans in a large bowl, cover with cold water and leave to soak overnight, then rinse under running water and drain. Kidney beans are poisonous unless they are properly cooked, so you need to boil the beans vigorously for 15 minutes, then change the water and simmer for about $1^3/_4$ hours until they are tender.

Lentils Red, green and brown lentils are all extremely versatile and do not require pre-soaking. Simply rinse under cold running water and add to a wide range of dishes.

Chickpeas These peas have a lovely creamy texture and hearty taste and can be used to make home-made hummus or to bulk out soups, stews and salads.

Canned goods

Although many foods taste best when they are fresh, there are some canned foods which are as good as or better than the fresh variety. These include canned tomatoes, which are usually cheaper and much more convenient to use than fresh tomatoes; canned beans, peas and lentils, which simply require rinsing before use; and some canned fish and shellfish, such as tuna and crab, which are significantly cheaper than the fresh varieties and make excellent additions to baked pasta dishes and salads.

Below: *Brown basmati rice.*

Left (from left to right): *Corn oil and vegetable oil are cheap and extremely versatile.*

Oils

Essential both for cooking and adding flavour, there are many different types of oil.

Corn oil Golden-coloured corn oil is inexpensive, has a strong flavour and can be used in most types of cooking.

Groundnut (peanut) oil This virtually flavourless oil is used for frying, baking and making dressings such as mayonnaise.

Olive oil Extra virgin olive oil is made from the first pressing of the olives. It has the best flavour but is the most expensive type, so it is best reserved for condiments or salad dressings. Ordinary olive oil is generally made from the third or fourth pressing of the olives, so it is cheaper and should be used for cooking.

Vegetable oil This is a blend of oils, usually including corn oil and other vegetable oils. It is cheap, flavourless and useful in most types of cooking.

Flavoured Oils

Herb-infused oil Half-fill a jar with washed and dried fresh herbs such as rosemary or basil. Pour over olive oil to cover, then seal the jar and place in a cool, dark place for 3 days. Strain the herb-flavoured oil into a clean jar or bottle and discard the herbs.

Chilli oil Add several dried chillies to a bottle of olive oil and leave to infuse for about 2 weeks before using. If the flavour is not sufficiently pronounced, leave for another week. The chillies can be left in the bottle and give a very decorative effect.

Garlic oil Add several whole garlic cloves to a bottle of olive oil and leave to infuse for about 2 weeks before using. If you like, you can strain the oil into a clean bottle and store in a cool, dark place.

Vinegars, sauces and condiments

Not only are vinegars, sauces and condiments perfect for serving with dishes at the table, they are also great for adding flavour and bite to simple dishes during cooking.

Vinegars It is worth buying a good-quality vinegar as it will keep better. White wine vinegar, cider vinegar, malt vinegar and balsamic vinegar are the most commonly used.

Soy sauce Made from fermented soy beans, soy sauce is salty and just a small amount adds a rich, rounded flavour to Asian-style stir-fries, glazes and sauces.

Tomato ketchup Add a splash of this strong table condiment to tomato sauces for a sweet-sour flavour.

Worcestershire sauce This brown, very spicy sauce brings a piquant flavour to casseroles, stews and soups.

Curry paste There are many ready-made curry pastes, including those for classic Indian and Thai curries. They can also be used to spice up burgers or meatballs.

Mustard Wholegrain mustard has a sweet taste and makes a mild salad dressing. French Dijon mustard has a piquant flavour which complements red meat. English mustard is excellent added to cheese dishes.

Passata/bottled strained tomatoes This Italian product, made of sieved tomatoes, has a fairly thin consistency and makes a good base for a tomato sauce.

Tomato purée/paste This concentrated purée is an essential in every storecupboard. It is great for adding flavour, and sometimes body, to sauces and stews.

Below: *Tomato purée (paste) can add extra flavour to tomato sauces, soups and stews of all types.*

Dried herbs and stock cubes

Dried herbs and stock (bouillon) cubes are cheap and convenient standbys when you don't have fresh herbs or stock to hand, although for some recipes you will only be able to use the fresh type. Dried herbs have a much more concentrated flavour than fresh, so be careful about how much you add or the flavour might be overpowering.

Basil This distinctive herb is the perfect partner to tomato-based dishes, and can be used in soups, stews and to make tomato sauces.

Bay Dried bay leaves are a perfectly satisfactory substitute for fresh bay leaves. They are used when making a bouquet garni and can be added to meat dishes, stews and casseroles before cooking. Remember to remove them from the dish before serving, as they are tough.

Oregano Dried oregano has a strong, pungent flavour that will permeate the whole dish, so use in moderation. It adds a distinctive aroma to Italian-style dishes, and is an integral part of a basic tomato sauce for spreading on pizzas or topping pasta dishes.

Rosemary This is another pungent herb that will enhance the flavour of many meat dishes, especially those made with lamb.

Below: *Store dried herbs, such as bay leaves, in airtight containers to help to preserve their flavour better.*

Above: *Rock or sea salt is generally regarded as the most superior type of salt available, and it is not treated with any chemicals. You will need to grind it in a mill or a mortar before adding to food.*

Sage Peppery-tasting sage has large, slightly furry leaves when fresh. Dried sage goes particularly well with pork, or in pasta sauces and in stuffings. It has a very strong flavour, so use in moderation or it will overpower the dish.

Tarragon This fragrant herb has a strong aniseed flavour, and is most often paired with fish and chicken dishes.

Stock (bouillon) cubes These handy cubes are an excellent way of adding flavour to a range of cooked meat and vegetable dishes, although if you are making soup, it is better to use home-made stock if you possibly can, because it is such a key ingredient and forms the basis of the dish. It is worth paying a little extra for good quality stock cubes because cheaper varieties tend to contain a lot of added salt and will give a less satisfactory result.

Salt

Salt can be used in moderation to add flavour and to bring out the taste of other foods. It also acts as a preservative when it is used in pickling and chutney-making, or when curing meats and fish, since it draws out the moisture and prevents decomposition. It is worth paying a little extra for rock or sea salt, since these types do not contain any added chemicals, which are often found in table salt. Sea salt has a stronger taste and seasoning potential than table salt, so use in moderation, and add a little at a time, tasting in between additions to prevent oversalting.

Spices

These flavourings play a very important role when cooking with relatively inexpensive ingredients, adding a warmth and roundness of flavour to simple dishes. It is difficult to have every spice to hand, but a few key spices will be enough to create culinary magic. Black pepper is an essential seasoning in every storecupboard; cumin seeds, coriander seeds, chilli flakes and turmeric are also good basics. Store spices in airtight containers in a cool, dark place. Buy small quantities that will be used up quickly, because flavours diminish with age.

Allspice This berry has a warm, slightly cinnamon-clove flavour. It is more readily available in its ground form and can be used in both savoury and sweet cooking.

Caraway seeds These small dark seeds have a fennel-like flavour and can be used in sweet and savoury dishes.

Cayenne pepper This fiery, piquant spice is made from dried hot red chillies, so use sparingly. It is excellent added to cheese dishes and creamy sauces and soups.

Chilli flakes Crushed dried red chillies can be added to, or sprinkled over, all kinds of dishes. You can easily make your own by drying fresh red chillies on a radiator and then crumbling them with your fingers.

Chinese five-spice powder This is a mixture of ground spices, including anise pepper, cassia, fennel seeds, star anise and cloves. It is a powerful mixture, so use sparingly.

Cinnamon This warm spice is available in sticks and ground into powder, and has many uses. Add sticks to Moroccan stews, and use powder in baking.

Cloves Available whole or ground, these dried flower buds are used in savoury and sweet dishes. Ground cloves are strong, so use sparingly.

Coriander Available whole or ground, this warm, aromatic spice is delicious with most meats, particularly lamb.

Cumin This warm, pungent spice works well with meats and a variety of vegetables.

Fennel seeds These little green seeds have a sweet, aniseed-like flavour that pairs well with chicken and fish.

Garam masala This mixture of ground roasted spices is made from cumin, coriander, cardamom and black pepper and is used in many Asian dishes. Ready-mixed garam masala is widely available, although the flavour is better when the spices are freshly roasted and ground.

Ginger The ground, dried spice is useful for baking. For a fresher flavour, it is best to use fresh root ginger.

Green cardamom The papery green pods enclose little black seeds that are easily scraped out and can be crushed.

Nutmeg This large aromatic seed is available in a ground form, but the flavour is better when it is freshly grated.

Paprika Used in many Spanish dishes, paprika is available in a mild and hot form. It has a slightly sweet flavour.

Pepper Black pepper is one of the most commonly used spices, and should always be freshly ground or it will lose its flavour. Green peppercorns have a mild flavour. They are available dried or preserved in brine. White pepper is hotter than green, but less aromatic than black.

Turmeric Made from dried turmeric root, the ground spice is bright yellow with a peppery, slightly earthy flavour and is used in many Indian dishes.

Vanilla Dried vanilla pods (beans) are long and black, encasing hundreds of tiny black seeds. Natural vanilla extract is distilled from vanilla pods and is a useful alternative to pods.

Above: *For the best flavour, grate whole nutmeg as and when you need the spice, using a special small grater.*

Seasonality Charts

Buying food when it is season ensures that you are getting the best-quality, best-value fresh produce. Although many products are available all year round, it is worth checking where they are grown and what condition they are in, and considering using a home-grown seasonal alternative instead. These charts provide a basic outline of when the food is in season in the country in which it is grown, and some of its culinary or nutritional properties and uses.

SPRING	
Apricots	Apricots appear in the shops in late spring. They are delicious poached with honey and lemon or made into tarts or sorbets.
Asparagus	Buy asparagus when it is on special offer. The stalks should snap easily and not be woody.
Aubergines (eggplants)	The first aubergines appear in mid-spring. The spongy flesh is very absorbent and carries the flavour of spices well – perfect for adding to curries and other robust dishes.
Broccoli	Dark green, vitamin-packed broccoli is a mainstay of the winter and early spring, and makes a cheap and very healthy accompaniment to most main dishes.
Broad (fava) beans	Pale green broad beans are available from the end of spring. Select firm pods.
Brussels sprouts	Small, round Brussels sprouts are available until early spring. Add to stir-fries or lightly steam or boil and serve with butter as an accompaniment.
Button (white) mushrooms	Although cultivated mushrooms are available all year, delicate button mushrooms are at their best in spring and are delicious served raw in salads or lightly sautéed.
Cabbage	Spring cabbage has tender young leaves and a mild flavour.
Carrots	Young carrots are at their best in spring and are delicious raw or lightly steamed.
Cauliflower	These are available in abundance from early spring. Pull back the leaves to check that the florets are creamy white with no discolouration.
Curly kale	Robust, dark green curly kale is available from early spring, and is packed with goodness and flavour.
Duck	Roast duck is traditionally eaten in mid-spring. The creamy flesh can be prepared in any number of ways, although since it is expensive, it is best eaten in a casserole to make it stretch further.
Greens	Spring greens are at their best towards the end of spring.
Guava	Exotic guava can be used raw in fruit salads or to make a delicate, fragrant jelly.
Halibut	These large, meaty fish are available in late spring/early summer.
Horseradish	Peel horseradish root before making into fiery horseradish sauce.
Lamb	New season lamb is the highlight of spring.
New potatoes	Many varieties are available in spring. Try to buy locally produced varieties to ensure that they are fresh.
Papaya	This tropical fruit is available most of the year round, but is particularly good in mid-spring.
Peas	Fresh peas are vibrant, sweet and tender in late spring. Select bright, firm pods.
Plaice	Buy this versatile white-fleshed fish when it is very fresh and cook it very gently.
Purple sprouting broccoli	This attractive leafy vegetable is at its best in spring and makes a change from standard green broccoli. It requires only minimal cooking.
Radishes	Crisp, fresh radishes are available from mid-spring right into the summer.
Rhubarb	The last of the forced and the first of the outdoor rhubarb is available in spring.
Rocket (arugula)	Peppery young leaves are in their prime and add a tang to salads.
Spinach	Spring heralds the arrival of baby spinach leaves, which are rich in vitamins and taste delicious .
Spring onions (scallions)	These pungent, tender onions are particularly flavoursome in late spring. Add them raw to salads, or lightly cook them by adding them to stir-fries.
Turnips	Spring turnips are small and very tender, requiring minimal cooking.

SUMMER

Apricots	These downy soft fruits do not ripen once they have been picked, so make sure they are ripe when you buy them.
Avocados	Meltingly soft, creamy and delicious, avocados are the perfect addition to any salad. Make sure that they are ripe before using, or the flavour and texture may be disappointing.
Basil	The flavour and aroma of basil is most intense during the summer months, when it is abundant.
Beef	Beef is available all year round, but make the most of tender steaks in the summer by marinading and cooking on a barbecue.
Blackcurrants	Tangy blackcurrants need to be cooked with a little sugar or mixed with other sweeter fruits.
Blueberries	Vitamin C-packed blueberries are at their best in late summer. They are very versatile, and can be added to fresh and cooked dishes.
Broad (fava) beans	Tender little broad beans are irresistible in soups, dips or steamed with a squeeze of lemon.
Cherries	Deep red, juicy cherries are divine eaten on their own, or mixed into summer fruit salads.
Corn	Freshly picked, local corn on the cob tastes fabulous when lightly steamed or baked on a barbecue and served just with some butter and ground black pepper.
Courgettes (zucchini)	Plump courgettes taste delicious and are very versatile – they can be baked, fried, cut into very thin slices and served raw or added to any number of summer soups and pasta sauces.
Crab	Make the most of the delicate flesh to make a really luxurious summer salad.
Cucumber	Although this salad vegetable is normally available all year, it is at its best during the summer.
Damsons	The intensely flavoured fruits are at their best in late summer, and can be used to make exquisite syrup, jelly, gin or cheese.
Fennel	Refreshing fennel has an aniseed flavour, and can be added raw to salads, blanched and chargrilled on a barbecue or tossed in stir-fries.
Garlic	Mild and aromatic, the first of the new season's garlic can be eaten raw in dips or marinades, or blanched and roasted for a creamy accompaniment to roast chicken.
Globe artichokes	Ideal for a lazy lunch, artichoke leaves taste delicious dipped in butter.
Gooseberries	The sharp taste and furry texture of gooseberries is unique, and since they are only around for a few weeks in mid-summer, make sure that you make the most of them.
Lettuce	Almost all varieties of lettuce are at their best in the summer. There are many different varieties, so try them out singly or in combination with other types to create a light, crisp salad.
Lovage	Leafy lovage tastes a bit like celery and can be added to salads, soups or as a flavouring for chicken or white fish.
Melons	Sweet, juicy and fragrant, melons are very versatile and can be served with cold meat and cheese as an appetizer, or simply eaten on their own as a refreshing dessert.
Mint	Most fresh herbs are at their best in the summer, and mint is no exception.
Nectarines	Allow nectarines to ripen fully before eating, so that their aromatic flavour is at its very best.
Peaches	Succulent peaches are best eaten raw, or sliced on top of natural (plain) yogurt.
Peas	Sweet new peas, straight from the pod are one of the highlights of the summer.
Peppers	Crisp and crunchy red, yellow and green (bell) peppers add flavour, texture and colour to pasta dishes and salads, or can be stuffed and baked in the oven or chargrilled on the barbecue.
Radishes	The potent, fiery flavour of radishes increases throughout the summer.
Raspberries	These soft, fragrant berries taste wonderful on their own, or mix them with peaches, nectarines and other soft summer fruits for a mouth-watering fruit salad.
Redcurrants	Jewel-like redcurrants can be served as an attractive topping to sponge cakes, as part of a mixed fruit salad or in a range of cooked summer desserts.
Strawberries	Juicy, sweet strawberries are the essence of summer, so enjoy them while they are in season.
Stringless beans	These plump beans can be cooked and eaten immediately as a side dish, or cooled and used as the basis of a substantial summer salad.
Tomatoes	All types of tomatoes are at their best in the summer. Enjoy them raw in salads or stuffed and baked. If you have a glut of tomatoes, or some that are over-ripe, convert them into sauces and soups to be enjoyed in the winter months.

AUTUMN

Apples	There are many varieties of apple available in supermarkets, but for the best locally grown varieties, buy them in greengrocers or your local food markets.
Bananas	Packed with potassium, bananas make the ideal economical snack or dessert.
Beetroot (beet)	Deep red beetroot can be boiled or baked to make a nutritious main dish or accompaniment.
Brussels sprouts	These small green brassicas are packed with vitamins. Take care not to overcook them.
Blackberries	Early autumn is the best time to go foraging in the hedgerows for wild blackberries.
Carrots	Infinitely versatile, carrots can be eaten on their own, or added to any number of soups, stews, casseroles or accompaniments.
Cauliflower	This staple autumn and winter vegetable is extremely versatile, and can be used to make creamy soups, appetizing cheese dishes or served simply boiled or steamed as an accompaniment.
Cavolo nero	Available throughout autumn and winter, cavolo nero tastes fabulous with bacon, cheese or meat.
Celery	Crisp young celery is incredibly versatile and has a subtle, sweet flavour.
Chanterelle mushrooms	Rich, earthy chanterelles require minimal preparation and are delicious added to risottos, soups and pasta. Store in a paper bag in the salad drawer of your refrigerator.
Crab apples	Tart and crisp, crab apples are ideal for converting into jams, jellies, sorbets and mousses.
Cranberries	Ruby red cranberries should be initially cooked without sugar – to prevent the waxy skin from toughening – before making into fruit tarts, or poaching and making into a piquant sauce.
Damsons	Early autumn is peak damson season, so make sure you make the most of them.
Dates	Sweet and succulent, dates are harvested in the autumn months. There are many varieties available, and their texture and sweetness ranges from toffee-like to plump and succulent.
Elderberries	Pick elderberries in early autumn and transform into cordials and jellies.
Figs	Always eat plump figs at room temperature as their flavour will be dulled if they are served chilled.
Game birds	Although usually quite expensive, the meat of game birds is rich and a little goes a long way.
Herring	Available most of the year, herring taste delicious fried or baked with a piquant citrus sauce.
Kale	Both plain and curly kale are available throughout autumn, and are packed with valuable nutrients and phytochemicals.
Leeks	Choose slender leeks whenever possible, as they will be less tough than thicker ones.
Mackerel	Omega 3-rich mackerel are at their best now. They are cheap, and easy to prepare and cook.
Marrow	Plump marrows are the ideal vessels for spicy fillings and taste wonderful baked with cheese.
Pears	Fragrant pears are the essence of autumn. Enjoy them raw, or poach them for a divine dessert.
Parsnips	These are another autumn and winter staple, and they can be used in many savoury dishes.
Passion fruit	Scrape out the flesh and seeds from these fragrant fruits and add to fruit salads for a special treat.
Pomegranates	Jewel-like pomegranates are grown in warmer climes, and are at their best now.
Pork	Pork is at its best in autumn, which coincides nicely with its traditional partner, apples.
Potatoes	Old potatoes are harvested before the cold weather really sets in, so there is an abundance of different varieties available in the autumn months.
Pumpkins	The sweet flesh can be used to create velvety soups, or can be added to stews and casseroles.
Quince	Golden yellow quinces have an aromatic flavour and are ideal for making into delicate jellies.
Rosemary	Woody-stemmed rosemary makes a great addition to many meat dishes.
Ruby chard	Red-stemmed ruby chard makes the perfect accompaniment to lamb, beef or fish dishes.
Sage	Strongly-flavoured sage is a great addition to meat dishes, and can be used to make stuffing.
Savoy cabbage	Dark green, crinkly-leaved savoy cabbage marks the start of the colder months. It can be steamed and served as an accompaniment, added to soups, or stuffed and baked.
Shallots	The first shallots come into season in early autumn.
Sloes	These grow wild in hedgerows and woodland. Use to make wonderful jellies, cordials, and sloe gin.
Squash	The many varieties of squash can be used to make a range of economical, tasty and filling dishes.
Swede (rutabaga)	Sustaining swede can be boiled and mashed, on its own or with carrots.
Swiss chard	Use the leaves of Swiss chard as you would spinach leaves, and lightly boil the white stems.

WINTER

Avocados	Creamy avocados come into season at the start of winter and last right through to the summer.
Beef	Cheaper cuts of beef, such as brisket, chuck or blade are perfectly suited to slow cooking and make warming, hearty, and economical casseroles and stews.
Brussels sprouts	Available from late autumn through to the early spring, Brussels sprouts are nutritious and cheap.
Carrots	Packed with vitamins and very economical, carrots are a key ingredient for the clever cook.
Cauliflower	The distinctive white florets of cauliflower are a mainstay on the winter menu.
Celeriac	Reminiscent of celery, celeriac has a mild flavour and can be mashed with potatoes or lightly fried.
Chicory (Belgian endive)	Red and white varieties of chicory are available during the winter months. The slightly bitter leaves can be used raw in salads, or baked with other leafy vegetables as a delicious accompaniment.
Clementines	These small, juicy fruits are delicious eaten raw and make a very handy snack food.
Cranberries	Poached cranberries can make a thick sauce that tastes wonderful with roasted game and turkey.
Goose	Some people like to eat goose during the festive period. It is reasonably expensive, so serve it with plenty of roast vegetables to make it stretch further.
Halibut	Halibut steaks or fillets are usually relatively inexpensive, and require very few additional ingredients to make them into a meal. Be careful not to overcook the flesh or it will become dry.
Leeks	These mild alliums have a delicate flavour that makes a great addition to winter soups and stews.
Mussels	These flavoursome morsels are cheap and abundant in winter.
Parsnips	Sweet white parsnips are cheap and can help to pad out a meat casserole or stew.
Physalis	Also known as Cape gooseberries, these small orange fruits make an unusual and delicious addition to fruit salads, pavlovas, sorbets and pies, and they are also very decorative.
Pomegranate	A flash of colour in the winter months, pomegranates are packed with iron and other beneficial compounds. To juice, simply press the flesh through a sieve (strainer) using the back of a ladle.
Field (portabello) mushrooms	Meaty and satisfying, field mushrooms can be grilled, stuffed and baked for a hearty vegetarian main meal, or added to any number of meat dishes.
Purple sprouting broccoli	Dramatic-looking purple sprouting broccoli makes a welcome change to green broccoli, which is available all year round.
Radicchio	The bitter white and magenta leaves of this brassica can be eaten raw or lightly cooked in a little butter. Store in a dark, dry place until required, and rinse thoroughly before use.
Red cabbage	Vibrant red cabbage can be shredded and eaten raw in salads, pickled in vinegar, or braised.
Seville oranges	These intensely-flavoured oranges are only around for a short period of time. Use for making marmalade, or adding flavour to vinaigrettes, marinades or puddings.
Squid	Unlike many other types of fish, squid prices are unaffected by bad weather since it can be caught and frozen during fair weather, so it usually good value for money.
Swede (rutabaga)	Usually white or yellow in colour, swedes can be served mashed or in stews and casseroles. They are normally very good value for money.
Sweet potatoes	Although they are available all year, sweet potatoes are particularly good in the winter months as they are both filling and warming, as well as being extremely versatile.
Turkey	Available for most of the year, but at its best during the festive months, turkey is very good value for money, and many different cuts are available, making it versatile and easy to use.
Turnips	The root of turnips can be mashed or added to slowly cooked meat dishes such as braises or casseroles, and the leaves can be steamed and eaten as an accompaniment.
Venison	Wild venison is available for most of the year as its availability varies according to the breed, sex and location of the animals. Go to your local market or butcher to get the best quality and price.
White cabbage	Extremely versatile and usually very cheap, white cabbage can be eaten raw in healthy salads, made into coleslaw, or lightly stir-fried for a warming and nutrient-packed Oriental meal.
White celery	Although green celery is available all year, frost-hardy white celery comes into its own in the winter months. Use in salads or for flavouring stocks, soups, casseroles and stuffings.
Yam	Similar in texture and flavour to sweet potatoes, yams are extremely filling and make an excellent addition to slowly cooked meat dishes, or can be served baked with butter.

 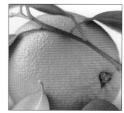   

Sample Menus

Whether you are planning a quick and easy mid-week family supper, a children's birthday party or an informal get-together, you can provide a dazzling array of delicious and varied dishes without blowing your budget. The key to success is to plan ahead – make sure that you know how many people are coming, if any of the guests have dietary requirements, and do as much preparation as you can ahead of time. These sample menus show what is possible, but you can easily adapt them.

Quick mid-week family dinner

After a busy day, the last thing you feel like doing is spending hours in the kitchen, so here is an example of a nutritious and easy meal that you can rustle up in next to no time at all.

Tortellini with Ham ✳✳

Pasta dishes are incredibly versatile, as well as being cheap and quick to prepare.

Mixed Green Leaf and Herb Salad ✳

Avoid buying vacuum packed ready-prepared salad leaves. Not only are they more expensive, but they are also less nutritious.

Baked Bananas with Toffee Sauce ✳

This simple dessert is warming, nutritious, and requires just 20 minutes cooking time.

Hearty winter warmer

During cold weather, there is nothing better than eating a really warming and sustaining meal that will help to drive out the chill.

Kale, Chorizo and Potato soup ✳✳

This filling and delicious soup is packed with essential nutrients and uses storecupboard staples.

Chilli Con Carne ✳✳

This spicy dish improves with keeping, so is ideal as a make-ahead dinner. Serve with rice and seasonal green vegetables.

Lemon Surprise Pudding ✳

Tangy, rich and warming, this delicious pudding is always popular. Serve with vanilla ice cream or cream.

Sunday lunch

Sunday lunch is a great opportunity to gather friends and family together around the table to enjoy a delicious meal together. For a vegetarian alternative, why not try Lentil and Nut Loaf in place of roasted meat?

Traditional Roast Chicken with Herb Stuffing ✳ ✳

Succulent, tender roast chicken is always a hit, especially when it is served with a herb stuffing and lashings of home-made gravy. To make the meat stretch further, serve with sausages and plenty of vegetables.

Potatoes, Peppers and Shallots Roasted with Rosemary ✳ ✳

Soft, floury potatoes absorb the flavour and aroma of fresh rosemary and sweet roasted shallots and peppers in this delicious accompaniment.

Steamed Seasonal Greens ✳

Choose any seasonal greens that are available and are good value, such as carrots, broccoli or cabbage.

Apple and Blackberry Crumble ✳

Fruit crumbles are very cheap and easy to make. When blackberries are out of season, simply use more apples, and add a handful of dried fruit and a pinch of cinammon.

Light summer supper

Salads and chilled desserts really come into their own during the summer months, and they provide the perfect opportunity to really make the most of all of the fresh produce on offer.

Salad Nicoise ✳ ✳ ✳

This luxurious salad is packed with flavour. Look out for special offers on fresh tuna steaks, as they can be expensive. You could use good-quality canned tuna as a cheaper alternative, if you prefer.

Pitta Bread ✳

Fresh, home-made pitta bread served warm from the oven makes the perfect accompaniment to a substantial salad. You could also serve with any Italian bread, such as foccacia or ciabatta, if you prefer.

Lemon Sorbet ✳

This tangy chilled dessert will cleanse the palate and makes the ideal end to a light summer supper. The simple ingredients are very cheap, and you can make it well in advance.

Casual entertaining

Entertaining on a budget needn't be a strain on your time or your wallet. Simply plan your menu in advance and choose simple yet stunning dishes that can easily be adapted according to the number of guests and the season.

Crème Fraîche and Coriander Chicken ✳✳

Succulent chicken thighs are used in this impressive dish, so it is inexpensive as well as being very easy to make.
Serve with fluffy rice or mashed potato

Fresh Fig Compote ✳✳✳

Simple yet stunning, this elegant dessert is sure to impress your guests. Serve with double cream or good-quality vanilla ice cream.

Finger buffet

The beauty of finger food is that you can do most of the preparation in advance, leaving you free to enjoy yourself.
It is a good idea to serve a wide range of dishes so that there is something for everyone.

Mushroom Caviar ✳

This impressive and tasty vegetarian caviar requires minimal preparation and tastes as amazing as it looks.

Hummus ✳

Creamy hummus is an ideal dip to accompany finger food, and it is sure to be popular so make sure that you make a lot!
Serve with raw vegetable crudités, such as celery, carrot and cucumber.

Focaccia

Home-made Italian bread tastes much better than store-bought varieties and requires just a little effort to make.

Courgette Fritters with Chilli Jam ✳

Fiery chilli jam complements the light and subtle flavour of the courgette (zucchini) fritters in this unusual dish.

Spicy Chickpea Samosas ✳✳

These light-as-air vegetarian samosas contain a simple yet delicious mixture of chickpeas, coriander (cilantro) and chilli oil,
and are sure to be popular, so make sure that you make enough.

Poppyseed Carrot Cake ✳

Slices of moist, tangy carrot cake spread with zesty mascarpone icing are the perfect way to end a finger buffet.
Just remember to have plenty of napkins to hand.

Family Barbecue

Simplicity and preparation are the key ingredients for a successful barbecue, so make sure that you have planned in advance – and hope for good weather.

Potato Skewers with Mustard Dip ✳

Sticky, sweet shallots are alternated with soft new potatoes and served with a tangy mustard dip in this delicious appetizer.

Barbecued Chicken ✳✳

Chicken pieces are marinated in a spicy lemon sauce before being cooked over the coals of a barbecue in this simple dish. Serve with warm pitta bread, lemon wedges and a mixed salad.

Oranges in Syrup ✳

Serve these sticky, sweet oranges chilled, accompanied by natural (plain) yogurt or vanilla ice cream.

Children's party

It is worth finding out about any food intolerances before you plan a menu for children. Keep the food simple and cut it into small pieces to avoid waste.

Potato, Onion and Broad Bean Tortilla ✳✳

Slice this simple broad (fava) bean and potato tortilla into child-friendly chunks. If the children are older than five, thread on to cocktail sticks (toothpicks).

Crab Cakes ✳

Ask your children to help you make these little crab cakes, which you can mould into a variety of shapes, such as fish or stars.

Turkey Patties ✳

Prepare these tasty patties in advance, so that you simply have to shallow fry them on the day of the party.

Oat Chocolate Chip Cookies ✳

These tasty little bites are sure to be popular, so make lots of little ones rather than several large ones. It may be a good idea to omit the pecan nuts if you are concerned about intolerances.

Victoria Sandwich Cake ✳

This simple classic makes an ideal birthday cake, as it is not too rich for young palates. You can use any flavour jam you like, and/or omit the cream, according to personal preference.

Sensational Soups

A STEAMING BOWL OF HEARTY SOUP IS THE ULTIMATE COMFORT FOOD ON A COLD DAY, AND IT MAKES THE IDEAL ALL-IN-ONE LIGHT MEAL AT OTHER TIMES OF THE YEAR TOO. SOUPS ARE AN EXCELLENT WAY TO TRANSFORM A GLUT OF SEASONAL INGREDIENTS INTO A DELICIOUS MEAL, AND THEY ARE INCREDIBLY VERSATILE. CHOOSE FROM ELEGANT CHILLED SOUPS, SUCH AS LEEK AND POTATO SOUP, OR EVERYDAY WARMERS, SUCH AS FRESH MUSHROOM SOUP WITH TARRAGON OR CURRIED CAULIFLOWER SOUP.

Leek and Potato Soup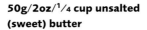

This classic, chilled summer soup is made from the simplest of ingredients and is very economical. Serve it garnished with fresh chives as an elegant appetizer to a special meal, or as a light lunch.

SERVES SIX

1 Melt the butter in a large, heavy pan. Add the leeks and shallots and cook gently, covered, for 15–20 minutes, until they are soft but not browned.

2 Add the potatoes and cook, uncovered, for a few minutes. Stir in the stock or water, 5ml/1 tsp salt and pepper to taste.

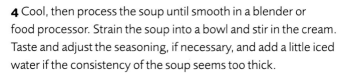

3 Bring to the boil, then reduce the heat and partly cover the pan. Simmer for 15 minutes, or until the potatoes are soft.

4 Cool, then process the soup until smooth in a blender or food processor. Strain the soup into a bowl and stir in the cream. Taste and adjust the seasoning, if necessary, and add a little iced water if the consistency of the soup seems too thick.

5 Chill the soup for at least 4 hours or until very cold. Taste the chilled soup for seasoning and add a squeeze of lemon juice, if required. Pour the soup into bowls and sprinkle with chopped chives. Serve immediately.

50g/2oz/¹⁄₄ cup unsalted (sweet) butter

450g/1lb leeks, white parts only, thinly sliced

3 large shallots, sliced

250g/9oz floury potatoes (such as King Edward or Idaho), peeled and cut into chunks

300ml/¹⁄₂ pint/1¹⁄₄ cups double (heavy) cream

iced water (optional)

a little lemon juice (optional)

chopped fresh chives, to garnish

FROM THE STORECUPBOARD

1 litre/1³⁄₄ pints/4 cups light chicken stock

salt and ground black pepper, to taste

VARIATIONS

• *For hot leek and potato soup, use 1 chopped onion instead of the shallots and 450g/1lb potatoes. Halve the quantity of double (heavy) cream and reheat the soup, adding milk if it seems too thick.*

• *To make chilled leek and sorrel soup, add about 50g/2oz/1 cup shredded sorrel at the end of cooking. Finish and chill as in the main recipe, then serve garnished with a little shredded sorrel.*

Energy 547Kcal/2260kJ; Protein 4.6g; Carbohydrate 17.7g, of which sugars 6.8g; Fat 51.4g, of which saturates 31.7g; Cholesterol 129mg; Calcium 79mg; Fibre 3.6g; Sodium 103mg

Avgolemono ✱

This is a great example of how a few ingredients can make a marvellous dish if carefully chosen and cooked. It is essential to use a well-flavoured stock. Add as little or as much rice as you like.

SERVES FOUR

1 Pour the chicken stock into a large pan, bring to simmering point, then add the drained rice.

2 Half cover the pan and cook for about 12 minutes until the rice is just tender. Season with salt and pepper to taste.

3 Whisk the egg yolks in a bowl, then add about 30ml/2 tbsp of the lemon juice, whisking constantly until the mixture is smooth and bubbly. Add a ladleful of soup and whisk again.

4 Remove the pan from the heat and slowly add the egg mixture to the soup, whisking all the time. The soup will turn a pretty lemon colour and will thicken slightly.

5 Taste the soup and add more lemon juice if necessary. Stir in the chopped parsley.

6 Serve at once, without reheating, garnished with lemon slices and parsley sprigs.

3 egg yolks

30–60ml/2–4 tbsp lemon juice

30ml/2 tbsp finely chopped fresh parsley

lemon slices and parsley sprigs, to garnish

FROM THE STORECUPBOARD

900ml/1 1/2 pints/3 3/4 cups chicken stock, preferably home-made

50g/2oz/generous 1/3 cup long grain rice

salt and ground black pepper, to taste

Energy 96Kcal/404kJ; Protein 3.3g; Carbohydrate 10.9g, of which sugars 0.2g; Fat 4.7g, of which saturates 1.2g; Cholesterol 151mg; Calcium 39mg; Fibre 0.4g; Sodium 10mg

Spiced Parsnip Soup ✳

This lightly spiced, creamy soup is perfect for a cold winter day. It is very easy and cheap to make, and is packed with flavour.

SERVES SIX

1 Peel and thinly slice the parsnips. Heat the butter in a large heavy pan and add the peeled parsnips and chopped onion with the crushed garlic.

2 Cook over a gently heat until the vegetables are softened but not coloured, stirring occasionally.

3 Add the ground cumin and ground coriander to the vegetable mixture and cook, stirring, for 1–2 minutes, and then gradually blend in the hot chicken stock and mix well.

4 Cover and simmer for about 20 minutes, or until the parsnip is soft. Remove from the heat and leave to cool slightly.

5 Purée the soup in a food processor or blender. Check the texture, and adjust with extra stock or water if it seems too thick.

6 Check the seasoning and adjust as required. Add the cream and reheat without boiling.

7 Serve immediately, sprinkled with chopped chives or parsley and/or croûtons, to garnish.

900g/2lb parsnips

50g/2oz/$^1/_4$ cup butter

1 onion, chopped

2 garlic cloves, crushed

150ml/$^1/_4$ pint/$^2/_3$ cup single (light) cream

chopped fresh chives and/or croûtons, to garnish

FROM THE STORECUPBOARD

10ml/2 tsp ground cumin

5ml/1 tsp ground coriander

about 1.2 litres/2 pints/ 5 cups hot chicken stock

salt and ground black pepper, to taste

Energy 215Kcal/899kJ; Protein 3.9g; Carbohydrate 21.3g, of which sugars 10.6g; Fat 13.3g, of which saturates 7.7g; Cholesterol 32mg; Calcium 92mg; Fibre 7.3g; Sodium 74mg

Curried Cauliflower Soup ✳

This simple yet delicious soup is perfect for lunch or as a light meal, served with warm, crusty bread and garnished with fresh coriander.

SERVES FOUR

1 Pour the milk into a large pan and place over a medium heat. Break or cut the cauliflower into florets and add to the milk with the garam masala and season with salt and pepper.

2 Bring the milk to the boil, then reduce the heat, partially cover the pan with a lid and simmer for about 20 minutes, or until the cauliflower is tender.

3 Let the mixture cool for a few minutes, then transfer to a food processor and process until smooth (you may have to do this in two separate batches).

4 Return the purée to the pan and heat through gently without boiling, checking and adjusting the seasoning to taste. Serve immediately, garnished with fresh coriander, if you like.

750ml/1¼ pints/3 cups full-fat (whole) milk

1 large cauliflower

15ml/1 tbsp garam masala

fresh coriander (cilantro) leaves, to garnish (optional)

FROM THE STORECUPBOARD

salt and ground black pepper, to taste

Energy 143Kcal/601kJ; Protein 12g; Carbohydrate 13.9g, of which sugars 12.6g; Fat 4.8g, of which saturates 2.3g; Cholesterol 11mg; Calcium 271mg; Fibre 3.2g; Sodium 104mg

Fresh Mushroom Soup with Tarragon ✳

The rich, earthy flavour of brown cap mushrooms in subtly enhanced with fresh tarragon to create a hearty and satisfying appetizer or lunch. Serve with bread and cold meats for a tasty light meal.

SERVES SIX

1 Finely chop the shallots. Melt the butter in a large pan, add the shallots and cook for 5 minutes, stirring occasionally.

2 Add the mushrooms and cook gently for 3 minutes, stirring, then the stock and milk. Bring to the boil, then cover the pan and simmer for about 20 minutes until the vegetables are soft.

3 Stir in the chopped tarragon and season to taste with salt and ground black pepper.

4 Allow the soup to cool slightly, then purée in a blender or food processor, in batches if necessary, until smooth. Return to the rinsed-out pan and reheat gently.

5 Ladle the soup into warmed soup bowls and serve garnished with sprigs of tarragon.

15g/¹⁄₂oz/1 tbsp butter

4 shallots, finely chopped

450g/1lb/6 cups brown cap (cremini) mushrooms, finely chopped

300ml/¹⁄₂ pint/1¹⁄₄ cups semi-skimmed (low-fat) milk

15–30 ml/1–2 tbsp chopped fresh tarragon

sprigs of fresh tarragon, to garnish

FROM THE STORECUPBOARD

300ml/¹⁄₂ pint/1¹⁄₄ cups vegetable stock

salt and ground black pepper, to taste

VARIATION *Depending on what is available, you can use a mixture of wild and button (white) mushrooms rather than just brown cap (cremini) mushrooms.*

COOK'S TIP *Brown cap (cremini) mushrooms have a more robust flavour than cultivated mushrooms, such as button (white), cap and flat mushrooms. Field (portabello) mushrooms are similar in appearance to cultivated flat mushrooms, but they are simply large brown cap mushrooms.*

Energy 58kcal/242kJ; Protein 3.4g; Carbohydrate 3.7g, of which sugars 3.3g; Fat 3.4g, of which saturates 1.9g; Cholesterol 8mg; Calcium 84mg; Fibre 1.4g; Sodium 44mg

Potato Soup ✳

This incredibly economical soup is not only excellent as it is, but it is very versatile too, as it can be used as a base for numerous other soups. Use a floury potato, such as Golden Wonder or russet.

SERVES EIGHT

1 Melt the butter in a large heavy pan and add the onions, turning them in the butter until well coated. Cover and leave to cook over a very low heat for about 10 mintues.

2 Add the potatoes to the pan, and mix well with the butter and onions. Season with salt and pepper to taste, cover and cook without colouring over a gentle heat for about 10 minutes.

3 Add most of the stock, bring to the boil and simmer for 25 minutes, or until the vegetables are tender.

4 Remove from the heat and allow to cool slightly. Purée the soup in batches in a blender or food processor.

5 Reheat over a low heat and adjust the seasoning. If it seems too thick, add extra stock to achieve the right consistency.

6 Serve the soup very hot with warm rustic bread, such as soda bread, sprinkled with chopped chives.

50g/2oz/¹⁄₄ cup butter

2 large onions, peeled and finely chopped

675g/1¹⁄₄lb potatoes, peeled and diced

a little milk, if necessary

chopped fresh chives, to garnish

FROM THE STORECUPBOARD

about 1.75 litres/ 3 pints/7¹⁄₂ cups hot chicken stock

salt and ground black pepper, to taste

Energy 167Kcal/699kJ; Protein 2.9g; Carbohydrate 23.5g, of which sugars 5.3g; Fat 7.5g, of which saturates 4.5g; Cholesterol 18mg; Calcium 26mg; Fibre 2.1g; Sodium 201mg

Carrot and Orange Soup **

This traditional light and summery soup is always popular for its wonderfully creamy consistency and vibrantly fresh citrus flavour. Use a good, home-made chicken or vegetable stock if you can.

SERVES FOUR

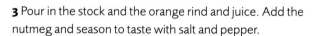

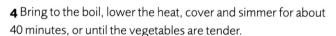

1 Melt the butter in a large pan. Add the leeks and carrots and stir well, coating the vegetables with the butter.

2 Cover and cook for about 10 minutes, until the vegetables are beginning to soften but not colour.

3 Pour in the stock and the orange rind and juice. Add the nutmeg and season to taste with salt and pepper.

4 Bring to the boil, lower the heat, cover and simmer for about 40 minutes, or until the vegetables are tender.

5 Leave to cool slightly, then purée the soup in a food processor or blender until smooth.

6 Return the soup to the pan and add 30ml/2 tbsp of the yogurt, then taste the soup and adjust the seasoning, if necessary. Reheat gently.

7 Ladle the soup into warm individual bowls and put a swirl of yogurt in the centre of each. Sprinkle the fresh sprigs of coriander over each bowl to garnish, and serve immediately.

50g/2oz/^{1}/$_4$ cup butter

3 leeks, sliced

450g/1lb carrots, sliced

rind and juice of 2 oranges

150ml/^{1}/$_4$ pint/^{2}/$_3$ cup Greek (US strained plain) yogurt

fresh sprigs of coriander (cilantro), to garnish

FROM THE STORECUPBOARD

1.2 litres/2 pints/5 cups chicken or vegetable stock

2.5ml/^{1}/$_2$ tsp freshly grated nutmeg

salt and ground black pepper, to taste

Energy 206Kcal/856kJ; Protein 5g; Carbohydrate 15.8g, of which sugars 14.2g; Fat 14.4g, of which saturates 8.3g; Cholesterol 27mg; Calcium 111mg; Fibre 5.8g; Sodium 131mg

Summer Minestrone **

This brightly coloured, fresh-tasting soup makes the most of delicious summer vegetables and fresh basil and is a meal in itself.

SERVES FOUR

1 large onion, finely chopped

450g/1lb ripe Italian plum tomatoes, peeled and finely chopped

225g/8oz green courgettes (zucchini), trimmed and roughly chopped

225g/8oz yellow courgettes, trimmed and roughly chopped

3 waxy new potatoes, washed and diced

2 garlic cloves, crushed

60ml/4 tbsp shredded fresh basil

50g/2oz/²/₃ cup grated grano padano cheese

FROM THE STORECUPBOARD

45ml/3 tbsp olive oil

15ml/1 tbsp sun-dried tomato purée (paste)

about 1.2 litres/2 pints/ 5 cups vegetable stock or water

salt and ground black pepper, to taste

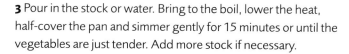

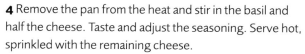

1 Heat the oil in a large, heavy pan, add the onion and cook gently for about 5 minutes, stirring constantly, until softened but not browned.

2 Stir in the sun-dried tomato purée, chopped tomatoes, courgettes, diced potatoes and garlic. Mix well and cook gently for 10 minutes, uncovered, shaking the pan frequently to stop the vegetables sticking to the base.

3 Pour in the stock or water. Bring to the boil, lower the heat, half-cover the pan and simmer gently for 15 minutes or until the vegetables are just tender. Add more stock if necessary.

4 Remove the pan from the heat and stir in the basil and half the cheese. Taste and adjust the seasoning. Serve hot, sprinkled with the remaining cheese.

COOK'S TIP
Grano padano cheese is similar in taste and texture to Parmesan cheese, although it has a slightly milder taste. It is usually considerably cheaper than Parmesan, and makes an economical alternative.

Energy 254kcal/1059kJ; Protein 10.2g; Carbohydrate 24.3g, of which sugars 11.1g; Fat 13.5g, of which saturates 4.1g; Cholesterol 13mg; Calcium 211mg; Fibre 4.1g; Sodium 167mg

Cappelletti in Broth ✴

This simple broth contains cappelletti, which are little stuffed pasta shapes that resemble hats. If you are unable to find capelleti, you could use stuffed tortellini or any dried pasta shapes, such as fusilli, penne, conchiglione or orechiette, depending on your personal preference.

SERVES FOUR

1 Pour the chicken stock into a large pan and bring to the boil. Add a little seasoning to taste, then drop in the pasta.

2 Stir well and bring back to the boil. Lower the heat to a simmer and cook according to the instructions on the packet, until the pasta is *al dente*, that is, tender but still firm to the bite.

3 Swirl in the finely chopped fresh flat leaf parsley, if using, then taste and adjust the seasoning, if necessary.

4 Ladle the broth into four warmed soup plates, then sprinkle with the freshly grated grano padano cheese and serve immediately with crusty bread.

45ml/3 tbsp chopped fresh flat leaf parsley (optional)

30ml/2 tbsp grated grano padano cheese

crusty bread, to serve

FROM THE STORECUPBOARD

1.2 litres/2 pints/ 5 cups chicken stock

salt and ground black pepper, to taste

90–115g/3^1/$_2$–4oz/1 cup fresh or dried cappelletti

Tiny Pasta in Broth ✴

This Italian soup is ideal for a light supper served with ciabatta bread and also makes a delicious first course for an *al fresco* supper. A wide variety of different types of *pastina* or soup pasta are available including stellette (stars), anellini (tiny thin rounds), risoni (rice-shaped) and farfalline (little butterflies). Choose just one shape or a combination of different varieties for an interesting result.

SERVES FOUR

2 pieces bottled roasted red (bell) pepper

shaved Parmesan cheese

FROM THE STORECUPBOARD

1.2 litres/2 pints/ 5 cups beef stock

75g/3oz/^{3}/$_4$ cup dried tiny soup pasta

salt and ground black pepper, to taste

1 Bring the beef stock to the boil in a large pan. Add seasoning to taste, then drop in the dried soup pasta. Stir well and bring the stock back to the boil.

2 Reduce the heat so that the soup simmers and cook for 7–8 minutes, or according to the packet instructions, until the pasta is tender but still firm to the bite.

3 Drain the pieces of roasted pepper and dice them finely. Place them in the base of four warmed soup plates.

4 Taste the soup for seasoning and adjust if necessary, then ladle it into the soup plates. Serve immediately, topped with shavings of Parmesan.

Top: Energy 111kcal/469kJ; Protein 5.9g; Carbohydrate 16.7g, of which sugars 0.8g; Fat 3g, of which saturates 1.6g; Cholesterol 8mg; Calcium 96mg; Fibre 0.7g; Sodium 265mg

Above: Energy 135kcal/567kJ; Protein 7.8g; Carbohydrate 16.7g, of which sugars 3.3g; Fat 4.7g, of which saturates 2.7g; Cholesterol 13mg; Calcium 159mg; Fibre 1.3g; Sodium 321mg

Chunky Tomato Soup with Noodles ✳✳✳

This full-flavoured Moroccan soup is given a warming kick by the ras el hanout, a spicy paste that you can buy in most supermarkets.

SERVES FOUR

2 onions, chopped

1 butternut squash, peeled, seeded and cut into small chunks

4 celery stalks, chopped

2 carrots, peeled and chopped

8 large, ripe tomatoes, skinned and roughly chopped

5–10ml/1–2 tsp store-bought ras el hanout

a big bunch of fresh coriander (cilantro), chopped (reserve a few sprigs for garnish)

60–75ml/4–5 tbsp creamy yogurt, to serve

FROM THE STORECUPBOARD

45–60ml/3–4 tbsp olive oil

3–4 cloves

5–10ml/1–2 tsp sugar

15ml/1 tbsp tomato purée (paste)

2.5ml/$^1/_2$ tsp ground turmeric

1.75 litres/3 pints/ 7$^1/_2$ cups vegetable stock

a handful dried egg noodles or capellini, broken into pieces

salt and ground black pepper, to taste

1 In a deep, heavy pan, heat the oil and add the cloves, onions, squash, celery and carrots. Fry until they begin to colour, then stir in the tomatoes and sugar. Cook the tomatoes until the water reduces and they begin to pulp.

2 Stir in the tomato purée, ras el hanout, turmeric and chopped coriander. Pour in the stock and bring to the boil. Reduce the heat and simmer for 30–40 minutes, until the vegetables are tender and the liquid has reduced a little.

3 To make a puréed soup, leave the liquid to cool slightly before processing in a food processor or blender, then pour back into the pan and add the pasta. Alternatively, to make a chunky soup, simply add the pasta to the unblended soup and cook for a further 8–10 minutes, or until the pasta is soft.

4 Season the soup to taste and ladle it into bowls. Spoon a swirl of yogurt into each one, garnish with the extra coriander and serve with freshly baked bread.

Energy 258kcal/1086kJ; Protein 7.6g; Carbohydrate 36.3g, of which sugars 18.3g; Fat 10.2g, of which saturates 1.7g; Cholesterol 0mg; Calcium 175mg; Fibre 6.9g; Sodium 72mg

Tuscan Cannellini Bean Soup with Cavolo Nero ✳

Cavolo nero is a very dark green cabbage with a nutty flavour that is available during the winter months. It is ideal for this Italian recipe, which is packed with flavour as well as being healthy and sustaining.

SERVES FOUR

250g/9oz cavolo nero leaves, or Savoy cabbage

FROM THE STORECUPBOARD

2 x 400g/14oz cans chopped tomatoes with herbs

400g/14oz can cannellini beans, drained and rinsed

60ml/4 tbsp extra virgin olive oil

salt and ground black pepper, to taste

1 Pour the tomatoes into a large pan and add a can of cold water. Season with salt and pepper to taste and bring to the boil, then reduce the heat to a simmer.

2 Roughly shred the cabbage leaves and add them to the pan. Partially cover the pan and simmer gently for about 15 minutes, or until the cabbage is tender.

3 Add the cannellini beans to the pan and warm through over a gentle heat for a few minutes.

4 Check and adjust the seasoning, then ladle the soup into bowls, drizzle each one with a little olive oil and serve.

Energy 227Kcal/950kJ; Protein 8.2g; Carbohydrate 22.3g, of which sugars 10.4g; Fat 12.2g, of which saturates 1.9g; Cholesterol 0mg; Calcium 60mg; Fibre 7.9g; Sodium 443mg

Chickpea Soup ✳

This nutritious soup is enjoyable in any season, even during the hot summer months. Compared to other soups based on beans, peas and lentils, which are often very hearty, this has a unique lightness in terms of both flavour and texture. It can be enjoyed as an appetizer, or can be a delicious healthy main meal when served with fresh bread and feta cheese.

SERVES FOUR

1 Heat the extra virgin olive oil in a heavy pan, add the onion and cook gently until it starts to colour.

2 Meanwhile, drain the chickpeas, rinse them under cold water and drain them thoroughly again. Add to the pan, coat them well in the oil, then pour in enough hot water to cover them by about 4cm/1^1/$_2$in. Slowly bring to the boil. Skim off and discard any white froth that rises to the surface. Lower the heat, add some freshly ground black pepper, cover and cook for 1–1^1/$_4$ hours, or until the chickpeas are soft.

3 Combine the flour and lemon juice. When the chickpeas are soft, add this mixture to them. Mix, then add seasoning to taste. Cover and cook for 5–10 minutes more, stirring occasionally.

4 To thicken the soup, take out about two cupfuls of the chickpeas and put them in a food processor or blender. Process briefly so that the chickpeas are broken up, then stir into the soup.

5 Add the parsley, then taste the soup and add more lemon juice if bland. Serve in heated bowls with a drizzle of olive oil on top.

1 large onion, chopped

juice of 1 lemon, or to taste

45ml/3 tbsp chopped fresh flat leaf parsley

FROM THE STORECUPBOARD

150ml/^{1}/$_4$ pint/^{2}/$_3$ cup extra virgin olive oil, plus extra for drizzling and serving

350g/12oz/1^3/$_4$ cups dried chickpeas, soaked in cold water overnight

15ml/1 tbsp plain (all-purpose) flour

salt and ground black pepper, to taste

Energy 544Kcal/2,274kJ; Protein 20.1g; Carbohydrate 51.6g, of which sugars 6.1g; Fat 30g, of which saturates 4g; Cholesterol 0mg; Calcium 184mg; Fibre 10.9g; Sodium 40mg

Lentil Soup ✳

Lentils do not need soaking, so they make an easy option for a quick meal. The secret of good lentil soup is to be generous with the olive oil. The soup can be served as a substantial appetizer, or as a warming lunch dish when accompanied by plenty of fresh bread.

SERVES SIX–EIGHT

1 Rinse the brown-green lentils thoroughly, drain them and put them in a large pan with cold water to cover.

2 Bring the water to the boil and boil for 3–4 minutes. Strain, discarding the liquid, and set the lentils aside.

3 Wipe the pan clean and add the extra virgin olive oil. Place it over a medium heat until hot and then add the thinly sliced onion and sauté until translucent.

4 Stir in the sliced garlic, then, as soon as it becomes aromatic, return the lentils to the pan.

5 Add the carrot, tomatoes, tomato purée and oregano. Stir in the hot water and a little ground black pepper to taste.

6 Bring the soup to the boil, then lower the heat, cover the pan and cook gently for 20–30 minutes, until the lentils feel soft but have not begun to disintegrate.

7 Add salt, if required, and the chopped herbs before serving.

1 onion, thinly sliced

2 garlic cloves, sliced into thin matchsticks

1 carrot, sliced into thin discs

1 litre/1³/₄ pints/4 cups hot water

30ml/2 tbsp roughly chopped fresh herb leaves, to garnish

FROM THE STORECUPBOARD

275g/10oz/1¹/₄ cups brown-green lentils, preferably the small variety

150ml/¹/₄ pint/²/₃ cup extra virgin olive oil

400g/14oz can chopped tomatoes

15ml/1 tbsp tomato purée (paste)

2.5ml/¹/₂ tsp dried oregano

salt and ground black pepper, to taste

Energy 462Kcal/1,935kJ; Protein 18.4g; Carbohydrate 40g, of which sugars 6.6g; Fat 26.6g, of which saturates 3.7g; Cholesterol 0mg; Calcium 86mg; Fibre 8g; Sodium 64mg

Smoked Mackerel and Tomato Soup ✳✳

All the ingredients for this unusual soup are cooked in a single pan, so it is not only quick and easy to prepare, but requires minimal clearing up.

SERVES FOUR

200g/7oz smoked mackerel fillets

4 tomatoes

1 lemon grass stalk, finely chopped

5cm/2in piece fresh galangal, finely diced

4 shallots, finely chopped

2 garlic cloves, finely chopped

45ml/3 tbsp thick tamarind juice, made by mixing tamarind paste with warm water

small bunch of fresh chives or spring onions (scallions), to garnish

FROM THE STORECUPBOARD

1 litre/1³/₄ pints/4 cups vegetable stock

2.5ml/¹/₂ tsp dried chilli flakes

15ml/1 tbsp Thai fish sauce

5ml/1 tsp light muscovado (brown) sugar

1 Prepare the smoked mackerel fillets. Remove and discard the skin, if necessary, then chop the flesh into large pieces. Remove any stray bones with your fingers or a pair of tweezers.

2 Cut the tomatoes in half, squeeze out most of the seeds with your fingers, then finely dice the flesh with a sharp knife. Set aside until required.

3 Pour the stock into a large pan and add the lemon grass, galangal, shallots and garlic. Bring to the boil, reduce the heat and simmer for 15 minutes.

4 Add the fish, tomatoes, chilli flakes, fish sauce, muscovado sugar and tamarind juice. Simmer for 4–5 minutes, until the fish and tomatoes are heated through.

5 Serve immediately, garnished with chives or spring onions, with some plain boiled noodles for a more substantial meal.

VARIATION *For a spicier soup, you could use smoked peppered mackerel fillets. These are usually available in many large supermarkets, and add a delicious peppery flavour.*

Energy 203Kcal/845kJ; Protein 10.3g; Carbohydrate 5.3g, of which sugars 5g; Fat 15.8g, of which saturates 3.3g; Cholesterol 53mg; Calcium 21mg; Fibre 1.2g; Sodium 385mg

Crab, Coconut, Chilli and Coriander Soup ✳✳✳

Although fresh crab meat has a better flavour, you can use canned crab meat in this sensational soup to keep the cost down.

SERVES FOUR

1 Heat the olive oil in a pan over a low heat. Stir in the chopped onion and celery, and sauté gently for 5 minutes, until the onion is soft and translucent.

2 Add the garlic and chilli, mix to combine well, and cook for a further 2 minutes.

3 Add the tomato and half the coriander and increase the heat. Cook, stirring, for 3 minutes, then add the stock. Bring to the boil, then simmer for 5 minutes.

4 Stir the crab, coconut milk and palm oil into the pan and simmer over a very low heat for a further 5 minutes. The consistency should be thick, but not stew-like, so add some water if needed.

5 Stir in the lime juice and remaining coriander, then season with salt to taste. Serve in heated bowls with the chilli oil and lime wedges on the side.

1 onion, finely chopped

1 celery stick, chopped

2 garlic cloves, crushed

1 fresh red chilli, seeded and chopped

1 large tomato, peeled and chopped

45ml/3 tbsp chopped fresh coriander (cilantro)

500g/1¼lb crab meat

250ml/8fl oz/1 cup coconut milk

30ml/2 tbsp palm oil

juice of 1 lime

hot chilli oil and lime wedges, to serve

FROM THE STORECUPBOARD

30ml/2 tbsp olive oil

1 litre/1³/₄ pints/4 cups fresh crab or fish stock

salt

Energy 228kcal/951kJ; Protein 23.6g; Carbohydrate 5.4g, of which sugars 5g; Fat 12.6g, of which saturates 3.7g; Cholesterol 90mg; Calcium 199mg; Fibre 1.1g; Sodium 767mg

Chicken, Leek and Celery Soup ✳✳

This makes a substantial main course soup in winter, served with fresh crusty bread. You will need nothing more than a mixed green salad or fresh winter fruit to follow, such as satsumas or tangerines.

SERVE FOUR TO SIX

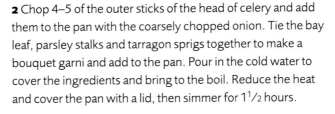

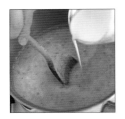

1 Cut the breasts off the chicken and set aside. Chop the rest of the chicken carcass into 8–10 pieces and place them in a large pan or stockpot.

2 Chop 4–5 of the outer sticks of the head of celery and add them to the pan with the coarsely chopped onion. Tie the bay leaf, parsley stalks and tarragon sprigs together to make a bouquet garni and add to the pan. Pour in the cold water to cover the ingredients and bring to the boil. Reduce the heat and cover the pan with a lid, then simmer for 1¹/₂ hours.

3 Remove the chicken from the pan using a slotted spoon and cut off and reserve the meat.

4 Strain the stock through a sieve (strainer), then return it to the cleaned pan and boil rapidly until it has reduced in volume to about 1.5 litres/2¹/₂ pints/6¹/₄ cups.

5 Meanwhile, set about 150g/5oz of the leeks aside. Slice the remaining leeks and the remaining celery, reserving any celery leaves. Chop the celery leaves and set them aside to garnish the soup, or reserve a few of the leek pieces.

6 Heat half the oil in a large, heavy pan. Add the sliced leeks and celery, cover and cook over a low heat for about 10 minutes, or until the vegetables are softened but not browned. Add the potatoes, wine and 1.2 litres/2 pints/5 cups of the stock.

7 Season with a little salt and plenty of black pepper, bring to the boil and reduce the heat. Part-cover the pan and simmer the soup for 15–20 minutes, or until the potatoes are cooked.

8 Check and adjust the seasoning as required, bring to the boil and reduce the heat. Part-cover the pan and simmer the soup for 15–20 minutes, or until the potatoes are cooked.

9 Thickly slice the reserved leeks, add to the frying pan and cook, stirring occasionally, for a further 3–4 minutes until they are just cooked.

10 Stir in the cream, if using, and the chicken and leek mixture. Reheat the soup gently.

11 Serve in warmed bowls. Crumble the pancetta over the soup and sprinkle with the celery leaves or reserved leek slices.

1.3kg/3lb chicken

1 small head of celery, trimmed

1 onion, coarsely chopped

1 fresh bay leaf

a few fresh parsley stalks

a few fresh tarragon sprigs

2.5 litres/4 pints/10 cups cold water

3 large leeks

2 potatoes, cut into chunks

150ml/¹/₄ pint/²/₃ cup dry white wine

30–45ml/2–3 tbsp single (light) cream

90g/3¹/₂oz pancetta, grilled until crisp, to garnish

FROM THE STORECUPBOARD

75ml/5 tbsp olive oil

salt and ground black pepper, to taste

VARIATIONS

• *If you prefer, you can use ready-cut chicken portions instead of jointing a whole chicken, although this may bump the cost up.*

• *Streaky (fatty) bacon can be used instead of pancetta to add a delicious flavour to the soup.*

Energy 253kcal/1056kJ; Protein 16.5g; Carbohydrate 10.3g, of which sugars 2.4g; Fat 14.7g, of which saturates 3.4g; Cholesterol 48mg; Calcium 31mg; Fibre 2g; Sodium 231mg

Moroccan Harira ✳✳

A cheaper cut of lamb, such as scrag end, middle neck or knuckle, would be ideal for this substantial meat and vegetable soup, which is a meal in itself.

SERVES FOUR

25g/1oz/2 tbsp butter

225g/8oz lamb, cut into 1cm/¹⁄₂in pieces

1 onion, chopped

450g/1lb tomatoes

60ml/4 tbsp chopped fresh coriander (cilantro)

30ml/2 tbsp chopped fresh parsley

600ml/1 pint/2¹⁄₂ cups cold water

4 baby onions or small shallots, peeled

FOR THE GARNISH

chopped fresh coriander (cilantro)

lemon slices

ground cinnamon

FROM THE STORECUPBOARD

2.5ml/1/2 tsp ground turmeric

2.5ml/¹⁄₂ tsp ground cinnamon

50g/2oz/¹⁄₄ cup red lentils

75g/3oz/¹⁄₂ cup chickpeas, soaked overnight

25g/1oz/¹⁄₄ cup soup noodles

salt and ground black pepper, to taste

1 Heat the butter in a large pan or flameproof casserole and fry the lamb and onion for 5 minutes, stirring frequently.

2 Peel the tomatoes, if you wish, by plunging them into boiling water to loosen the skins. Wait for them to cool a little before peeling off the skins. Then cut them into quarters and add to the lamb with the herbs and spices.

3 Place the lentils in a sieve (strainer) and rinse under cold running water, then drain the chickpeas. Add both to the pan with the water. Season with salt and pepper to taste. Bring to the boil, cover and simmer gently for 1¹⁄₂ hours.

4 Add the baby onions or small shallots and cook for a further 30 minutes. Add the noodles 5 minutes before the end of the cooking time.

5 Serve the soup when the noodles are tender, garnished with the coriander, lemon slices and cinnamon.

COOK'S TIP

This nourishing soup is traditionally eaten in the evening during the month of Ramadan, when the Muslim population fasts between sunset and sunrise. It is packed with goodness and is an ideal main-course dish.

Energy 303kcal/1271kJ; Protein 19.8g; Carbohydrate 27.6g, of which sugars 6.2g; Fat 13.2g, of which saturates 6.4g; Cholesterol 56mg; Calcium 78mg; Fibre 4.7g; Sodium 113mg

Kale, Chorizo and Potato Soup ✳✳

This hearty, warming winter soup has a spicy kick to it, which comes from the chorizo sausage, and it is a meal in itself. The spicy flavour becomes more potent if the soup is chilled overnight.

SERVES EIGHT

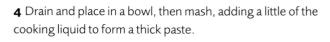

1 Place the kale in a food processor and process for a few seconds to chop it finely.

2 Prick the sausages and place in a pan with enough water to cover. Simmer for 15 minutes. Drain and cut into thin slices.

3 Cook the potatoes in a pan boiling water for about 15 minutes or until tender.

4 Drain and place in a bowl, then mash, adding a little of the cooking liquid to form a thick paste.

5 Bring the vegetable stock to the boil and add the kale. Add the chorizo and simmer for 5 minutes.

6 Add the mashed potato gradually, and simmer for 20 minutes. Season with black and cayenne pepper to taste.

7 Place bread slices in each bowl, and pour over the soup. Serve, generously sprinkled with pepper.

225g/8oz kale, stems removed

225g/8oz chorizo sausage

675g/1¹/₂lb red potatoes

12 slices French bread, grilled

FROM THE STORECUPBOARD

1.75 litres/3 pints/ 7¹/₂ cups vegetable stock

pinch cayenne pepper (optional)

salt and ground black pepper, to taste

Energy 290kcal/1228kJ; Protein 11.6g; Carbohydrate 49.3g, of which sugars 3.4g; Fat 6.5g, of which saturates 1.8g; Cholesterol 32mg; Calcium 120mg; Fibre 3.4g; Sodium 619mg

First Courses and Finger Food

IT IS ALWAYS A TREAT TO HAVE A FIRST COURSE TO
WHET THE APPETITE, AND THERE ARE A WIDE RANGE
OF DELICIOUS, ECONOMICAL RECIPES SUITABLE FOR
EVERY OCCASION, WHETHER YOU ARE PLANNING
A SUSTAINING FAMILY MEAL, AN INFORMAL GATHERING
OR AN ELEGANT DINNER PARTY. CHOOSE FROM
EASY-TO-MAKE DIPS, SUCH AS HUMMUS, OR
FOR SOMETHING MORE SUBSTANTIAL, TRY CRAB
CAKES, SPICY CHICKPEA SAMOSAS OR BAKED
EGGS WITH CREAMY LEEKS.

Chicken Liver and Brandy Pâté ∗

This pâté really could not be simpler to make, and tastes so much better than anything you can buy ready-made in the supermarkets. Serve with crispy toast for an elegant appetizer.

SERVES FOUR

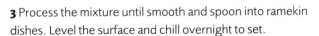

1 Heat the butter in a large frying pan until it is foamy. Add the chopped chicken livers and cook them over a medium heat for 3–4 minutes, or until they are browned and cooked through.

2 Add the brandy and allow it to bubble for a few minutes. Remove the pan from the heat, allow the mixture to cool slightly, then tip it into a food processor with the cream and some salt and pepper to taste.

3 Process the mixture until smooth and spoon into ramekin dishes. Level the surface and chill overnight to set.

4 Serve garnished with sprigs of parsley to add a little colour, and some lightly toasted bread.

50g/2oz/¹⁄₄ cup butter

350g/12oz chicken livers, trimmed and roughly chopped

30ml/2 tbsp brandy

30ml/2 tbsp double (heavy) cream

FROM THE STORECUPBOARD

salt and ground black pepper, to taste

Energy 227kcal/942kJ; Protein 15.7g; Carbohydrate 0.2g, of which sugars 0.2g; Fat 16.3g, of which saturates 9.6g; Cholesterol 369mg; Calcium 13mg; Fibre 0g; Sodium 144mg

Mushroom Caviar ✳

The name caviar refers to the dark colour and texture of this dish of chopped mushrooms. Serve with toasted rye bread, and garnish with chopped hard-boiled egg, spring onion and parsley, if you like.

SERVES FOUR

1 Heat the oil in a large pan, add the chopped mushrooms, shallots and garlic, and cook gently for about 5 minutes, stirring occasionally, until browned.

2 Season the mixture with salt and pepper to taste, then continue cooking until the mushrooms give up their liquor.

3 Continue cooking, stirring frequently, until the liquor has evaporated and the mushrooms are brown and dry.

4 Leave the mixture to cool slightly, then scrape it in to a food processor or blender and process briefly until a chunky paste is formed.

5 Spoon the mushroom caviar into dishes and serve with plenty of toasted bread.

450g/1lb mushrooms, coarsely chopped

5–10 shallots, chopped

4 garlic cloves, chopped

FROM THE STORECUPBOARD

45ml/3 tbsp olive or vegetable oil

salt and ground black pepper, to taste

COOK'S TIP *For a rich wild mushroom caviar, soak 10–15g/ ¼–½oz dried porcini in about 120ml/4fl oz/ ½ cup water for about 30 minutes. Add the porcini and their soaking liquid to the browned mushrooms in step 2. Continue as in the recipe.*

Energy 116kcal/479kJ; Protein 2.9g; Carbohydrate 6.4g, of which sugars 4.4g; Fat 9g, of which saturates 1.3g; Cholesterol 0mg; Calcium 26mg; Fibre 2.3g; Sodium 8mg

Baba Ganoush with Flatbread ✳✳

Baba Ganoush is a delectable aubergine dip from the Middle East. It makes a very good appetizer served with raw vegetable crudités or bread for a party, or serve it at a barbecue as a side dish.

SERVES SIX

1 Start by making the Lebanese flatbread. Split the pitta breads through the middle and carefully open them out. Mix the sesame seeds, chopped thyme and poppy seeds in a mortar. Work them lightly with a pestle to release the flavour.

2 Stir in 150ml/$^1/_4$ pint/$^2/_3$ cup olive oil. Spread the mixture over the cut sides of the pitta bread. Grill (broil) until golden brown and crisp. When cool, break into pieces and set aside.

3 Grill the aubergines, turning them frequently, until the skin is blackened and blistered. Remove the peel, chop the flesh roughly and leave to drain in a colander.

4 Squeeze out as much liquid from the aubergine as possible. Place the flesh in a blender or food processor, then add the garlic, tahini, ground almonds, lemon juice and cumin, with salt to taste. Process to a smooth paste, then roughly chop half the mint and stir into the dip.

5 Spoon the paste into a bowl, scatter the remaining mint leaves on top and drizzle with the remaining olive oil. Serve with the Lebanese flatbread.

2 small aubergines (eggplants)

1 garlic clove, crushed

60ml/4 tbsp tahini

25g/1oz/$^1/_4$ cup ground almonds

juice of $^1/_2$ lemon

30ml/2 tbsp fresh mint leaves

FOR THE FLATBREAD

4 pitta breads

45ml/3 tbsp sesame seeds

45ml/3 tbsp fresh thyme leaves

45ml/3 tbsp poppy seeds

FROM THE STORECUPBOARD

175ml/6fl oz/$^3/_4$ cup olive oil

2.5ml/$^1/_2$ tsp ground cumin

salt, to taste

COOK'S TIPS
• *Tahini is a paste that is made from sesame seeds, cumin and sesame oil. It is used in many Middle Eastern recipes, including hummus and tahini yogurt dip, so it is a useful ingredient to have to hand.*

• *Run the prongs of a fork down the woody stem to remove the leaves from fresh thyme.*

Energy 129Kcal/535kJ; Protein 3.3g; Carbohydrate 1.9g, of which sugars 1.6g; Fat 12.2g, of which saturates 1.6g; Cholesterol 0mg; Calcium 85mg; Fibre 2.5g; Sodium 4mg

Hummus ✳

Blending chickpeas with garlic and oil creates a surprisingly creamy purée that is delicious as part of a Turkish-style mezze, or as a dip with bread and cherry tomatoes. Leftovers make a good sandwich filler.

SERVES FOUR TO SIX

juice of 2 lemons

2 garlic cloves, sliced

150ml/¼ pint/⅔ cup tahini paste

flat leaf parsley sprigs, to garnish

FROM THE STORECUPBOARD

150g/5oz/¾ cup dried chickpeas

30ml/2 tbsp olive oil

pinch of cayenne pepper

salt and ground black pepper, to taste

extra olive oil and cayenne pepper, for sprinkling

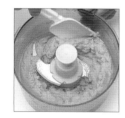

1 Put the chickpeas in a large bowl with plenty of cold water and leave them to soak overnight.

2 Thoroughly rinse and drain the chickpeas, then place them in a large pan and cover with fresh water. Bring to the boil and boil rapidly for 10 minutes. Reduce the heat and simmer gently for 1¼–2 hours until soft.

3 Drain the chickpeas in a colander, then purée in a food processor until they form a smooth paste.

4 Add the lemon juice, garlic, olive oil, cayenne pepper and tahini paste and blend until creamy, scraping the mixture down from the sides of the bowl.

5 Season the purée with plenty of salt and ground black pepper and transfer to a serving dish.

6 Sprinkle with a little olive oil and cayenne pepper, and garnish with a few parsley sprigs. Serve with pitta bread and cherry tomatoes, if you like.

Energy 453Kcal/1887kJ; Protein 15.7g; Carbohydrate 32.1g, of which sugars 13.8g; Fat 30g, of which saturates 4.2g; Cholesterol 0mg; Calcium 345mg; Fibre 10.5g; Sodium 49mg

Falafel with Tahini Dip ✳

Sesame seeds are used to give a delightfully crunchy coating to these spicy chickpea patties. Serve them with the tahini yogurt dip, and some warmed pitta bread for a delicious appetizer or warming snack.

SERVES SIX

1 Place the chickpeas in a large bowl, cover with cold water and leave to soak overnight.

2 Drain and rinse the chickpeas, then place them in a large pan and cover with cold water. Bring to the boil and boil rapidly for 10 minutes. Reduce the heat and simmer for 1¹/₄–2 hours until the chickpeas are tender.

3 Meanwhile, make the tahini yogurt dip. Mix together the tahini, yogurt, cayenne pepper and mint in a small bowl. Sprinkle the spring onion and extra cayenne pepper on top and chill in the refrigerator until required.

4 Combine the chickpeas with the garlic, chilli, ground spices, herbs, spring onions and seasoning, then mix in the egg. Place in a food processor and blend until the mixture forms a coarse paste. If the paste seems too soft, chill it for 30 minutes.

5 Form the chilled chick-pea paste into 12 patties with your hands, then roll each one in the sesame seeds to coat evenly.

6 Heat enough oil to cover the base of a large frying pan. Fry the falafel, in batches if necessary, for 6 minutes, turning once. Serve with the tahini yogurt dip garnished with fresh herbs.

2 garlic cloves, crushed

1 fresh red chilli, seeded and finely sliced

15ml/1 tbsp chopped fresh mint

15ml/1 tbsp chopped fresh parsley

2 spring onions (scallions), finely chopped

1 large egg, beaten

sesame seeds, for coating

FOR THE TAHINI YOGURT DIP

30ml/2 tbsp light tahini

200g/7oz/scant 1 cup natural (plain) yogurt

15ml/1 tbsp chopped fresh mint

1 spring onion (scallion), finely sliced

fresh herbs, to garnish

FROM THE STORECUPBOARD

250g/9oz/1¹/₃ cups dried chickpeas

5ml/1 tsp cayenne pepper, plus extra for sprinkling

5ml/1 tsp ground coriander

5ml/1 tsp ground cumin

sunflower oil, for frying

salt and ground black pepper, to taste

Energy 372Kcal/1557kJ; Protein 19.3g; Carbohydrate 35.3g, of which sugars 5.8g; Fat 18.1g, of which saturates 2.6g; Cholesterol 48mg; Calcium 280mg; Fibre 8g; Sodium 89mg

Potato Skewers with Mustard Dip ✳

Tender new potatoes cooked on the barbecue have a great flavour and crisp skin, but you could also cook these simple skewers under a hot grill (broiler). Serve with a creamy mustard and garlic dip at a family barbecue or as an appetizer at a summer dinner party.

SERVES FOUR

FOR THE DIP

4 garlic cloves, crushed

2 egg yolks

30ml/2 tbsp freshly squeezed lemon juice

FOR THE SKEWERS

1kg/2¼lb small new potatoes

200g/7oz shallots

FROM THE STORECUPBOARD

350ml/12fl oz/1½ cups extra virgin olive oil

10ml/2 tsp wholegrain mustard

salt and ground black pepper, to taste, plus 15ml/1 tbsp salt

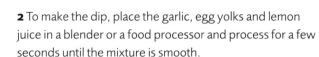

1 Prepare and light the barbecue or preheat the grill (broiler) to high.

2 To make the dip, place the garlic, egg yolks and lemon juice in a blender or a food processor and process for a few seconds until the mixture is smooth.

3 Keep the blender motor running and add 300ml/ ½ pint/1¼ cups of the olive oil very gradually, pouring it in a thin stream, until the mixture forms a thick, glossy cream.

4 Add the mustard and stir the ingredients together, then season with salt and pepper. Chill until ready to use.

5 Skin the shallots and then cut them in half. Par-boil the potatoes in their skins in a pan of boiling water for 5 minutes.

6 Drain well and then thread the potatoes on to metal skewers, alternating with the shallots.

7 Brush the skewers with the remaining olive oil and sprinkle with 15ml/1 tbsp salt. Cook over a barbecue or under a hot grill for 10–12 minutes, turning occasionally. Serve the skewers immediately with the dip.

COOK'S TIPS

• Early or "new" potatoes, and salad potatoes have the firmness and waxy texture that is necessary for the potatoes to stay on the skewer. Don't be tempted to use other types of small potato, since they will probably split or fall off the skewers during cooking.

• If you do not like mustard, you can omit it from this creamy home-made mayonnaise dip. You could add a dash of paprika instead.

Energy 2731kcal/11338kJ; Protein 28g; Carbohydrate 181.3g, of which sugars 25g; Fat 215.4g, of which saturates 32.8g; Cholesterol 403mg; Calcium 174mg; Fibre 14.3g; Sodium 297mg

Courgette Fritters with Chilli Jam ✳

Chilli jam is hot, sweet and sticky – rather like a thick chutney. It adds a delicious piquancy to these light fritters, which are always popular with adults and children alike.

SERVES SIX

450g/1lb/3¹/₂ cups coarsely grated courgettes (zucchini)

50g/2oz/²/₃ cup freshly grated grano padano cheese

2 eggs, beaten

FOR THE CHILLI JAM

4 large onions, diced

4 garlic cloves, chopped

1–2 green chillies, seeded and sliced

FROM THE STORECUPBOARD

75ml/5 tbsp olive oil

30ml/2 tbsp soft dark brown sugar

60ml/4 tbsp plain flour

vegetable oil, for frying

salt and ground black pepper, to taste

COOK'S TIP *Stored in an airtight jar in the refrigerator, the chilli jam will keep for up to 1 week.*

1 First make the chilli jam. Heat the olive oil in a frying pan until hot, then add the onions and the garlic. Reduce the heat to low, then cook for 20 minutes, stirring frequently, until the onions are very soft.

2 Leave the onion mixture to cool, then transfer to a food processor or blender. Add the chillies and sugar and blend until smooth, then return the mixture to the pan. Cook for a further 10 minutes, stirring frequently, until the liquid evaporates and the mixture has the consistency of jam. Cool slightly.

3 To make the fritters, squeeze the courgettes in a dish towel to remove any excess liquid, then combine with the grano padano, eggs, flour and salt and pepper.

4 Heat enough oil to cover the base of a large frying pan. Add 30ml/2 tbsp of the mixture for each fritter and cook three fritters at a time. Cook for 2–3 minutes on each side until golden, then keep warm while you cook the rest of the fritters. Drain on kitchen paper and serve warm with a spoonful of the chilli jam.

Energy 326kcal/1355kJ; Protein 10g; Carbohydrate 22.3g, of which sugars 13.2g; Fat 22.6g, of which saturates 4.7g; Cholesterol 103mg; Calcium 177mg; Fibre 2.6g; Sodium 131mg

Crab Cakes ✳

Definitely one for younger members of the family who like flavourful fish cakes. They may even help you make some fish-shaped cakes.

SERVES FOUR

1 Put the crab meat in a bowl and stir in the mayonnaise with the mustard and egg. Season with Tabasco, salt, pepper and cayenne.

2 Stir in the parsley, spring onions, if using, and 50g/2oz/^{1}/$_2$ cup of the breadcrumbs. The mixture should be just firm enough to hold together; you may need to add some more breadcrumbs.

3 Divide the mixture into eight portions, roll each into a ball and flatten slightly to make a thick flat disc. Spread out the crab cakes on a platter and put in the refrigerator for 30 minutes before frying.

4 Pour the oil into a pan to a depth of about 5mm/^{1}/$_4$ in. Cook the crab cakes, in two batches, until golden brown. Drain on kitchen paper and keep hot. Serve with a spring onion garnish and red onion marmalade.

30ml/2 tbsp mayonnaise

2.5–5ml/^{1}/$_2$–1 tsp mustard powder

1 egg, lightly beaten

45ml/3 tbsp chopped fresh parsley

4 spring onions (scallions), finely chopped (optional)

50–75g/2–3oz/^{1}/$_2$–^{3}/$_4$ cup dried breadcrumbs, preferably home-made

chopped spring onions (scallions), to garnish

red onion marmalade, to serve

FROM THE STORECUPBOARD

450g/1lb canned crab meat

Tabasco sauce

salt, ground black pepper and cayenne pepper

sunflower oil, for frying

Energy 285kcal/1187kJ; Protein 23.9g; Carbohydrate 10.3g, of which sugars 0.9g; Fat 16.7g, of which saturates 2.4g; Cholesterol 134mg; Calcium 178mg; Fibre 0.8g; Sodium 768mg

Mini Baked Potatoes with Sour Cream and Blue Cheese ✳

These attractive miniature baked potatoes are packed with flavour and can be eaten with the fingers. They provide an economical and unusual way of starting off an informal supper party.

MAKES 20

1 Preheat the oven to 180°C/350°F/Gas 4. Wash and dry the potatoes. Toss with the oil in a bowl to coat.

2 Dip the potatoes in the salt to coat lightly, then spread them out on a large baking sheet. Bake for 45–50 minutes until they are tender.

3 In a small bowl, combine the sour cream and blue cheese, mixing together well to combine thoroughly.

4 Cut a cross in the top of each potato. Press gently with your fingers to open the potatoes. Top each one with a dollop of the blue cheese mixture.

5 Place on a serving dish and garnish with the chives.

20 small new or salad potatoes

120ml/4fl oz/^{1}/$_2$ cup sour cream

25g/1oz blue cheese, crumbled

30ml/2 tbsp snipped fresh chives, to garnish

FROM THE STORECUPBOARD

60ml/4 tbsp vegetable oil

pinch of salt

Energy 71kcal/299kJ; Protein 1.3g; Carbohydrate 8.3g, of which sugars 0.9g; Fat 3.9g, of which saturates 1.3g; Cholesterol 5mg; Calcium 15mg; Fibre 0.5g; Sodium 23mg

Mushrooms with Garlic and Chilli Sauce ✳

These spicy, garlic-flavoured mushrooms make an ideal vegetarian alternative for a dinner party or summer barbecue.

SERVES FOUR

COOK'S TIP *If you like really spicy foods, do not remove the seeds from the red chilli.*

1 If using wooden skewers, soak eight of them in cold water for at least 30 minutes before making the kebabs. This will prevent them from burning over the barbecue or under the grill (broiler).

2 Make the dipping sauce by heating 15ml/1 tbsp of the sugar, rice vinegar and salt in a small pan, stirring occasionally until the sugar and salt have dissolved. Add the garlic and chilli, pour into a serving dish and keep warm.

3 Thread three mushroom halves on to each skewer. Lay the skewers side by side in a shallow dish.

4 In a mortar or spice grinder, pound or blend the garlic and coriander roots. Scrape into a bowl and mix with the remaining sugar, soy sauce and a little pepper.

5 Brush the soy sauce mixture over the mushrooms and leave to marinate for 15 minutes. Prepare the barbecue or preheat the grill, and cook the mushrooms for 2–3 minutes on each side. Serve with the dipping sauce.

12 large field (portabello), brown cap (cremini) or oyster mushrooms, or a mixture of the three, halved

4 garlic cloves, coarsely chopped

6 coriander (cilantro) roots, coarsely chopped

FOR THE DIPPING SAUCE

1 garlic clove, crushed

1 small fresh red chilli, seeded and finely chopped

FROM THE STORECUPBOARD

30ml/2 tbsp sugar

90ml/6 tbsp rice vinegar

5ml/1 tsp salt

30ml/2 tbsp light soy sauce

ground black pepper, to taste

Energy 78kcal/329kJ; Protein 5.8g; Carbohydrate 11.5g, of which sugars 9.1g; Fat 1.3g, of which saturates 0.3g; Cholesterol 0mg; Calcium 23mg; Fibre 3.3g; Sodium 1039mg

Spicy Chickpea Samosas *

A blend of crushed chickpeas and coriander sauce makes an interesting alternative to the more familiar meat or vegetable fillings in these crisp little pastries. The samosas look pretty garnished with fresh coriander leaves and finely sliced onion and are delicious served with a simple dip such as Fresh Tomato Sauce, Hummus or a mixture of Greek (US strained plain) yogurt and chopped fresh mint leaves.

MAKES EIGHTEEN

120ml/4fl oz/¹/₂ cup hara masala or coriander (cilantro) sauce

275g/10oz filo pastry

FROM THE STORECUPBOARD

2 x 400g/14oz cans chickpeas, drained and rinsed

60ml/4 tbsp chilli and garlic oil (*see* page 31)

1 Preheat the oven to 220°C/425°F/Gas 7. Process half the chickpeas to a paste in a food processor. Tip into a bowl and add the whole chickpeas, the hara masala or coriander sauce, and a little salt. Mix until well combined.

2 Cut a sheet of filo pastry into three strips. Brush with a little of the oil. Place 10ml/2 tsp of the filling at one end of a strip. Turn one corner diagonally over the filling to meet the long edge. Continue folding the filling and the pastry along the length of the strip, keeping the triangular shape.

3 Transfer to a baking sheet and repeat with the remaining filling and pastry. Brush with any remaining oil and bake for 15 minutes. Serve garnished with coriander and sliced red onion.

Energy 119kcal/499kJ; Protein 4.1g; Carbohydrate 13.7g, of which sugars 0.4g; Fat 5.7g, of which saturates 0.8g; Cholesterol 0mg; Calcium 36mg; Fibre 2.2g; Sodium 99mg

Red Onion and Goat's Cheese Pastries ✳✳

These attractive little tartlets couldn't be easier to make. Garnish them with fresh thyme sprigs and serve with a selection of salad leaves and a tomato and basil salad for a light lunch or quick supper. A wide variety of different types of goat's cheeses are available – the creamy log-shaped types without a rind are most suitable for these pastries. Ordinary onions can be used instead of red, if you prefer.

SERVES FOUR

1 Heat the oil in a large, heavy frying pan, add the onions and cook over a gentle heat for 10 minutes, or until softened, stirring occasionally to prevent them from browning.

2 Add seasoning to taste and cook for a further 2 minutes. Remove the pan from the heat and leave to cool.

3 Preheat the oven to 220°C/425°F/Gas 7. Roll out the puff pastry on a lightly floured board and cut out four rounds, using a 15cm/6in plate as a guide.

4 Place the pastry rounds on a dampened baking sheet and, using the point of a sharp knife, score a border, 2cm/¾in inside the edge of each pastry round.

5 Divide the cooked onions among the pastry rounds and top with the cubed goat's cheese.

6 Bake the pastries for 25–30 minutes, until the pastry is golden brown and the goat's cheese has melted. Serve immediately, garnished with thyme sprigs, if you like.

450g/1lb red onions, peeled and sliced

425g/15oz packet puff pastry

115g/4oz/1 cup goat's cheese, cubed

thyme sprigs, to garnish (optional)

FROM THE STORECUPBOARD

15ml/1 tbsp olive oil

salt and ground black pepper, to taste

Energy 554kcal/2308kJ; Protein 13.5g; Carbohydrate 48.5g, of which sugars 8g; Fat 36.4g, of which saturates 5.6g; Cholesterol 27mg; Calcium 128mg; Fibre 1.6g; Sodium 506mg

Potato, Onion and Broad Bean Tortilla ✳✳

The classic tortilla is simple to make and tastes fabulous. Serve it as a light summer lunch dish with a green leafy salad, or cut it into pieces, thread on to cocktail sticks (toothpicks) and serve as an appetizer.

SERVES SIX

1 Heat 30ml/2 tbsp of the oil in a deep 23cm/9in non-stick frying pan. Add the onions and potatoes and season with salt and pepper to taste. Stir to mix, then cover and cook gently, stirring, for 20–25 minutes.

2 Meanwhile, cook the beans in lightly salted, boiling water for 5 minutes. Drain well and set aside to cool. When the beans are cool enough to handle, peel off the grey outer skins. Add to the frying pan, together with the thyme or summer savory. Stir and cook for a further 2–3 minutes.

3 Beat the eggs with salt and pepper to taste and the mixed fresh herbs, then pour over the potatoes and onions and increase the heat slightly. Cook gently until the egg on the base sets and browns, gently pulling the omelette away from the sides of the pan and tilting it to allow the uncooked egg to run underneath.

4 Invert the tortilla on to a plate. Add the remaining oil to the pan and heat. Slip the tortilla back into the pan, uncooked side down, and cook for another 3–5 minutes. Slide the tortilla out on to a plate. Divide as you like, and serve warm rather than piping hot.

2 Spanish (Bermuda) onions, thinly sliced

300g/11oz waxy potatoes, cut into 1cm/¹⁄₂ in dice

250g/9oz/1³⁄₄ cups shelled broad (fava) beans

5ml/1 tsp chopped fresh thyme or summer savory

6 large (US extra large) eggs

45ml/3 tbsp chopped mixed fresh chives and flat leaf parsley

FROM THE STORECUPBOARD

45ml/3 tbsp olive oil

salt and ground black pepper, to taste

Energy 673kcal/2812kJ; Protein 34.9g; Carbohydrate 59.2g, of which sugars 18.1g; Fat 35.2g, of which saturates 7.3g; Cholesterol 571mg; Calcium 272mg; Fibre 14.3g; Sodium 252mg

Baked Eggs with Creamy Leeks ✳

This simple but elegant appetizer is perfect for last-minute entertaining or quick dining. It is extremely economical, as well as being nourishing, sustaining and delicious.

SERVES FOUR

15g/¹/₂oz/1 tbsp butter, plus extra for greasing

225g/8oz small leeks, thinly sliced

75–90ml/5–6 tbsp whipping cream

4 small-medium (US medium-large) eggs

crisp, fried sage leaves, to garnish

FROM THE STORECUPBOARD

salt and ground black pepper, to taste

1 Preheat the oven to 190°C/375°F/Gas 5. Generously butter the base and sides of four small ramekins or individual soufflé dishes.

2 Melt the butter in a frying pan and cook the leeks over a medium heat, stirring frequently, for 3–5 minutes, until softened and translucent, but not browned.

3 Add 45ml/3 tbsp of the cream and cook over a low heat for 5 minutes, until the leeks are very soft and the cream has thickened a little. Season to taste.

4 Place the ramekins in a small roasting pan and divide the cooked leeks among them. Break an egg into each, spoon over the remaining cream and season with salt and pepper.

5 Pour boiling water into the roasting pan to come about halfway up the sides of the ramekins. Transfer the pan to the preheated oven and bake for about 10 minutes, until just set. Garnish with fried bay leaves and serve immediately.

Energy 149kcal/614kJ; Protein 4.4g; Carbohydrate 2.2g, of which sugars 1.8g; Fat 13.7g, of which saturates 7.5g; Cholesterol 123mg; Calcium 39mg; Fibre 1.3g; Sodium 64mg

Pasta, Pulses and Grains

PASTA, BEANS, LENTILS, RICE AND COUSCOUS ARE LOW IN FAT, SUSTAINING AND EXTREMELY GOOD VALUE FOR MONEY, AS WELL AS BEING INCREDIBLY VERSATILE. USE THEM TO CREATE WHOLESOME VEGETARIAN DISHES, SUCH AS MACARONI CHEESE, PORCINI RISOTTO, OR CASABLANCAN COUSCOUS WITH ROASTED VEGETABLES, OR TO BULK OUT MORE EXPENSIVE INGREDIENTS SUCH AS MEAT AND FISH, AS IN TURKEY LASAGNE, FARFALLE WITH TUNA, OR TORTELLINI WITH HAM.

Spaghetti with Fresh Tomato Sauce ✳✳

This is an ideal dish to make in the summer when you have a glut of soft, ripe, juicy tomatoes. Do not be tempted to use under-ripe tomatoes, as they will have an inferior flavour and be too firm.

SERVES FOUR

1 Cut a cross in the base end of each tomato, then plunge into a bowl of boiling water. Leave for around 30 seconds, then lift them out with a slotted spoon and drop them into a bowl of cold water. Drain well, then remove the skins from the tomatoes. Place on a chopping board and cut them into quarters, then eighths, and chop as finely as possible.

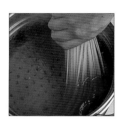

2 Heat the oil in a large pan, add the onion and cook gently for 5 minutes, until softened and lightly coloured.

3 Add the tomatoes, season with salt and pepper, bring to a simmer, then turn the heat down to low and cover. Cook, stirring occasionally, for 30–40 minutes, until the mixture is thick.

4 Meanwhile, cook the pasta according to the instructions on the packet. Shred the basil leaves or tear them into small pieces.

5 Remove the sauce from the heat, stir in the basil and check the seasoning. Drain the pasta, then tip into a warmed bowl. Pour the sauce over and toss the mixture well. Serve immediately, with shaved Parmesan handed around in a separate bowl.

675g/1¹⁄₄lb ripe Italian plum tomatoes or sweet cherry tomatoes

1 onion, finely chopped

a small handful of fresh basil leaves

coarsely shaved Parmesan cheese, to serve

FROM THE STORECUPBOARD

60ml/4 tbsp extra virgin olive oil or sunflower oil

350g/12oz dried spaghetti

salt and ground black pepper, to taste

Energy 436kcal/1840kJ; Protein 12.2g; Carbohydrate 71.5g, of which sugars 9.2g; Fat 13.2g, of which saturates 1.9g; Cholesterol 0mg; Calcium 58mg; Fibre 4.9g; Sodium 22mg

Macaroni Cheese **

Rich and creamy, this is a deluxe macaroni cheese. It goes well with either a tomato and basil salad or a leafy green salad.

SERVES FOUR

1 Preheat the oven to 180°C/350°F/Gas 4. Cook the macaroni according to the instructions on the packet.

2 Meanwhile, gently melt the butter in a pan, add the flour and cook, stirring, for 1–2 minutes.

3 Add the milk a little at a time, whisking vigorously after each addition. Stir in the cream, then the dry white wine. Bring to the boil. Cook, stirring constantly, until the sauce thickens. Remove from the heat.

4 Add the Gruyère or Emmenthal, Gorgonzola and about a third of the grated grano padano cheese to the sauce. Stir well to mix in the cheeses, then taste for seasoning and add salt and pepper if necessary.

5 Thoroughly drain the macaroni and tip it into a baking dish. Pour the sauce over the pasta and mix well, then sprinkle the remaining grano padano over the top.

6 Place in the preheated oven and bake for 25–30 minutes or until golden brown. Serve immediately.

50g/2oz/$^{1}/_{4}$ cup butter

600ml/1 pint/2$^{1}/_{2}$ cups milk

100ml/3$^{1}/_{2}$ fl oz/scant $^{1}/_{2}$ cup double (heavy) cream

100ml/3$^{1}/_{2}$ fl oz/scant $^{1}/_{2}$ cup dry white wine

100g/4oz/1 cup grated Gruyère or Emmenthal cheese

50g/2oz Gorgonzola cheese, crumbled

75g/3oz/1 cup freshly grated grano padano cheese

FROM THE STORECUPBOARD

250g/9oz/2$^{1}/_{4}$ cups short-cut macaroni

50g/2oz/$^{1}/_{2}$ cup plain (all-purpose) flour

salt and ground black pepper, to taste

Energy 743Kcal/3104kJ; Protein 30.3g; Carbohydrate 52.1g, of which sugars 8.9g; Fat 45.4g, of which saturates 27.8g; Cholesterol 123mg; Calcium 673mg; Fibre 0.4g; Sodium 593mg

Farfalle with Tuna ✳

Passata and canned tuna are very good value for money and endlessly versatile for making weekday suppers. A variety of herbs can be added – choose from basil, marjoram or oregano – and use fresh herbs, as the short cooking time does not allow the flavour of dried herbs to develop fully.

SERVES FOUR

1 Cook the pasta in a large pan of lightly salted boiling water according to the instructions on the packet.

2 Meanwhile, gently heat the passata in a separate pan and add the olive rings.

3 Drain the canned tuna and flake it with a fork. Add the tuna to the sauce with about 60ml/4 tbsp of the hot water used for cooking the pasta. Mix well to combine. Taste and adjust the seasoning, as necessary.

4 Drain the pasta thoroughly and tip it into a large, warmed serving bowl. Pour the tuna sauce over the top and toss lightly to mix. Serve immediately.

8–10 pitted black olives, cut into rings

175g/6oz can tuna in olive oil

FROM THE STORECUPBOARD

400g/14oz/3¹/₂ cups dried farfalle

600ml/1 pint/2¹/₂ cups passata (bottled strained tomatoes)

Energy 459kcal/1949kJ; Protein 25.2g; Carbohydrate 78.6g, of which sugars 7.8g; Fat 7.1g, of which saturates 1.1g; Cholesterol 22mg; Calcium 53mg; Fibre 4.2g; Sodium 756mg

Turkey Lasagne ✳✳

This easy-to-make baked pasta dish is delicious made with cooked turkey left over from a roast dinner and broccoli florets in a rich, creamy cheese sauce. It is a good way to include an extra portion of vegetables.

SERVES FOUR

1 Preheat the oven to 180°C/350°F/Gas 4. Heat the oil in a pan and cook the onion and garlic until softened but not coloured. Remove from the heat and stir in the diced turkey, mascarpone and tarragon and season with salt and pepper to taste.

2 Blanch the broccoli for 1 minute, then drain and rinse under cold water. Drain well and set aside.

3 To make the sauce, melt the butter in a pan, stir in the flour and cook for 1 minute, still stirring. Remove from the heat and gradually stir in the milk.

4 Return to the heat and bring the sauce to the boil, stirring constantly. Simmer for 1 minute, then add 50g/2oz/²/₃ cup of the grano padano and seasoning to taste.

5 Spoon a layer of the turkey mixture into a large, shallow ovenproof dish. Add a layer of broccoli and cover with sheets of lasagne. Coat with cheese sauce.

6 Repeat these layers, finishing with a layer of cheese sauce on top. Sprinkle with the remaining grano padano and bake for 35–40 minutes.

1 onion, chopped

2 garlic cloves, chopped

450g/1lb cooked turkey meat, finely diced

225g/8oz/1 cup mascarpone cheese

30ml/2 tbsp chopped fresh tarragon

300g/11oz broccoli, broken into florets

FOR THE SAUCE

50g/2oz/1/4 cup butter

600ml/1 pint/2¹/₂ cups milk

75g/3oz/1 cup freshly grated grano padano cheese

FROM THE STORECUPBOARD

30ml/2 tbsp light olive oil

salt and ground black pepper, to taste

30ml/2 tbsp plain (all-purpose) flour

115g/4oz no pre-cook lasagne verdi

Energy 673kcal/2819kJ; Protein 49.4g; Carbohydrate 44.3g, of which sugars 11g; Fat 34.4g, of which saturates 18.4g; Cholesterol 142mg; Calcium 471mg; Fibre 2.5g; Sodium 409mg

Tortellini with Ham ✳✳

This is a very easy recipe that can be made quickly from storecupboard ingredients. It is therefore ideal for an after-work supper.

SERVES FOUR

1 Cook the pasta according to the instructions on the packet. Meanwhile, heat the oil in a large pan, add the onion and cook over a low heat, stirring frequently, for about 5 minutes until softened. Add the ham and cook, stirring occasionally, until it darkens.

2 Add the passata to the pan. Stir well, then add salt and pepper to taste. Bring to the boil, lower the heat and simmer the sauce for a few minutes, stirring occasionally, until it has reduced slightly. Stir in the cream. Drain the pasta well and add it to the sauce.

COOK'S TIP *Passata (bottled strained tomatoes) is handy for making quick sauces.*

3 Add a handful of grated grano padano to the pan. Stir to combine well and taste for seasoning. Serve in warmed bowls, topped with the remaining grano padano.

250g/9oz meat-filled tortellini

¹/₄ large onion, finely chopped

115g/4oz cooked ham, diced

100ml/3¹/₂fl oz/scant ¹/₂ cup double (heavy) cream

about 90g/3¹/₂oz/generous 1 cup freshly grated grano padano cheese

FROM THE STORECUPBOARD

30ml/2 tbsp olive oil

150ml/¹/₄ pint/²/₃ cup passata (bottled strained tomatoes)

salt and ground black pepper, to taste

Bolognese Sauce ✳✳

This is a versatile meat sauce. You can toss it with freshly cooked pasta or, alternatively, you can layer it in a baked dish like lasagne.

SERVES FOUR

1 Heat the oil in a large pan, then add the chopped onion, carrot, celery and garlic and cook over a low heat, stirring frequently, for 5–7 minutes until softened.

2 Add the minced beef and cook for 5 minutes, stirring frequently and breaking up any lumps in the meat with a wooden spoon. Stir in the red wine and mix well.

3 Cook for 1–2 minutes, then add the passata, tomato purée, fresh parsley, dried oregano and 60ml/4 tbsp of the stock. Season with salt and pepper to taste. Stir well and bring the mixture to the boil.

4 Cover the pan, and cook gently for 30 minutes, stirring from time to time and adding more stock as necessary.

5 Taste for seasoning and toss with hot, freshly cooked pasta, or use in baked pasta dishes.

1 onion, finely chopped

1 small carrot, finely chopped

1 celery stick, finely chopped

2 garlic cloves, finely chopped

400g/14oz minced (ground) beef

120ml/4fl oz/¹/₂ cup red wine

15ml/1 tbsp chopped fresh flat leaf parsley

FROM THE STORECUPBOARD

45ml/3 tbsp olive oil

200ml/7fl oz/scant 1 cup passata (strained bottled tomatoes)

15ml/1 tbsp tomato purée (paste)

5ml/1 tsp dried oregano

about 350ml/12fl oz/1¹/₂ cups beef stock

salt and ground black pepper

Top: Energy 373kcal/1549kJ; Protein 17.4g; Carbohydrate 10.9g, of which sugars 3.5g; Fat 29.2g, of which saturates 14.8g; Cholesterol 79mg; Calcium 302mg; Fibre 1g; Sodium 1025mg

Above: Energy 340kcal/1410kJ; Protein 20.6g; Carbohydrate 4.3g, of which sugars 3.9g; Fat 24.5g, of which saturates 8.1g; Cholesterol 60mg; Calcium 27mg; Fibre 1g; Sodium 214mg

Indian Mee Goreng ✳✳

This is a truly international dish combining Indian, Chinese and Western ingredients. It is a delicious and nutritious treat for lunch or supper.

SERVES SIX

1 Bring a large pan of water to the boil, add the fresh or dried egg noodles and cook according to the packet instructions. Drain the noodles and immediately rinse them under cold water to halt cooking. Drain again and set aside.

2 Heat 30ml/2 tbsp of the oil in a large frying pan. Cut the tofu into cubes and cook until brown, then lift it out with a slotted spoon and set aside.

3 Beat the eggs with the water and seasoning. Add to the oil in the frying pan and cook without stirring until set. Flip over, cook the other side, then slide out of the pan, roll up and slice thinly.

4 Heat the remaining oil in a wok or large frying pan and cook the onion and garlic for 2–3 minutes. Add the drained noodles, soy sauce, ketchup and chilli sauce. Toss well over medium heat for 2 minutes, then add the diced potato.

5 Reserve a few spring onions to garnish, and stir the rest into the noodles with the chilli, if using, and the tofu.

6 Stir in the sliced omelette. Serve immediately on a hot plate, garnished with the remaining spring onion.

150g/5oz firm tofu

2 eggs

30ml/2 tbsp water

1 onion, sliced

1 garlic clove, crushed

1 large cooked
potato, diced

4 spring onions
(scallions), shredded

1–2 fresh green chillies,
seeded and thinly
sliced (optional)

FROM THE STORECUPBOARD

450g/1lb fresh or 225g/8oz
dried egg noodles

60–90ml/4–6 tbsp
vegetable oil

15ml/1 tbsp light
soy sauce

30–45ml/2–3 tbsp
tomato ketchup

15ml/1 tbsp chilli sauce
(or to taste)

Energy 421kcal/1772kJ; Protein 13.7g; Carbohydrate 59g, of which sugars 4.2g; Fat 16.2g, of which saturates 3.2g; Cholesterol 85mg; Calcium 165mg; Fibre 2.7g; Sodium 416mg

½ cucumber, sliced
lengthways, seeded and diced

4–6 spring onions (scallions)

a bunch of radishes,
about 115g/4oz

225g/8oz mooli
(daikon), peeled

115g/4oz/2 cups beansprouts,
rinsed then left in iced water
and drained

2 garlic cloves, crushed

45ml/3 tbsp toasted
sesame paste

roasted peanuts or cashew
nuts, to garnish

FROM THE STORECUPBOARD

225g/8oz dried egg noodles

60ml/4 tbsp groundnut
(peanut) oil or sunflower oil

15ml/1 tbsp sesame oil

15ml/1 tbsp light soy sauce

5–10ml/1–2 tsp chilli sauce,
to taste

15ml/1 tbsp rice vinegar

120ml/4fl oz/½ cup chicken
stock or water

5ml/1 tsp sugar, or to taste

salt and ground black pepper,
to taste

Sichuan Noodles ✳ ✳

This tasty vegetarian dish combines egg noodles with plenty of fresh
vegetables in a rich, nutty sauce, with just a hint of chilli.

SERVES FOUR

1 Bring a large pan of water to the boil, add the noodles and
cook according to the packet instruction. Drain and rinse
them under cold water. Drain again and set aside.

2 Sprinkle the cucumber with salt, leave for 15 minutes,
rinse well, then drain and pat dry on kitchen paper. Place
in a large salad bowl.

3 Cut the spring onions into fine shreds. Cut the radishes
in half and slice finely. Coarsely grate the mooli, using a
mandolin or a food processor. Add all the vegetables to the
cucumber and toss gently.

4 Heat half the oil in a wok or large frying pan and stir-fry the
noodles for about 1 minute. Using a slotted spoon, transfer
the noodles to a large serving bowl and keep warm.

5 Heat the remaining oil in the wok or frying pan and add the
garlic to flavour the oil. Stir in the sesame paste, sesame oil,
soy and chilli sauces, vinegar and chicken stock or water.
Add a little sugar and season. Warm over a gentle heat.

6 Pour the sauce over the noodles and toss well. Garnish
with peanuts or cashew nuts and serve with the vegetables.

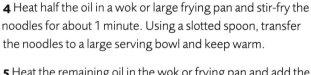

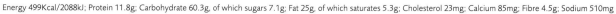

Energy 499Kcal/2088kJ; Protein 11.8g; Carbohydrate 60.3g, of which sugars 7.1g; Fat 25g, of which saturates 5.3g; Cholesterol 23mg; Calcium 85mg; Fibre 4.5g; Sodium 510mg

Rosemary Risotto ✳✳

This is a classic risotto with a subtle and complex taste. It is very filling and quite rich, so it only requires a simple side salad as an accompaniment.

SERVES FOUR

1 onion, chopped

2 garlic cloves, crushed

175ml/6fl oz/^{3}/$_4$ cup dry white wine

60ml/4 tbsp mascarpone cheese

65g/2^1/$_2$oz/scant 1 cup freshly grated Parmesan cheese, plus extra, to serve (optional)

5ml/1 tsp chopped fresh rosemary

FROM THE STORECUPBOARD

400g/14oz can borlotti beans

30ml/2 tbsp olive oil

275g/10oz/1^1/$_2$ cups risotto rice

900ml–1 litre/ 1^1/$_2$–1^3/$_4$ pints/ 3^3/$_4$–4 cups simmering vegetable or chicken stock

salt and ground black pepper, to taste

1 Drain the beans, rinse under cold water and drain again. Purée about two-thirds of the beans fairly coarsely in a food processor or blender. Set the remaining beans aside.

2 Heat the oil in a large pan and gently fry the onion and garlic for 6–8 minutes until very soft. Add the rice and cook over a medium heat for a few minutes, stirring constantly, until the grains are thoroughly coated in oil and are slightly translucent.

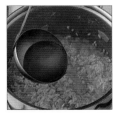

3 Pour in the wine. Cook over a medium heat for 2–3 minutes, stirring all the time, until the wine has been absorbed. Add the stock a ladleful at a time, waiting for each quantity to be absorbed before adding more, and continuing to stir.

4 When the rice is three-quarters cooked, stir in the bean purée. Continue to cook, adding the remaining stock, until it is creamy and the rice is tender but still has a bit of "bite". Add the reserved beans, with the mascarpone, Parmesan and rosemary, then season to taste. Stir thoroughly, then cover and leave to stand for about 5 minutes. Serve with extra Parmesan.

COOK'S TIPS

• Arborio rice is the best type of rice to use for making a rissotto because it has shorter, fatter grains than other short grain rices, and a high starch content, which makes for a creamier risotto. By being coated in oil, the grains of rice absorb the liquid slowly and release their starch gradually, which helps to produce a creamy end result.

• You should use a large pan for making risotto, as it makes it easier to stir and allows the grains of rice to cook evenly and more quickly.

Energy 531Kcal/2220kJ; Protein 20g; Carbohydrate 74.6g, of which sugars 5.2g; Fat 14g, of which saturates 5.6g; Cholesterol 23mg; Calcium 287mg; Fibre 6.4g; Sodium 569mg

Porcini Risotto ✳✳

This risotto is easy to make because you don't have to stand over it stirring constantly as it cooks, as you do with a traditional risotto. Serve with steamed green vegetables for a sustaining main meal.

SERVES FOUR

25g/1oz/¹/₂ cup dried
porcini mushrooms

1 onion, finely chopped

FROM THE STORECUPBOARD

225g/8oz/generous 1 cup
risotto rice

30ml/2 tbsp garlic-infused
olive oil

salt and ground black
pepper, to taste

1 Soak the mushrooms for 30 minutes in 750ml/1¹/₄ pints/ 3 cups boiling water. Drain through a sieve (strainer) lined with kitchen paper, reserving the soaking liquor. Rinse and pat dry.

2 Preheat the oven to 180°C/350°F/Gas 4. Heat the oil in a roasting pan on the hob (stovetop) and add the onion. Cook for 2–3 minutes, or until softened but not coloured.

3 Add the rice and stir for 2 minutes, then add the mushrooms. Mix in the mushroom liquor, then season, and cover with foil.

4 Bake in the oven for 30 minutes, stirring occasionally, until all the stock has been absorbed and the rice is tender. Divide between warm serving bowls and serve immediately.

Energy 258kcal/1074kJ; Protein 4.5g; Carbohydrate 46.1g, of which sugars 0.9g; Fat 5.8g, of which saturates 0.8g; Cholesterol 0mg; Calcium 15mg; Fibre 0.3g; Sodium 1mg

Barley Risotto with Roasted Squash and Leeks ✳✳✳

This healthy risotto is made with slightly chewy, nutty-flavoured pearl barley, which is perfectly complemented by leeks and roasted squash.

SERVES FOUR

1 Rinse the barley, then cook it in simmering water, keeping the pan part-covered, for 35–45 minutes, or until tender. Drain. Preheat the oven to 200°C/400°F/Gas 6.

2 Place the squash in a roasting pan with half of the thyme. Season with pepper and toss with half the oil. Roast, stirring once, for 30–35 minutes, until the squash is tender and beginning to brown.

3 Heat half the butter with the remaining olive oil in a large frying pan. Cook the leeks and garlic gently for 5 minutes. Add the mushrooms and remaining thyme, then cook until the liquid from the mushrooms evaporates and they begin to fry.

4 Stir in the carrots and cook for about 2 minutes, then add the barley and most of the vegetable stock. Season well and part-cover the pan. Cook for a further 5 minutes. Pour in the remaining stock if the mixture seems dry.

5 Stir in the parsley, the remaining butter and half the cheese, then stir in the squash. Add seasoning to taste and serve immediately, sprinkled with the toasted pumpkin seeds or walnuts and the remaining cheese.

200g/7oz/1 cup pearl barley

1 butternut squash, peeled, seeded and cut into chunks

10ml/2 tsp chopped fresh thyme

25g/1oz/2 tbsp butter

4 leeks, cut into fairly thick diagonal slices

2 garlic cloves, chopped

175g/6oz/2^1/$_2$ cups brown cap (cremini) mushrooms, sliced

2 carrots, coarsely grated

30ml/2 tbsp chopped fresh flat leaf parsley

50g/2oz/^{2}/$_3$ cup grano padano cheese, grated

45ml/3 tbsp pumpkin seeds, toasted, or chopped walnuts

FROM THE STORECUPBOARD

60ml/4 tbsp olive oil

about 120ml/4fl oz/^{1}/$_2$ cup vegetable stock

salt and ground black pepper, to taste

VARIATIONS

• *You could make the risotto with brown rice instead of barley – cook following the packet instructions and continue from step 2.*

• *Any type of fresh mushrooms can be used in this recipe – try sliced field (portabello) mushrooms, or rehydrated dried shiitake mushrooms for a rich, hearty flavour.*

Energy 398Kcal/1670kJ; Protein 9.1g; Carbohydrate 52.8g, of which sugars 7.7g; Fat 18.1g, of which saturates 2.4g; Cholesterol 0mg; Calcium 121mg; Fibre 5g; Sodium 21mg

1 small onion,
finely chopped

2 fresh green
chillies, seeded
and finely chopped

25g/1oz garlic chives,
roughly chopped

15g/^{1}/$_2$oz fresh coriander
(cilantro) sprigs

250g/9oz mixed
mushrooms, wiped
clean and thickly sliced

50g/2oz cashew nuts,
fried in 15ml/1 tbsp
olive oil until
golden brown

FROM THE STORECUPBOARD

350g/12oz/generous
1^3/$_4$ cups long grain rice

60ml/4 tbsp groundnut
(peanut) oil

600ml/1 pint/2^1/$_2$ cups
good-quality vegetable
or mushroom stock, hot

salt and ground black
pepper, to taste

Garlic Chive Rice with Mixed Mushrooms ✳✳

A mixture of fresh mushrooms combines well with rice and garlic chives
to make a tasty accompaniment to vegetarian dishes, fish or chicken.

SERVES FOUR

1 Wash and drain the rice in a sieve (strainer). Heat half the oil in a pan and cook the onion and chillies over a gentle heat, stirring occasionally, for 10–12 minutes until soft.

2 Set half the garlic chives aside. Cut the stalks off the coriander and set the leaves aside. Purée the remaining chives and the coriander stalks with the stock in a food processor or blender.

3 Add the rice to the onions and fry gently for 4–5 minutes. Pour in the stock mixture, then season to taste. Bring to the boil, then stir and reduce the heat to very low. Cover and cook for 15–20 minutes, or until the rice has absorbed all the liquid.

4 Remove from the heat and lay a clean dish towel over the pan, under the lid, and press on the lid to wedge it firmly in place. Leave to stand for a further 10 minutes.

5 Meanwhile, heat the remaining oil and cook the mushrooms for 5–6 minutes, then add the remaining garlic chives and cook for another 1–2 minutes. Stir the mushroom mixture and coriander leaves into the rice. Adjust the seasoning to taste, then transfer to a warmed serving dish. Serve immediately, scattered with the fried cashew nuts.

Energy 535kcal/2227kJ; Protein 11g; Carbohydrate 74.7g, of which sugars 1.9g; Fat 21g, of which saturates 3g; Cholesterol 0mg; Calcium 37mg; Fibre 1.8g; Sodium 41mg

Thai Rice ✳

This is soft, fluffy rice dish is perfumed with fresh lemon grass and limes, and is ideal as a light vegetarian supper dish.

SERVES FOUR

2 limes

1 lemon grass stalk

1 onion, chopped

2.5cm/1in piece of fresh root ginger, peeled and finely chopped

60ml/4 tbsp chopped fresh coriander (cilantro)

spring onion (scallion) green, toasted coconut strips and lime wedges, to serve

FROM THE STORECUPBOARD

225g/8oz/generous 1 cup brown long grain rice

15ml/1 tbsp olive oil

7.5ml/1$\frac{1}{2}$ tsp coriander seeds

7.5ml/1$\frac{1}{2}$ tsp cumin seeds

750ml/1$\frac{1}{4}$ pints/3 cups vegetable stock

1 Pare the limes using a canelle knife or grate them using a fine grater, taking care to avoid cutting the bitter pith. Set aside the rind. Finely chop the lower portion of the lemon grass stalk and set aside.

2 Rinse the rice in plenty of cold water until the water runs clear. Tip into a sieve (strainer) and drain thoroughly.

3 Heat the olive oil in a large pan. Add the onion, ginger, spices, lemon grass and lime rind and fry gently over a low heat for 2–3 minutes.

4 Add the drained rice and cook for 1 minute, then pour in the stock and bring to the boil. Reduce the heat to very low and cover the pan. Cook gently for 30 minutes, then check the rice. If it is still crunchy, cover the pan and leave for 3–5 minutes more. Remove the pan from the heat.

5 Stir in the fresh coriander, fluff up the grains of rice, cover and leave for about 10 minutes. Garnish the rice with spring onion green and toasted coconut strips, and serve with lime wedges, if you like.

VARIATION *Spicy stir-fried prawns (shrimp) would make an excellent addition to this dish. To make, simply thaw, peel and devein 150g/5oz frozen prawns, then fry in 30ml/ 2 tbsp hot oil for 4 minutes. Sprinkle with 5ml/1 tsp dried chilli flakes and serve with the Thai Rice.*

Energy 234kcal/992kJ; Protein 4.3g; Carbohydrate 47.2g, of which sugars 1.8g; Fat 4.5g, of which saturates 0.8g; Cholesterol 0mg; Calcium 30mg; Fibre 1.8g; Sodium 6mg

75g/3oz/6 tbsp butter

**1 small onion,
finely chopped**

**150ml/¹/₄ pint/²/₃ cup dry
white wine**

**225g/8oz/2 cups frozen
peas, thawed**

**115g/4oz cooked
ham, diced**

**50g/2oz/²/₃ cup freshly
grated Parmesan cheese,
to serve**

FROM THE STORECUPBOARD

**about 1 litre/1³/₄ pints/
4 cups simmering
chicken stock**

**275g/10oz/1¹/₂ cups
risotto rice**

**salt and ground black
pepper, to taste**

COOK'S TIPS

• *Always use fresh
Parmesan cheese, grated
off a block. It has a far
superior flavour to
ready-grated Parmesan
and is usually better
value for money.*

• *Frozen peas are much
cheaper than fresh peas,
and have the added
bonus of being available
all year round. They also
often have a better flavour
than fresh ones, since
they are frozen at source
immediately after being
picked, which helps to
preserve their sweet taste
and their freshness.*

• *Serve this tasty risotto
with generous hunks
of warm crusty bread
and some butter for a
delicious, warming
supper dish.*

Risi e Bisi ✳✳

Use good quality ham in this classic Italian risotto; you only need a small amount, and the overall flavour of the dish will be greatly improved.

SERVES FOUR

1 Melt 50g/2oz/4 tbsp of the butter in a large heavy pan until foaming. Add the onion and cook gently for about 3 minutes, stirring frequently, until softened. Have the hot stock ready in an adjacent pan.

2 Add the rice to the onion mixture. Stir until the grains start to swell, then pour in the wine. Stir until the wine stops sizzling and most of it has been absorbed, then pour in a little hot stock, with salt and pepper to taste. Stir continuously, over a low heat, until all the stock has been absorbed.

3 Add the remaining stock, a little at a time, allowing the rice to absorb all the liquid before adding more, and stirring constantly. Add the peas after about 20 minutes. After 25–30 minutes, the the risotto should be moist and creamy.

4 Gently stir in the diced cooked ham and the remaining butter. Heat through until the butter has melted, then taste for seasoning and adjust as necessary. Transfer the risotto to a warmed serving bowl. Grate or shave a little Parmesan over the top and serve the rest separately.

Energy 545kcal/2268kJ; Protein 19.3g; Carbohydrate 61.9g, of which sugars 1.9g; Fat 21.6g, of which saturates 12.8g; Cholesterol 69mg; Calcium 184mg; Fibre 2.7g; Sodium 597mg

Spiced Vegetable Stew with Chickpeas and Couscous ✳✳

This tasty, satisfying vegetarian main course is cheap and easy to make and can be prepared with any number of seasonal vegetables such as spinach, peas, broad (fava) beans or baby corn.

SERVES SIX

1 Heat 30ml/2 tbsp olive oil in a large pan, add the onion and garlic and cook until soft. Stir in the tomato purée, turmeric, cayenne, ground coriander and cumin. Cook for 2 minutes.

2 Add the cauliflower, carrots and pepper, with enough water to come halfway up the vegetables. Bring to the boil, then lower the heat, cover and simmer for 10 minutes. Add the courgettes, chickpeas and tomatoes and cook for 10 minutes. Stir in the fresh coriander and season. Keep hot.

3 To cook the couscous, bring about 475ml/16fl oz/2 cups water to the boil in a large pan. Add the remaining olive oil and a pinch of salt. Remove from the heat and add the couscous. Allow to swell for 2 minutes, then add the sunflower oil and heat through, stirring to separate the grains.

4 Turn the couscous out on to a warm serving dish, and spoon the cooked vegetables on top, pouring over any liquid. Garnish with coriander and serve immediately.

1 large onion, finely chopped

2 garlic cloves, crushed

225g/8oz/1¹/₂ cups cauliflower florets

225g/8oz baby carrots, washed and trimmed

1 red (bell) pepper, seeded and diced

225g/8oz courgettes (zucchini), sliced

4 beefsteak tomatoes, skinned and sliced

45ml/3 tbsp chopped fresh coriander (cilantro)

coriander sprigs, to garnish

FROM THE STORECUPBOARD

45ml/3 tbsp olive oil

15ml/1 tbsp tomato purée (paste)

2.5ml/¹/₂ tsp ground turmeric

2.5ml/¹/₂ tsp cayenne pepper

5ml/1 tsp ground coriander

5ml/1 tsp ground cumin

400g/14oz can chickpeas, drained and rinsed

salt and ground black pepper, to taste

450g/1lb/2²/₃ cups couscous

50ml/3¹/₂ tbsp sunflower oil

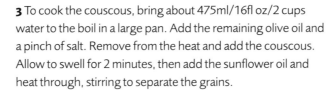

Energy 419kcal/1749kJ; Protein 12.9g; Carbohydrate 61.8g, of which sugars 11.8g; Fat 14.8g, of which saturates 1.9g; Cholesterol 0mg; Calcium 87mg; Fibre 6.7g; Sodium 178mg

3 red onions, peeled
and quartered

2–3 courgettes (zucchini),
halved lengthways and cut
across into 2–3 pieces

2–3 red, green or yellow
(bell) peppers, seeded
and quartered

2 aubergines (eggplants), cut
into 6–8 long segments

2–3 leeks, trimmed and cut
into long strips

2–3 sweet potatoes, peeled,
halved lengthways and cut
into long strips

4–6 tomatoes, quartered

6 garlic cloves, crushed

25g/1oz fresh root
ginger, sliced

a few large fresh
rosemary sprigs

natural (plain) yogurt or
harissa and bread, to serve

FOR THE COUSCOUS

600ml/1 pint/2^1/$_2$ cups
warm water

about 25g/1oz/2 tbsp
butter, diced

FROM THE STORECUPBOARD

about 150ml/^{1}/$_4$ pint/
^{2}/$_3$ cup olive oil

10ml/2 tsp sugar or
clear honey

salt and ground black
pepper, to taste, plus a
pinch of salt

500g/1^1/$_4$lb/3 cups
medium couscous

45ml/3 tbsp sunflower oil

Casablancan Couscous with Roasted Vegetables ✳✳✳

This delicious summer dish is packed with seasonal vegetables. Serve with yogurt and bread for a stunning vegetarian dinner-party dish and follow with a simple lemon sorbet for dessert.

SERVES SIX

1 Preheat the oven to 200°C/400°F/Gas 6. Arrange all the vegetables in a roasting pan. Tuck the garlic, ginger and rosemary around the vegetables. Pour the olive oil over the vegetables, sprinkle with the sugar or honey, and salt and pepper to taste, and roast, turning occasionally, for about 1^1/$_2$ hours until they are tender and slightly caramelized.

2 When the vegetables are nearly ready, put the couscous in a bowl. Stir a pinch of salt into the water, then pour it over the couscous, stirring to make sure it is absorbed evenly. Leave to stand for 10 minutes, then, using your fingers, rub the sunflower oil into the grains and break up any lumps. Tip into an ovenproof dish, arrange the butter over the top, cover with foil and heat in the oven for about 20 minutes.

3 To serve, use your fingers to work the melted butter into the couscous and fluff it up, then pile it on a large dish and shape into a mound with a pit at the top. Spoon some vegetables into the pit and arrange the rest around the dish. Pour the oil from the pan over the couscous. Serve immediately with yogurt, or harissa if you prefer, and bread for mopping up the juices.

Energy 607kcal/2531kJ; Protein 11.3g; Carbohydrate 81.3g, of which sugars 22.2g; Fat 28.3g, of which saturates 5.7g; Cholesterol 9mg; Calcium 115mg; Fibre 9.2g; Sodium 76mg

Mixed Bean and Aubergine Tagine with Mint Yogurt ✳✳

Beans are not only cheap, but they are also a very good source of protein. Here they are combined with aubergine (eggplant), fresh herbs, garlic and chillies to make a very healthy dish that is perfect for a cold winter's day.

SERVES FOUR

1 Place the soaked and drained kidney beans in a large pan of unsalted boiling water. Bring back to the boil and boil rapidly for 10 minutes, then drain.

2 Place the soaked and drained black-eyed or cannellini beans in a separate large pan of boiling unsalted water and boil rapidly for 10 minutes, then drain.

3 Place 600ml/1 pint/2¹/₂ cups of water in a large tagine or casserole, and add the bay leaves, celery and beans. Cover and place in an unheated oven.

4 Set the oven to 190°C/375°F/Gas 5. Cook for 1–1¹/₂ hours or until the beans are tender, then drain.

5 Heat 60ml/4 tbsp of the oil in a large frying pan or cast-iron tagine base. Pat the aubergine chunks dry, then add to the pan and cook, stirring, for 4–5 minutes. Remove and set aside.

6 Add the remaining oil to the tagine base or frying pan, then add the sliced onion and cook, stirring, for about 4–5 minutes, until softened. Add the crushed garlic and chopped red chillies and cook for a further 5 minutes, stirring frequently, until the onion is golden and has softened.

7 Reset the oven temperature to 160°C/325°F/Gas 3. Add the tomato purée and paprika to the onion mixture and cook for 1–2 minutes. Add the tomatoes, aubergine, beans and stock, then season to taste.

8 Cover the tagine base with the lid or, if using a frying pan, transfer the contents to a clay tagine or casserole. Place in the oven and cook for 1 hour.

9 Meanwhile, mix together the yogurt, mint and spring onions. Just before serving, add the fresh mint, parsley and coriander to the tagine and lightly mix through the vegetables.

10 Garnish with fresh herb sprigs and serve immediately with the mint yogurt and some couscous or brown rice.

---

2 bay leaves

2 celery sticks, each cut into 4 matchsticks

1 aubergine (eggplant), about 350g/12oz, cut into chunks

1 onion, thinly sliced

3 garlic cloves, crushed

1–2 fresh red chillies, seeded and chopped

2 large tomatoes, roughly chopped

15ml/1 tbsp each chopped fresh mint, parsley and coriander (cilantro)

fresh herb sprigs, to garnish

FOR THE MINT YOGURT

150ml/¹/₄ pint/²/₃ cup natural (plain) yogurt

30ml/2 tbsp chopped fresh mint

2 spring onions (scallions), chopped

FROM THE STORECUPBOARD

115g/4oz/generous ¹/₂ cup dried red kidney beans, soaked overnight in cold water and drained

115g/4oz/generous ¹/₂ cup dried black-eyed beans (peas) or cannellini beans, soaked overnight in cold water and drained

75ml/5 tbsp olive oil

30ml/2 tbsp tomato purée (paste)

5ml/1 tsp paprika

300ml/¹/₂ pint/1¹/₄ cups vegetable stock

salt and ground black pepper, to taste

Energy 209Kcal/890kJ; Protein 16.6g; Carbohydrate 33.9g, of which sugars 9.4g; Fat 1.9g, of which saturates 0.5g; Cholesterol 1mg; Calcium 173mg; Fibre 12.3g; Sodium 62mg

Creamy Puy Lentils ✳✳

Wholesome lentils are filling, nutritious, and very good value for money. A poached egg is the perfect companion to the creamy lentils, making this a very healthy and tasty supper dish.

SERVES SIX

1 Put the Puy lentils and bay leaf in a large pan, cover with cold water, and slowly bring to the boil. Reduce the heat and simmer, partially covered, for about 25 minutes, or until the lentils are tender. Stir the lentils occasionally and add more water, if necessary. Drain.

2 Heat the oil in a frying pan and cook the spring onions and garlic for 1 minute. Add the mustard, lemon rind and juice, tomatoes and seasoning, then mix together and cook gently for 1–2 minutes until the tomatoes are heated through. Add a little water if the mixture becomes too dry.

3 Meanwhile, poach the eggs in a pan of lightly salted barely simmering water for 4 minutes, adding them one at a time.

4 Stir the lentils and crème fraiche into the tomato mixture, remove and discard the bay leaf, then heat through for 1 minute. Divide among six serving plates. Top each portion with a poached egg, and sprinkle with parsley.

4 spring onions (scallions), sliced

2 large garlic cloves, chopped

finely grated rind and juice of 1 large lemon

4 plum tomatoes, seeded and diced

6 eggs

60ml/4 tbsp crème fraîche

30ml/2 tbsp chopped fresh flat leaf parsley, to garnish

FROM THE STORECUPBOARD

250g/9oz/generous 1 cup Puy lentils

1 bay leaf

30ml/2 tbsp olive oil

15ml/1 tbsp Dijon mustard

salt and ground black pepper, to taste

Energy 281kcal/1179kJ; Protein 17.2g; Carbohydrate 22.8g, of which sugars 3g; Fat 14.2g, of which saturates 4.9g; Cholesterol 202mg; Calcium 71mg; Fibre 4.5g; Sodium 84mg

Lentil and Nut Loaf ✶✶

For a vegetarian alternative at a special celebration, serve this with all the trimmings, including a vegetarian gravy. Garnish with fresh cranberries and flat leaf parsley for a really festive effect.

SERVES SIX

1 Cover the lentils with cold water and soak for 1 hour. Grind the nuts in a food processor, then place them in a large bowl. Coarsely chop the carrot, celery, onion and mushrooms, add to the food processor and process until finely chopped.

2 Heat the butter in a large pan. Add the vegetables and fry gently over a low heat, stirring occasionally, for 5 minutes. Stir in the curry powder and cook for 1 minute more. Remove from the heat and set aside to cool.

3 Drain the lentils and stir them into the ground nuts. Add the vegetables, ketchup, vegetarian Worcestershire sauce, egg, salt, chopped parsley and water.

4 Preheat the oven to 190°C/375°F/Gas 5. Grease a 1kg/2¹⁄₄lb loaf tin (pan) and line with baking parchment or foil. Press the mixture into the tin.

5 Bake for 1–1¹⁄₄ hours, until just firm, covering the top with foil if it starts to burn. Leave to stand for 15 minutes, turn out, and peel off the paper. Serve immediately in slices.

115g/4oz/1 cup hazelnuts

115g/4oz/1 cup walnuts

1 large carrot

2 celery sticks

1 large onion

115g/4oz/1¹⁄₂ cups fresh mushrooms

50g/2oz/¹⁄₄ cup butter, plus extra for greasing

1 egg, beaten

60ml/4 tbsp chopped fresh parsley

150ml/¹⁄₄ pint/²⁄₃ cup water

FROM THE STORECUPBOARD

115g/4oz/¹⁄₂ cup red lentils

10ml/2 tsp mild curry powder

30ml/2 tbsp tomato ketchup

30ml/2 tbsp vegetarian Worcestershire sauce

10ml/2 tsp salt

Energy 410kcal/1703kJ; Protein 11.9g; Carbohydrate 16.5g, of which sugars 5.2g; Fat 33.5g, of which saturates 6.6g; Cholesterol 49mg; Calcium 81mg; Fibre 3.6g; Sodium 222mg

Fabulous Fish and Shellfish

The cost of fish and shellfish can vary
tremendously, depending on where you live,
the type of fish, and what season it is. Oily fish,
such as sardines and mackerel, firm-fleshed
white fish such as halibut and haddock, and
squid are all usually good value for money.
So why not indulge yourself without breaking
the bank with delicate Smoked Haddock Flan,
super-healthy Pan-fried Mackerel with
Ratatouille and Lemon, or Spicy Squid Stew?

Hake with Lemon Sauce ✳✳✳

This healthy dish is perfect on its own as a light lunch, or can be served with steamed new potatoes for a more substantial main course.

500g/1¹⁄₄lb fresh spinach, trimmed of thick stalks

4 x 200g/7oz fresh hake steaks

175ml/6fl oz/³⁄₄ cup white wine

3–4 strips of pared lemon rind

FOR THE EGG AND LEMON SAUCE

2 large (US extra large) eggs, at room temperature

juice of ¹⁄₂ lemon

FROM THE STORECUPBOARD

30ml/2 tbsp plain (all-purpose flour)

75ml/5 tbsp olive oil

salt and ground black pepper, to taste

2.5ml/¹⁄₂ tsp cornflour (cornstarch)

SERVES FOUR

1 Place the spinach leaves in a large pan with just the water that clings to the leaves after washing. Cover and cook over a medium heat for 5–7 minutes, then drain and set aside.

2 Dust the fish with the flour. Heat the oil in a large frying pan, add the fish and sauté gently for 2–3 minutes on each side. Pour in the wine, and add the lemon rind and some seasoning. Lower the heat and simmer gently for a few minutes, then add the spinach, and let it simmer for 3–4 minutes more. Remove from the heat.

3 To make the sauce, mix the cornflour to a paste with a little water. Beat the eggs in a bowl, then add the lemon juice and the cornflour mixture and beat until smooth. Gradually beat in a ladleful of the liquid from the fish pan, then beat for 1 minute. Add a second ladleful in the same way, and continue until all of the liquid is incorporated.

4 Pour the sauce over the fish and spinach, and return the pan to the hob. Allow to cook gently for 2–3 minutes, then serve immediately.

COOK'S TIP *Spinach can have a gritty texture if it is not washed properly. The best way to wash it is to swirl the leaves gently with your hand in a large bowl of cold water, then lift them out by hand into a colander positioned over a sink. Repeat the process until the water that drains from the colander runs clear.*

Energy 441Kcal/1,839kJ; Protein 43.6g; Carbohydrate 10.6g, of which sugars 2.3g; Fat 22.1g, of which saturates 3.5g; Cholesterol 141mg; Calcium 273mg; Fibre 2.9g; Sodium 413mg

1 large red (bell) pepper

4 rashers (strips) streaky (fatty) bacon, roughly chopped

4 garlic cloves, finely chopped

1 onion, sliced

5ml/1 tsp hot pimentón (smoked Spanish paprika)

large pinch of saffron threads or 1 sachet powdered saffron, soaked in 45ml/3 tbsp hot water

6 plum tomatoes, quartered

350g/12oz fresh skinned cod fillet, cut into large chunks

45ml/3 tbsp chopped fresh coriander (cilantro), plus a few sprigs to garnish

crusty bread, to serve

FROM THE STORECUPBOARD

45ml/3 tbsp olive oil

10ml/2 tsp paprika

400g/14oz can haricot (navy) beans, drained and rinsed

about 600ml/1 pint/ 2½ cups fish stock

salt and ground black pepper, to taste

COOK'S TIP

Cod is a popular white fish despite having been over-fished. Ensure that you buy fish that comes from a carefully controlled source, or else use an alternative white fish, such as hoki, hake, haddock, whiting, coley or pollack.

Cod and Bean Stew ✳✳

Everything is cooked in one pot in this divine dish, which combines fresh cod with luxurious saffron and smoked paprika-spiced beans.

SERVES EIGHT

1 Preheat the grill (broiler) and line the pan with foil. Halve the red pepper and scoop out the seeds. Place the halves, cut-side down, in the grill pan and grill (broil) under a hot heat for about 10–15 minutes, until the skin is charred.

2 Put the pepper into a plastic bag, seal and leave for 10 minutes to steam. Remove from the bag, peel off the skin and discard. Chop the pepper into large pieces.

3 Heat the oil in a pan, then add the bacon and garlic. Fry for 2 minutes, then add the onion. Cover and cook for 5 minutes until the onion is soft. Stir in the paprika and pimentón, the saffron and its soaking water, and salt and pepper to taste.

4 Stir in the beans and add just enough stock to cover. Bring to the boil and simmer, uncovered, for about 15 minutes, stirring to prevent sticking. Stir in the chopped pepper and tomato quarters. Drop in the cubes of cod and bury them in the sauce.

5 Cover and simmer for 5 minutes. Stir in the chopped coriander. Serve in warmed soup plates or bowls, garnished with the coriander sprigs. Eat with lots of crusty bread.

Energy 181kcal/757kJ; Protein 14.4g; Carbohydrate 13.4g, of which sugars 6g; Fat 8.1g, of which saturates 1.8g; Cholesterol 28mg; Calcium 59mg; Fibre 4.6g; Sodium 388mg

Halibut with Leek and Ginger ✳✳✳

Generally fish needs to be absolutely fresh, but halibut needs to mature for a day or two to bring out the flavour. In this simple recipe the delicate flavour is subtly complemented by leeks and fresh root ginger.

SERVES FOUR

1 Trim the leeks, discarding the coarse outer leaves, the very dark green tops and the root end. Cut them into 5cm/2in lengths then slice into thin matchsticks. Wash thoroughly.

2 Peel the fresh ginger as best you can then slice it very thinly and cut the slices into thin matchsticks.

3 Pat the halibut steaks dry on kitchen paper. Heat a large pan with the olive oil and add 50g/2oz/$^1/_4$ cup of the butter. As it begins to bubble place the fish steaks carefully in the pan, skin side down. Allow the halibut to colour – this will take 3–4 minutes. Then turn the steaks over, reduce the heat and cook for about a further 10 minutes.

4 Remove the fish from the pan, set aside and keep warm. Add the leek and ginger to the pan, stir to mix then allow the leek to soften (they may colour slightly but this is fine). Once softened, season with a little salt and ground black pepper. Cut the remaining butter into small pieces then, off the heat, gradually stir into the pan. Serve immediately.

2 leeks

50g/2oz piece fresh root ginger

4 halibut steaks, approximately 175g/6oz each (*see* Cook's Tip)

75g/3oz/6 tbsp butter

FROM THE STORECUPBOARD

15ml/1 tbsp olive oil

COOK'S TIP
Look out for flattish, reasonably thin halibut steaks, as you want to cook them quite quickly in a pan on the stove rather than in the oven.

Energy 364kcal/1520kJ; Protein 39.1g; Carbohydrate 2.7g, of which sugars 2.1g; Fat 21.9g, of which saturates 10.8g; Cholesterol 101mg; Calcium 75mg; Fibre 1.9g; Sodium 221mg

Haddock with Fennel Butter ✳✳✳

Fresh fish tastes fabulous cooked in a simple herb butter. Here the liquorice flavour of fennel complements the haddock beautifully to make a simple dish that is ideal for a dinner party.

SERVES FOUR

1 Preheat the oven to 220°C/425°F/Gas 7. Season the fish on both sides with salt and pepper. Melt one-quarter of the butter in a non-stick frying pan and cook the fish over a medium heat briefly on both sides.

2 Transfer the fish to a shallow ovenproof dish. Cut four wafer-thin slices from the lemon and squeeze the juice from the remainder over the fish. Place the lemon slices on top and then bake for 15–20 minutes, or until the fish is cooked.

3 Meanwhile, melt the remaining butter in the frying pan and add the fennel and a little seasoning.

4 Transfer the cooked fish to plates and pour the cooking juices into the herb butter. Heat the butter gently for a few seconds, then pour over the fish. Serve immediately.

675g/1¹/₂ lb haddock fillet, skinned and cut into 4 portions

50g/2oz/¹/₄ cup butter

1 lemon

45ml/3 tbsp chopped fennel

Energy 269kcal/1125kJ; Protein 36.5g; Carbohydrate 0.4g, of which sugars 0.3g; Fat 13.5g, of which saturates 7g; Cholesterol 86mg; Calcium 54mg; Fibre 0.3g; Sodium 178mg

Smoked Haddock Flan ✳✳✳

The classic combination of potatoes and smoked fish is reworked in pastry. Always ask your fishmonger for "pale" smoked rather than "yellow" haddock as the latter tends to have been dyed to look bright and often has not been smoked properly at all. It is worth paying the extra for the real thing.

SERVES FOUR

1 Preheat the oven to 200°C/400°F/Gas 6. Use a food processor to make the pastry. Put the flour, salt and butter into the food processor bowl and process until the mixture resembles fine breadcrumbs. Pour in a little cold water (you will need about 40ml/8 tsp but see Cook's Tip) and continue to process until the mixture forms a ball. If this takes longer than 30 seconds add a dash or two more water.

2 Take the pastry ball out of the food processor, wrap it in clear film (plastic wrap) and leave it to rest in a cool place for about 30 minutes.

3 Roll out the pastry and use it to line a 20cm/8in flan tin (quiche pan). Prick the base of the pastry all over with a fork then bake blind in the preheated oven for 20 minutes.

4 Put the haddock fillets in a pan with the milk, peppercorns and thyme. Poach for 10 minutes. Remove the fish from the pan using a slotted spoon and flake the flesh into small chunks. Allow the poaching liquor to cool.

5 Whisk the cream and eggs together in a large bowl, then whisk in the cooled poaching liquid.

6 Arrange the flaked fish and diced potato in the base of the pastry case, and season to taste with black pepper. Pour the cream mixture over the top.

7 Put the flan in the oven and bake for 40 minutes, until lightly browned on top and set.

VARIATION

This recipe is also delicious if you add roughly chopped hard-boiled eggs when you arrange the fish and potatoes in the base of the pastry case.

FOR THE PASTRY

115g/4oz/1¹/₂ cup cold butter, cut into chunks

cold water, to mix

FOR THE FILLING

2 pale smoked haddock fillets (approximately 200g/7oz)

600ml/1 pint/2¹/₂ cups full-fat (whole) milk

150ml/¹/₄ pint/²/₃ cup double (heavy) cream

2 eggs

200g/7oz potatoes, peeled and diced

FROM THE STORECUPBOARD

225g/8oz/2 cups plain (all-purpose) flour

pinch of salt

3–4 black peppercorns

sprig of fresh thyme

ground black pepper, to taste

Energy 734kcal/3064kJ; Protein 23.8g; Carbohydrate 58.4g, of which sugars 8.2g; Fat 46.8g, of which saturates 27.9g; Cholesterol 225mg; Calcium 280mg; Fibre 2.3g; Sodium 636mg

Crispy Fried Whitebait with Sherry Salsa ✳

Whitebait are the small fry of herring and sprats, and are especially delicious when fried and eaten whole. Frozen varieties are good value for money and are particularly useful if you are unable to buy fresh ones from your local supermarket or fishmonger.

SERVES FOUR

1 Preheat the oven to 150°C/300°F/Gas 2. Wash the fresh or thawed whitebait thoroughly, drain well and dry on kitchen paper, then dust in the seasoned flour.

2 To make the salsa, place the chopped shallot, garlic, tomatoes, chilli and 30ml/2 tbsp olive oil in a pan. Cover with a lid and cook gently for about 10 minutes.

3 Pour the sherry into the pan and season with salt and pepper to taste. Stir in the herbs and breadcrumbs, then cover and keep the salsa hot until the whitebait are ready.

4 Heat the oils together in a heavy frying pan and cook the fish in batches until crisp and golden. Drain on kitchen paper and keep warm until all the fish are cooked. Serve immediately with the salsa and crusty bread.

225g/8oz whitebait, thawed if frozen

FOR THE SALSA

1 shallot, finely chopped

2 garlic cloves, finely chopped

4 ripe tomatoes, chopped

1 small red chilli, seeded and finely chopped

60ml/4 tbsp sweet sherry

30–45ml/2–3 tbsp chopped mixed fresh herbs, such as parsley or basil

25g/1oz/1/2 cup stale white breadcrumbs

FROM THE STORECUPBOARD

30ml/2 tbsp seasoned plain (all-purpose) flour

90ml/6 tbsp olive oil

60ml/4 tbsp sunflower oil

salt and ground black pepper, to taste

Energy 360kcal/1498kJ; Protein 12.6g; Carbohydrate 13.2g, of which sugars 5.2g; Fat 27.2g, of which saturates 0.1g; Cholesterol 0mg; Calcium 504mg; Fibre 1.5g; Sodium 188mg

Pan-fried Mackerel with Ratatouille and Lemon ✳✳✳

Make this colourful dish during the summer when peppers and tomatoes have the sweetest flavour and are better value for money. Ratatouille is rather like a chunky vegetable stew. This version is particularly lemony, to offset the richness of the mackerel.

SERVES FOUR

2 large mackerel, filleted, or 4 fillets

lemon wedges, to serve

FOR THE RATATOUILLE

1 large aubergine (eggplant), sliced

1 large onion, chopped

2 garlic cloves, finely chopped

1 large courgette (zucchini), sliced

1 red and 1 green (bell) pepper, seeded and chopped

800g/1³/₄lb ripe tomatoes, roughly chopped

FROM THE STORECUPBOARD

90ml/6 tbsp olive oil

1 bay leaf

plain (all-purpose) flour, for dusting

salt and ground black pepper, to taste

COOK'S TIP *Sprinkling the slices of aubergine (eggplant) with salt helps to draw out the bitter juices and allows the aubergine to absorb more flavour.*

1 Sprinkle the aubergine slices with salt and leave to stand in a colander for 30 minutes.

2 Heat 15ml/3 tsp of the olive oil in a large flameproof casserole. Gently fry the onion until it colours slightly. Add the garlic, then the courgette and peppers and stir-fry. Add the tomatoes and bay leaf, partially cover and simmer until the tomatoes just soften.

3 Rinse off the salt from the aubergine. Using kitchen paper, squeeze the slices dry, then cut into cubes. Heat 15ml/3 tsp of the olive oil in a frying pan until smoking. Add the aubergine cubes a handful at a time and cook, stirring over a high heat until the cubes are brown on all sides. Stir into the tomato sauce.

4 Cut each mackerel fillet into three, then dust the filleted side with flour. Heat 60ml/4 tbsp of the oil in a frying pan and fry the fish, floured side down, for 3 minutes. Turn and cook for a further minute, then slip into the sauce and simmer, covered, for 5 minutes. Check the seasoning before serving hot or cold.

Energy 544kcal/2260kJ; Protein 28.4g; Carbohydrate 22.9g, of which sugars 17.9g; Fat 38.2g, of which saturates 6.9g; Cholesterol 68mg; Calcium 78mg; Fibre 6.3g; Sodium 104mg

Grilled Mackerel with Spicy Dhal ✳✳✳

Oily fish like mackerel are essential as part of a balanced diet and are good value for money. Here they are complemented by tamarind-flavoured dhal, chopped fresh tomatoes, onion salad and flat bread.

SERVES FOUR

1 Rinse the lentils, drain them well and put them in a pan. Pour in 1 litre/1³/₄ pints/4 cups water and bring to the boil. Lower the heat, partially cover the pan and simmer the lentils for about 30–40 minutes, stirring occasionally, until they are tender and soft.

2 Heat the oil in a wok or shallow pan. Add the mustard seeds, then cover and cook for a few seconds, until they pop. Remove the lid, add the rest of the seeds, with the turmeric and chillies and cook for a few more seconds.

3 Stir in the lentils, with salt to taste. Mix well, then stir in the tamarind paste and sugar. Bring to the boil, then simmer for 10 minutes, until thick. Stir in the chopped fresh coriander.

4 Meanwhile, clean the fish then heat a ridged griddle pan or the grill (broiler) until very hot. Make six diagonal slashes on either side of each fish and remove the head if you like. Season inside and out, then cook for 5–7 minutes on each side, until the skin is crisp. Serve with the dhal, flat bread and tomatoes, garnished with chilli and coriander.

3–4 dried red chillies, crumbled

30ml/2 tbsp tamarind paste

30ml/2 tbsp chopped fresh coriander (cilantro)

4 mackerel or 8 large sardines

fresh red chilli slices and finely chopped coriander (cilantro), to garnish

flat bread and tomatoes, to serve

FROM THE STORECUPBOARD

250g/9oz/1 cup red lentils

30ml/2 tbsp sunflower oil

2.5ml/¹/₂ tsp each mustard seeds, cumin seeds, fennel seeds, and fenugreek or cardamom seeds

5ml/1 tsp ground turmeric

5ml/1 tsp soft brown sugar

salt and ground black pepper, to taste

Energy 586kcal/2453kJ; Protein 43.3g; Carbohydrate 36.5g, of which sugars 2.8g; Fat 30.6g, of which saturates 5.7g; Cholesterol 81mg; Calcium 72mg; Fibre 3.6g; Sodium 121mg

Grilled Sardines with Chilli and Onion Marinade ✳✳

This unusual dish is packed with flavour and is an ideal make-ahead dish for a summer dinner party or *al fresco* meal. Serve with roasted summer vegetables and flatbread to mop up the marinade.

SERVES FOUR

1 Cut the heads off the sardines and split each of them along the belly. Turn the fish over so that the backbone is uppermost. Press down along the backbone to loosen it, then carefully lift out the backbone and as many of the remaining little bones as possible. Close the sardines up again and dust them with seasoned flour.

2 Heat 30ml/2 tbsp of the olive oil in a frying pan and fry the sardines for 2–3 minutes on each side. With a metal spatula, remove the fish from the pan to a plate and allow to cool, then pack them in a single layer in a large shallow dish.

3 To make the marinade, add the remaining olive oil to the oil in the frying pan. Fry the onion and garlic for 5–10 minutes until translucent. Add the bay leaves, cloves, chilli and paprika, with pepper to taste. Fry for another 1–2 minutes.

4 Stir in the vinegar, wine and a little salt. Allow to bubble up, then pour over the sardines to cover the fish completely. When cool, cover and chill overnight or for up to three days. Serve garnished with the onion, pepper and tomatoes.

12–16 sardines, cleaned

roasted red onion, green (bell) pepper and tomatoes, to garnish

FOR THE MARINADE

1 onion, sliced

1 garlic clove, crushed

1 dried red chilli, seeded and chopped

120ml/4fl oz/^{1}/$_2$ cup white wine

FROM THE STORECUPBOARD

seasoned plain (all-purpose) flour, for dusting

90 ml/6 tbsp olive oil

3–4 bay leaves

2 cloves

5ml/1 tsp paprika

120ml/4fl oz/^{1}/$_2$ cup wine or sherry vinegar

salt and ground black pepper, to taste

Energy 353kcal/1467kJ; Protein 23.7g; Carbohydrate 4.2g, of which sugars 1g; Fat 26g, of which saturates 5.1g; Cholesterol 0mg; Calcium 124mg; Fibre 0.3g; Sodium 129mg

Barbecued Sardines with Orange and Parsley ✳

Sardines are ideal for the barbecue – the meaty flesh holds together and the skin crisps nicely – but they are equally delicious cooked under a grill (broiler). Serve them with boiled potatoes and a green salad.

SERVES SIX

6 whole sardines, gutted

1 orange, sliced

a small bunch of fresh flat leaf parsley, chopped

FROM THE STORECUPBOARD

60ml/4 tbsp extra virgin olive oil

salt and ground black pepper, to taste

1 Arrange the sardines and orange slices in a single layer in a shallow, non-metallic dish. Sprinkle over the chopped parsley and season with salt and pepper, to taste.

2 Drizzle the oil over the sardines and orange slices and stir to coat. Cover with clear film (plastic wrap) and chill for 2 hours.

3 Meanwhile, prepare the barbecue or preheat the grill (broiler) to high. Remove the sardines and orange slices from the marinade and place them directly on to a grill rack.

4 Cook the fish over the barbecue or under the hot grill for 7–8 minutes on each side, until the fish are cooked through. Serve immediately.

Energy 156kcal/649kJ; Protein 13.1g; Carbohydrate 1.7g, of which sugars 1.7g; Fat 10.8g, of which saturates 2.3g; Cholesterol 0mg; Calcium 73mg; Fibre 0.3g; Sodium 72mg

Fish Curry with Shallots and Lemon Grass ✳✳✳

This is a thin fish curry made with salmon fillets. It has wonderfully strong, aromatic flavours, and it should ideally be served in small bowls with plenty of crusty bread or plain boiled rice.

SERVES FOUR

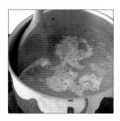

1 Place the salmon fillets in the freezer for about 30–40 minutes to firm up the flesh slightly. Remove and discard the skin, then use a sharp knife to cut the fish into 2.5cm/1in cubes, removing any stray bones as you do so.

2 Pour the vegetable stock into a pan and bring it slowly to the boil. Add the chopped shallots, garlic, ginger, lemon grass, dried chilli flakes, fish sauce and sugar. Bring back to the boil, stir well to ensure the ingredients are thoroughly mixed, then reduce the heat and simmer gently for about 15 minutes.

3 Add the fish pieces, bring back to the boil, then turn off the heat. Leave the curry to stand for 10–15 minutes, then serve in small bowls.

450g/1lb salmon fillets

4 shallots, finely chopped

2 garlic cloves, finely chopped

2.5cm/1in piece fresh root ginger, finely chopped

1 lemon grass stalk, finely chopped

2.5ml/^{1}/$_2$ tsp dried chilli flakes

FROM THE STORECUPBOARD

500ml/17fl oz/2^1/$_4$ cups vegetable stock

15ml/1 tbsp Thai fish sauce

5ml/1 tsp light muscovado (brown) sugar

Energy 218kcal/910kJ; Protein 23.4g; Carbohydrate 3.1g, of which sugars 2.7g; Fat 12.6g, of which saturates 2.2g; Cholesterol 56mg; Calcium 51mg; Fibre 0.8g; Sodium 322mg

Prawn and New Potato Stew ✳✳

New potatoes with plenty of flavour, such as Jersey Royals, Maris Piper or Nicola, are essential for this effortless seasonal stew. Use fresh prawns if they are on special offer, otherwise use good-quality frozen ones as they will usually be much more economical and taste almost as good.

SERVES FOUR

1 Cook the new potatoes in lightly salted, boiling water for 15 minutes, until tender. Drain and return to the pan.

2 Meanwhile, finely chop the coriander and crumble the dried chilli. Heat the oil in large pan and fry the garlic for 1 minute. Pour in the chopped tomatoes, and add the chilli, coriander and 90ml/6 tbsp water. Bring to the boil, reduce the heat, cover and simmer gently for 5 minutes.

3 Stir in the prawns and the cooked new potatoes and heat briefly until they are warmed through. Be careful not to overcook the prawns or they will quickly shrivel, becoming tough and tasteless.

4 Spoon the stew into shallow bowls and serve sprinkled with the remaining coriander, torn into pieces. Serve with bread and salad, or steamed seasonal vegetables.

675g/1¹/₂lb small new potatoes, scrubbed

15g/¹/₂ oz/¹/₂ cup fresh coriander (cilantro)

1 garlic clove

300g/11oz cooked peeled prawns (shrimp), thawed and drained if frozen

FROM THE STORECUPBOARD

15ml/1 tbsp olive oil

400g/14oz can chopped tomatoes

1 dried red chilli, crumbled

Energy 218kcal/924kJ; Protein 16.9g; Carbohydrate 30.4g, of which sugars 5.4g; Fat 4.1g, of which saturates 0.7g; Cholesterol 146mg; Calcium 84mg; Fibre 2.9g; Sodium 171mg

Prawn, Tomato and Potato Omelette ✳✳

This simple dish makes a delicious lunch when served with a fresh leafy green salad, or a healthy light meal when served with steamed seasonal vegetables. The sweet prawns are cooked gently inside the omelette, which helps them to stay tender and succulent.

SERVES FOUR

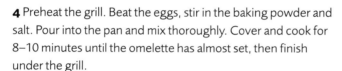

1 Cook the potatoes in a pan of salted boiling water for about 10 minutes or until tender.

2 Meanwhile, pour the oil into a 23cm/9in frying pan which can safely be used under the grill (broiler). Place over a medium heat. Add the onion slices and stir well to coat evenly in the oil. Cook for 5 minutes until the onions begin to soften. Sprinkle over the paprika and cook for 1 minute more.

3 Stir in the tomatoes. Drain the cooked potatoes thoroughly and add to the pan. Stir gently to mix. Increase the heat and cook for 10 minutes, or until the mixture has thickened and the potatoes have absorbed the flavour of the tomatoes. Remove from the heat and stir in the prawns.

4 Preheat the grill. Beat the eggs, stir in the baking powder and salt. Pour into the pan and mix thoroughly. Cover and cook for 8–10 minutes until the omelette has almost set, then finish under the grill.

200g/7oz potatoes, peeled and diced

1 onion, finely sliced

2 large tomatoes, peeled, seeded and chopped

200g/7oz frozen peeled raw prawns (shrimp), thawed

6 eggs

FROM THE STORECUPBOARD

30ml/2 tbsp olive oil

2.5ml/$^1/_2$ tsp paprika

2.5ml/$^1/_2$ tsp baking powder

a pinch of salt

Energy 247kcal/1031kJ; Protein 19.6g; Carbohydrate 10.8g, of which sugars 3.1g; Fat 14.5g, of which saturates 3.3g; Cholesterol 383mg; Calcium 93mg; Fibre 1.2g; Sodium 211mg

Spicy Squid Stew ✳✳✳

This hearty stew is ideal on a cold evening, served with plenty of fresh crusty bread or steamed rice. The potatoes disintegrate to thicken and enrich the sauce, making a warming, comforting main course.

SERVES SIX

1 Clean the squid under cold water. Pull the tentacles away from the body. The squid's entrails will come out easily.

2 Remove the cartilage from inside the body cavity and discard it. Wash the body thoroughly.

3 Pull away the membrane that covers the body. Cut between the tentacles and head, discarding the head and entrails. Leave the tentacles whole but discard the hard beak in the middle. Cut the body into thin rounds.

4 Heat the oil, add the garlic, chillies and celery and cook gently over a low heat for 5 minutes.

5 Stir in the potatoes, then add the wine and stock. Bring to the boil, then simmer, covered, for 25 minutes.

6 Remove from the heat and stir in the squid, tomatoes and parsley. Cover the pan and leave to stand until the squid is cooked. Serve immediately.

600g/1lb 6oz squid

5 garlic cloves, crushed

4 fresh jalapeño chillies, seeded and finely chopped

2 celery sticks, diced

500g/1^{1}/4lb small new potatoes scrubbed, scraped or peeled and quartered

400ml/14fl oz/1^{2}/3 cups dry white wine

4 tomatoes, diced

30ml/2 tbsp chopped fresh flat leaf parsley

white rice or arepas (corn breads), to serve

FROM THE STORECUPBOARD

45ml/3 tbsp olive oil

400ml/14fl oz/1^{2}/3 cups fish stock

salt

Energy 247kcal/1041kJ; Protein 17.6g; Carbohydrate 17.4g, of which sugars 3.8g; Fat 7.8g, of which saturates 1.3g; Cholesterol 225mg; Calcium 48mg; Fibre 2g; Sodium 136mg

Crab and Tofu Stir-fry ✳✳✳

For a year-round light meal, this stir-fry is a delicious choice. Use canned crab meat, as it is much more economical than fresh. Serve with fine egg noodles, if you like, as a special supper for two.

SERVES TWO

200g/7oz silken tofu

2 garlic cloves, finely chopped

115g/4oz canned crab meat

100g/3³/₄oz baby corn, halved lengthways

2 spring onions (scallions), chopped

1 fresh red chilli, seeded and finely chopped

juice of 1 lime

small bunch fresh coriander (cilantro), chopped, to garnish

lime wedges, to serve

FROM THE STORECUPBOARD

60ml/4 tbsp vegetable oil

30ml/2 tbsp soy sauce

15ml/1 tbsp Thai fish sauce (nam pla)

5ml/1 tsp light muscovado (brown) sugar

1 Drain the silken tofu, if necessary. Using a sharp knife, cut the tofu into 1cm/¹/₂in cubes.

2 Heat the oil in a wok or large, heavy frying pan. Add the tofu cubes and stir-fry until golden. Remove the tofu with a slotted spoon and set aside.

3 Add the garlic to the wok or pan and stir-fry for about 1 minute, or until golden. Add the crab meat, tofu, corn, spring onions, chilli, soy sauce, fish sauce and sugar. Cook, stirring constantly, until the vegetables are just tender.

4 Stir in the lime juice, sprinkle with coriander and serve in dishes with lime wedges, and fine egg noodles, if you like.

COOK'S TIPS
• Store fresh tofu in plenty of water in the refrigerator and use within three days. Change the water daily. Follow the use-by dates on cartoned or vacuum-packed tofu.

• Silken tofu is delicate, so handle it with care.

Energy 357kcal/1478kJ; Protein 21.5g; Carbohydrate 6.6g, of which sugars 5.6g; Fat 27.3g, of which saturates 3.2g; Cholesterol 41mg; Calcium 637mg; Fibre 2g; Sodium 2501mg

Perfect Poultry

CHICKEN, TURKEY AND DUCK ARE VERY POPULAR
AND INFINITELY VERSATILE. THE SUCCULENT FLESH
IS THE PERFECT PARTNER FOR A WIDE RANGE OF
DIVERSE INGREDIENTS, AND CAN BE COOKED IN
MANY DIFFERENT WAYS. FROM QUICK AND EASY STIR-
FRIED CHICKEN WITH THAI BASIL OR CHARGRILLED
CHICKEN WITH GARLIC AND PEPPERS TO ROASTED
DUCKLING WITH POTATOES OR TURKEY AND
CRANBERRY FILO PASTRY BUNDLES, THERE IS A RECIPE
TO SUIT EVERY BUDGET, TASTE AND OCCASION.

Stir-fried Chicken with Thai Basil ✳✳✳

Thai basil, sometimes called holy basil, has purple-tinged leaves and a more pronounced, slightly aniseedy flavour than the usual varieties. It is available in most Asian food stores but if you can't find any, use a handful of ordinary basil instead. Serve this fragrant stir-fry with plain steamed rice or boiled noodles and soy sauce on the side as a quick and easy supper dish.

SERVES SIX

1 Using a sharp knife, slice the chicken breast portions into strips. Halve the peppers, remove the seeds, then cut each piece of pepper into strips.

2 Heat the oil in a wok or large frying pan. Add the chicken and red peppers and stir-fry over a high heat for about 3 minutes, until the chicken is golden and cooked through. Season with salt and ground black pepper to taste.

3 Roughly tear up the basil leaves, add to the chicken and peppers and toss briefly to combine. Serve immediately with rice or noodles.

4 skinless chicken breast fillets

2 red (bell) peppers

1 small bunch of fresh Thai basil

FROM THE STORECUPBOARD

30ml/2 tbsp garlic-infused olive oil

salt and ground black pepper, to taste

Crème Fraîche and Coriander Chicken ✳✳

Boneless chicken thighs are usually better value for money than chicken breast fillets, and the meat has a stronger taste. There is no need to buy ready-skinned thighs, since it takes seconds to skin them yourself. Be generous with the coriander leaves, as they have a wonderful fragrant flavour, or use chopped parsley instead. Serve with creamy mashed potatoes or steamed rice, and steamed vegetables.

SERVES FOUR

1 Remove the skin from the chicken thighs, then cut each into three or four pieces.

2 Heat the oil in a wok or large frying pan, add the chicken and cook for about 6 minutes, turning occasionally, until cooked through.

3 Add the crème fraîche to the pan and stir until melted, then allow to bubble for 1–2 minutes.

4 Add the chopped coriander to the chicken and stir to combine. Season with salt and ground black pepper to taste, and serve immediately with mashed potatoes or rice, and steamed seasonal green vegetables.

6 boneless chicken thighs

60ml/4 tbsp crème fraîche

1 small bunch of fresh coriander (cilantro), roughly chopped

FROM THE STORECUPBOARD

15ml/1 tbsp sunflower oil

salt and ground black pepper, to taste

Top: Energy 161kcal/675kJ; Protein 24.8g; Carbohydrate 4g, of which sugars 3.8g; Fat 5.1g, of which saturates 0.9g; Cholesterol 70mg; Calcium 26mg; Fibre 1.4g; Sodium 65mg

Above: Energy 222kcal/927kJ; Protein 26.8g; Carbohydrate 0.7g, of which sugars 0.6g; Fat 12.4g, of which saturates 5.4g; Cholesterol 148mg; Calcium 43mg; Fibre 0.6g; Sodium 120mg

Barbecued Chicken ✳✳

In this simple recipe, chicken pieces are marinated in a strongly-scented marinade made with garlic, lemon juice, cumin, cinnamon and paprika, and then cooked on a barbecue or under a hot grill.

SERVES FOUR

1 In a bowl, combine the garlic, cumin, cinnamon, paprika, lemon juice, oil, and salt and pepper to taste. Add the chicken and turn to coat thoroughly in the marinade.

2 Leave to marinate for at least 1 hour or cover with clear film (plastic wrap) and leave in the refrigerator overnight.

3 Prepare and light the barbecue or preheat a grill (broiler). Place the dark meat on the grill pan and cook for 10 minutes, turning once.

4 Place the remaining chicken on the grill pan and cook for 7–10 minutes, turning occasionally, until golden brown and the juices run clear when pricked with a skewer. Serve immediately, with pitta breads, lemon wedges and salad.

5 garlic cloves, chopped

juice of 1 lemon

1.3kg/3lb chicken, cut into 8 portions

fresh coriander (cilantro) leaves, to garnish

warmed pitta bread, salad and lemon wedges, to serve

FROM THE STORECUPBOARD

30ml/2 tbsp ground cumin

7.5ml/1¹/₂ tsp ground cinnamon

5ml/1 tsp paprika

30ml/2 tbsp olive oil

salt and ground black pepper, to taste

Energy 313kcal/1315kJ; Protein 52.7g; Carbohydrate 0.9g, of which sugars 0g; Fat 11g, of which saturates 2.3g; Cholesterol 219mg; Calcium 20mg; Fibre 0g; Sodium 188mg

finely grated rind and
juice of 1 lemon

2 garlic cloves,
finely chopped

10ml/2 tsp crumbled dried
red chillies

8 boneless chicken
thighs, skinned and each
cut into 3 or 4 pieces

flat leaf parsley leaves,
to garnish

lemon wedges, to serve

FROM THE STORECUPBOARD

60ml/4 tbsp olive oil

salt and ground black
pepper, to taste

Devilled Chicken ✳✳

Grilling is a very healthy, low-fat way of cooking meat, and these spicy chicken skewers are a good source of protein. Serve them with a crisp leaf salad and pitta bread for a nutritious main meal.

SERVES FOUR

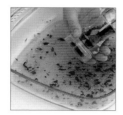

1 In a shallow dish, combine the oil, lemon rind and juice, garlic, dried chillies and seasoning. Add the chicken pieces and turn to coat thoroughly in the marinade. Cover and place in the refrigerator for at least 4 hours, or overnight.

2 When ready to cook, thread the marinated chicken on to eight oiled skewers and cook under a pre-heated grill (broiler) for 6–8 minutes, turning frequently. Garnish with parsley and serve with lemon wedges.

Energy 320kcal/1339kJ; Protein 42.1g; Carbohydrate 0.3g, of which sugars 0.2g; Fat 16.7g, of which saturates 3.2g; Cholesterol 210mg; Calcium 34mg; Fibre 0.5g; Sodium 183mg

Chargrilled Chicken with Garlic and Peppers ✳✳✳

An imaginative marinade can make all the difference to the sometimes bland flavour of chicken. This garlicky marinade, with mustard and chilli, gives tender chicken a real punch. Make sure the chicken has plenty of time to absorb the flavours before cooking.

SERVES SIX

1½ chickens, total weight about 2.25kg/5lb, jointed, or 12 chicken pieces

2 red or green (bell) peppers, quartered and seeded

5 ripe tomatoes, halved horizontally

lemon wedges, to serve

FOR THE MARINADE

juice of 1 large lemon

4 garlic cloves, crushed

2 fresh red or green chillies, seeded and chopped

FROM THE STORECUPBOARD

90ml/6 tbsp extra virgin olive oil

5ml/1 tsp French mustard

5ml/1 tsp dried oregano

salt and ground black pepper, to taste

1 Beat together the oil, lemon juice, garlic, chilli, mustard, oregano and seasoning in a large bowl. Add the chicken pieces and turn to coat thoroughly in the marinade. Cover with clear film (plastic wrap) and place in the refrigerator for 4–8 hours.

2 Prepare the barbecue or preheat a grill (broiler). When the barbecue or grill is hot, lift the chicken pieces out of the marinade and place them on the grill rack. Add the pepper pieces and the tomatoes to the marinade and set aside for 15 minutes. Grill the chicken pieces for 20–25 minutes.

3 Turn the chicken pieces over and cook for 20–25 minutes more. Meanwhile, thread the peppers on two metal skewers. Add them to the grill rack, with the tomatoes, for the last 15 minutes of cooking. Serve with the lemon wedges.

COOK'S TIP *If you are jointing the chicken yourself, divide the legs into two and make slits in the deepest part of the flesh. This will help the marinade to be absorbed more and let the chicken cook thoroughly.*

Energy 760Kcal/3,156kJ; Protein 61.7g; Carbohydrate 11.1g, of which sugars 10.8g; Fat 52.2g, of which saturates 13.3g; Cholesterol 313mg; Calcium 40mg; Fibre 3.1g; Sodium 235mg

Chicken and Preserved Lemon Tagine ✳✳

This fragrant Moroccan dish is perfect for a casual dinner party. Slowly cooked chicken pieces are served in an aromatic sauce, which melds the mellow flavour of the preserved lemons with the earthiness of the olives.

SERVES FOUR

1 onion, chopped

3 garlic cloves

1cm/¹/₂in fresh root ginger, peeled and grated,

pinch of saffron threads

4 chicken quarters, halved if liked

30ml/2 tbsp chopped fresh coriander (cilantro)

30ml/2 tbsp chopped fresh parsley

1 preserved lemon

115g/4oz/²/₃ cup Moroccan tan olives

lemon wedges and fresh coriander (cilantro) sprigs, to garnish

FROM THE STORECUPBOARD

30ml/2 tbsp olive oil

2.5–5ml/¹/₂–1 tsp ground cinnamon

750ml/1¹/₄ pints/3 cups chicken stock

salt and ground black pepper, to taste

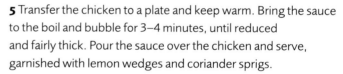

1 Heat the oil in a large flameproof casserole and fry the onion for 6–8 minutes over a moderate heat until lightly golden.

2 Meanwhile, crush the garlic and blend with the ginger, cinnamon, saffron and a little salt and pepper. Stir into the pan and fry for 1 minute. Add the chicken in batches and fry over a medium heat for 2–3 minutes, until browned.

3 Add the stock, coriander and parsley, bring to the boil, then cover and simmer for 45 minutes, until the chicken is tender.

4 Rinse the preserved lemon, discard the flesh and cut the peel into small pieces. Stir into the pan with the olives and simmer for a further 15 minutes, until the chicken is very tender.

5 Transfer the chicken to a plate and keep warm. Bring the sauce to the boil and bubble for 3–4 minutes, until reduced and fairly thick. Pour the sauce over the chicken and serve, garnished with lemon wedges and coriander sprigs.

COOK'S TIP
The salty, well-flavoured juice that is used to preserve the lemons can also be used to flavour salad dressings or added to hot sauces.

Energy 474Kcal/1967kJ; Protein 36.3g; Carbohydrate 5.3g, of which sugars 3.8g; Fat 34.3g, of which saturates 8.1g; Cholesterol 209mg; Calcium 83mg; Fibre 2.6g; Sodium 807mg

Chicken Casserole ✻✻

This is a very simple and economical dish to prepare and cook, and with its strong Mediterranean undertones it is also packed with colour and flavour. It is delicious served with French fries or plain boiled rice, but it goes equally well with steamed new potatoes.

SERVES FOUR

1 Preheat the oven to 180°C/350°F/Gas 4. Heat the olive oil in a wide flameproof casserole and brown the chicken pieces on both sides. Lift them out and set them aside.

2 Add the shallots, carrots and celery to the oil remaining in the casserole and sauté them for a few minutes. Stir in the garlic. As soon as it becomes aromatic, return the chicken to the pan and pour the lemon juice over the mixture. Let it bubble for a few minutes, then add the water and season with salt and pepper.

3 Cover the casserole and bake for 1 hour, turning the chicken pieces over occasionally.

4 Remove the casserole from the oven and stir in the parsley and olives. Re-cover the casserole and return it to the oven for about 30 minutes more. Check that it is cooked by piercing with a sharp knife. The juices should run clear. Serve immediately.

1 chicken, about 1.6kg/3¹/₂lb, jointed

3 or 4 shallots, finely chopped

2 carrots, sliced

1 celery stick, roughly chopped

2 garlic cloves, chopped

juice of 1 lemon

300ml/¹/₂ pint/1¹/₄ cups hot water

30ml/2 tbsp chopped flat leaf parsley

12 black or green olives

FROM THE STORECUPBOARD

75ml/5 tbsp extra virgin olive oil

salt and ground black pepper, to taste

Energy 726Kcal/3,008kJ; Protein 54.9g; Carbohydrate 3.8g, of which sugars 3.5g; Fat 54.5g, of which saturates 13.1g; Cholesterol 289mg; Calcium 55mg; Fibre 1.9g; Sodium 435mg

Spicy Chicken Casserole ✹✹

This spicy take on classic chicken casserole combines a rich red wine sauce with warming cinnamon and allspice, to create an aromatic dish that will be a treat for all the senses. Serve with orzo, plain boiled rice, or thick-cut fried potatoes for a satisfying supper.

SERVES FOUR

1.6kg/3¹/₂lb chicken, jointed

1 large onion, peeled and roughly chopped

250ml/8fl oz/1 cup red wine

boiled rice, orzo or fried potatoes, to serve

FROM THE STORECUPBOARD

75ml/5 tbsp extra virgin olive oil

30ml/2 tbsp tomato purée (paste) diluted in 450ml/³/₄ pint/ scant 2 cups hot water

1 cinnamon stick

3 or 4 whole allspice

2 bay leaves

salt and ground black pepper, to taste

1 Heat the oil in a large pan and brown the chicken pieces on all sides, ensuring that the skin is cooked and lifts away from the flesh slightly. Lift the chicken pieces out, set them aside on a plate, and keep them warm.

2 Add the chopped onion to the hot oil in the same pan and stir it over a medium heat until it becomes translucent.

3 Return the chicken pieces to the pan, pour over the wine and cook for 2–3 minutes, until it has reduced. Add the tomato purée mixture, cinnamon, allspice and bay leaves. Season well with salt and pepper.

4 Cover the pan and cook gently for 1 hour or until the chicken is tender. Serve with rice, orzo or fried potatoes.

Energy 767Kcal/3,195kJ; Protein 53.3g; Carbohydrate 32.5g, of which sugars 2.9g; Fat 47.7g, of which saturates 11.8g; Cholesterol 264mg; Calcium 51mg; Fibre 2.6g; Sodium 206mg

Chicken, Split Pea and Aubergine Koresh ✳✳

Koresh is traditionally a hearty meat dish, but here it has been transformed to a lighter chicken and vegetable stew.

SERVES FOUR

1 Put the split peas in a bowl, pour over cold water to cover, then leave to soak for about 4 hours. Drain well.

2 Heat a little of the oil in a pan, add two-thirds of the onions and cook for about 5 minutes. Add the chicken and cook until golden brown on all sides.

3 Add the soaked split peas to the chicken mixture, then the stock, turmeric, cinnamon and nutmeg. Cook over a medium-low heat for about 40 minutes, until the split peas are tender.

4 Heat the remaining oil in a pan, add the aubergines and remaining onions and cook until lightly browned. Add the tomatoes, garlic and mint. Season.

5 Just before serving, stir the aubergine mixture into the chicken and split pea stew. Garnish with fresh mint leaves and serve with boiled rice.

1 large or 2 small onions, finely chopped

500g/1¼lb boneless chicken thighs

2 aubergines (eggplants), roughly diced

8–10 ripe tomatoes, diced

2 garlic cloves, crushed

fresh mint, to garnish

FROM THE STORECUPBOARD

50g/2oz/¼ cup green split peas

45–60ml/3–4 tbsp olive oil

500ml/17fl oz/2¼ cups chicken stock

5ml/1 tsp ground turmeric

2.5ml/½ tsp ground cinnamon

1.5ml/¼ tsp grated nutmeg

30ml/2 tbsp dried mint

salt and ground black pepper, to taste

boiled rice, to serve

VARIATION *To make a traditional lamb koresh, use 675g/1½lb stewing lamb, cut into chunks, in place of chicken. Add to the onions, pour over water to cover and cook for 1½ hours until tender, then proceed as above.*

Energy 324kcal/1359kJ; Protein 32.4g; Carbohydrate 20.4g, of which sugars 12.6g; Fat 13.1g, of which saturates 2.5g; Cholesterol 131mg; Calcium 61mg; Fibre 6.2g; Sodium 136mg

3 onions, sliced

4 boneless chicken thighs

3 garlic cloves, chopped

5ml/1 tsp chopped fresh
root ginger

juice of 1 lemon

4 tomatoes, sliced

30ml/2 tbsp chopped fresh
coriander (cilantro)

150ml/^{1}/$_4$ pint/^{2}/$_3$ cup
natural (plain) yogurt, plus
extra to serve

4–5 saffron threads,
soaked in 10ml/2 tsp
hot milk

150ml/^{1}/$_4$ pint/^{2}/$_3$ cup
cold water

toasted flaked (sliced)
almonds and fresh
coriander (cilantro)
sprigs, to garnish

FROM THE STORECUPBOARD

10 whole green
cardamom pods

275g/10oz/1^1/$_2$ cups
basmati rice, soaked
and drained

2.5ml/^{1}/$_2$ tsp salt

2–3 whole cloves

5cm/2in cinnamon stick

45ml/3 tbsp vegetable oil

1.5ml/^{1}/$_4$ tsp
ground cloves

1.5ml/^{1}/$_4$ tsp hot
chilli powder

5ml/1 tsp ground cumin

5ml/1 tsp ground
coriander

2.5ml/^{1}/$_2$ tsp ground
black pepper

Chicken Biryani with Saffron Milk and Coriander **

Easy to make and very tasty, this delicious, fairly mild curry is bursting with flavours and is ideal for a family supper or relaxed dinner party.

SERVES FOUR

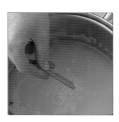

1 Preheat the oven to 190°C/375°F/ Gas 5. Remove the seeds from half the cardamom pods and grind them finely, using a mortar and pestle. Set them aside. Bring a pan of water to the boil and add the rice, salt, whole cardamom pods, cloves and cinnamon stick. Boil for 2 minutes, then drain, leaving the whole spices in the rice.

2 Heat the oil in a frying pan and cook the onions for 8 minutes, until softened and browned. Add the chicken and the ground spices, including the ground cardamom seeds. Mix well, then add the garlic, ginger and lemon juice. Stir-fry for 5 minutes.

3 Transfer the chicken mixture to a casserole and arrange the tomatoes on top. Sprinkle on the fresh coriander, spoon the yogurt evenly on top and cover with the drained rice.

4 Drizzle the saffron milk over the rice and pour over the water. Cover tightly and bake for 1 hour.

5 Transfer to a warmed serving platter and remove the whole spices from the rice. Garnish with toasted almonds and fresh coriander sprigs and serve with extra yogurt.

Energy 536kcal/2243kJ; Protein 31.3g; Carbohydrate 74.2g, of which sugars 14.6g; Fat 13g, of which saturates 2.1g; Cholesterol 105mg; Calcium 163mg; Fibre 3.6g; Sodium 139mg

1 large chicken, about 1.8kg/4lb, with giblets and neck if possible

1 small onion, sliced

1 small carrot, sliced

small bunch of fresh parsley and thyme

15g/¹⁄₂oz/1 tbsp butter

30ml/2 tbsp vegetable oil

6 rashers (strips) of streaky (fatty) bacon

FOR THE STUFFING

1 onion, finely chopped

50g/2oz/¹⁄₄ cup butter

150g/5oz/2¹⁄₂ cups fresh white breadcrumbs

15ml/1 tbsp fresh chopped parsley

15ml/1 tbsp fresh chopped mixed herbs, such as thyme, marjoram and chives

finely grated rind and juice of¹⁄₂ lemon

1 small egg, lightly beaten

FROM THE STORECUPBOARD

salt and ground black pepper, to taste

15ml/1 tbsp plain (all-purpose) flour

Traditional Roast Chicken with Herb Stuffing ✳✳

Nothing beats a roast chicken for Sunday lunch. Traditional accompaniments include roast potatoes, sausages and bacon rolls, bread sauce and a fruit sauce or jelly, such as cranberry sauce or elderberry jelly.

SERVES SIX

1 Remove the giblets from the chicken. Wipe out the inside of the bird thoroughly. Separate the liver from the rest of the giblets, chop it and set it aside to use in the gravy.

2 Put the giblets and the neck into a pan with the onion, carrot, parsley, thyme and some salt and pepper. Add cold water to cover, bring to the boil and simmer for 1 hour. Strain the stock and discard the giblets. Preheat the oven to 200°C/400°F/Gas 6.

3 Meanwhile, make the herb stuffing: cook the chopped onion in the butter in a large pan over a low heat for a few minutes. Remove from the heat, and add the breadcrumbs, herbs and lemon rind. Mix thoroughly. Mix in the lemon juice, beaten egg and a generous amount of salt and pepper.

4 Spoon the stuffing into the neck cavity of the chicken, without packing it in too tightly, and secure the opening with a small skewer. Spread the breast with the butter, then put the oil into a roasting pan and lay the bird in it. Season and lay the bacon rashers over the top of the bird to protect it in the oven.

5 Weigh the stuffed chicken and work out the cooking time (*see* Cook's Tip), then put into the oven. After 20 minutes, reduce the temperature to 180°C/350°F/Gas 4 and cook for another 45–60 minutes, or until cooked. Test by inserting a knife between the body and thigh: if the juices run clear, it is cooked. Transfer to a serving dish and allow it to rest for 10 minutes.

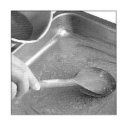

6 To make the gravy, pour off the excess fat from the roasting pan, then add the finely chopped liver and stir over a low heat for 1 minute. Sprinkle in just enough flour to absorb the remaining chicken fat and cook gently, stirring to blend, for 2 minutes. Gradually add some of the giblet stock, scraping the pan to dissolve the residues and stirring well to make a smooth gravy. Bring to the boil, stirring, gradually adding more stock until the consistency is as you like it. Adjust the seasoning, and then pour into a heated sauceboat to hand round separately.

7 Carve the chicken. Serve on heated plates with the herb stuffing and gravy, and any other accompaniments you like.

Energy 562Kcal/2342kJ; Protein 40.9g; Carbohydrate 23.2g, of which sugars 2.7g; Fat 34.5g, of which saturates 11.9g; Cholesterol 216mg; Calcium 72mg; Fibre 1.5g; Sodium 381mg

Baked Chicken with Fennel ✻✻✻

This simple dish is perfect as a make-ahead meal. It combines succulent chicken pieces with garlic, shallots and the aniseed flavour of fennel, and is served in a delicious creamy herb sauce.

SERVES FOUR

1 Place the chicken pieces, shallots and all but one of the garlic cloves in a flameproof dish or roasting pan. Add the oil, vinegar, wine or vermouth, if using, and fennel seeds. Season with pepper, then marinate for at least 2–3 hours.

2 Preheat the oven to 190°C/375°F/Gas 5. Add the fennel to the chicken, season with salt and stir to mix. Cook the chicken in the oven for 50–60 minutes, stirring once or twice. The chicken juices should run clear, not pink, when the thick thigh meat is pierced with a skewer.

3 Transfer the chicken and vegetables to a serving dish and keep them warm. Skim off some of the fat and bring the cooking juices to the boil, then pour in the cream. Stir, then whisk in the redcurrant jelly followed by the mustard. Check the seasoning.

4 Chop the remaining garlic clove with the feathery fennel tops and mix with the chopped parsley. Pour the sauce over the chicken and sprinkle the chopped garlic and herb mixture over the top. Serve immediately.

1.6–1.8kg/3¹/₂–4lb chicken, cut into 8 pieces or 8 chicken portions

250g/9oz shallots, peeled

1 garlic bulb, separated into cloves and peeled

45ml/3 tbsp white wine or vermouth (optional)

2 bulbs fennel, cut into wedges, feathery tops reserved

150ml/¹/₄ pint/²/₃ cup double (heavy) cream

5ml/1 tsp redcurrant jelly

30ml/2 tbsp chopped fresh parsley

FROM THE STORECUPBOARD

60ml/4 tbsp olive oil

45ml/3 tbsp tarragon vinegar

5ml/1 tsp fennel seeds, crushed

salt and ground black pepper

15ml/1 tbsp tarragon mustard

COOK'S TIPS

• *The cut surfaces of fennel quickly discolour, so make sure that you cook it soon after you have prepared it.*

• *Use new season garlic if possible, as the cloves will be more tender.*

Energy 568Kcal/2349kJ; Protein 24.3g; Carbohydrate 6.5g, of which sugars 5.3g; Fat 49.6g, of which saturates 19.4g; Cholesterol 163mg; Calcium 76mg; Fibre 2.9g; Sodium 112mg

Roasted Duckling with Potatoes ✳✳✳

The rich flavour of duck combined with these sweetened potatoes glazed with honey makes an excellent treat for a dinner party or special occasion. Serve with steamed seasonal green vegetables.

SERVES FOUR

1 Preheat the oven to 200°C/400°F/ Gas 6. Place the duckling in a roasting pan. Prick the skin well. Combine the soy sauce and orange juice and pour over the duck. Cook for 20 minutes.

2 Place the potato chunks in a bowl, stir in the honey and toss to mix well. Remove the duckling from the oven and spoon the potatoes all around and under the duckling.

3 Roast for 35 minutes, then remove from the oven. Toss the potatoes in the juices and turn the duck over. Put back in the oven and cook for a further 30 minutes.

4 Remove the duckling from the oven and carefully scoop off the excess fat, leaving the juices behind. Sprinkle the sesame seeds over the potatoes, season and turn the duckling back over, breast side up, and cook for a further 10 minutes. Remove from the oven and keep warm.

5 Pour off the excess fat and simmer the juices on the hob (stovetop). Serve the juices with the duckling and potatoes.

**1 duckling,
giblets removed**

**150ml/¹/₄ pint/²/₃ cup
fresh orange juice**

**3 large floury potatoes,
cut into chunks**

30ml/2 tbsp clear honey

15ml/1 tbsp sesame seeds

FROM THE STORECUPBOARD

**60ml/4 tbsp light
soy sauce**

**salt and ground
black pepper**

Energy 363kcal/1523kJ; Protein 23.3g; Carbohydrate 30.4g, of which sugars 11.8g; Fat 18.7g, of which saturates 4.9g; Cholesterol 108mg; Calcium 50mg; Fibre 1.6g; Sodium 198mg

VARIATIONS

These crisp, tasty little parcels can be made with a variety of fillings and they are a great way of using up a range of left-over cooked meats and the sauces that accompany them.

• To make ham and Cheddar bundles, replace the turkey with cubed cooked ham and use Cheddar cheese in place of the brie. A fruit-flavoured chutney would make a good alternative to the cranberry sauce, if you like.

• To make chicken and Stilton bundles, use diced cooked chicken in place of the cooked turkey and white Stilton instead of brie. Replace the cranberry sauce with mango chutney.

Turkey Filo Pastry Bundles ✳✳

After the traditional Christmas or Thanksgiving meal, it is easy to end up with lots of turkey leftovers. These delicious filo pastry parcels are a marvellous way of using up the small pieces of cooked turkey.

SERVES SIX

1 Preheat the oven to 200°C/400°F/Gas 6. Mix the turkey, diced brie, cranberry sauce and chopped parsley. Season with salt and pepper.

2 Cut the filo sheets in half widthways and trim to make 18 squares. Layer three pieces of pastry together, brushing them with a little melted butter so that they stick together. Repeat with the remaining filo squares to give six pieces.

3 Divide the turkey mixture among the pastry, making neat piles on each piece. Gather up the pastry to enclose the filling in bundles. Place on a baking sheet, brush with a little melted butter and bake for 20 minutes, or until the pastry is crisp and golden. Serve hot or warm with a green salad.

450g/1lb cooked turkey, cut into chunks

115g/4oz/1 cup diced brie cheese

30ml/2 tbsp cranberry sauce

30ml/2 tbsp chopped fresh parsley

9 sheets filo pastry, 45 x 28cm/18 x 11in each, thawed if frozen

50g/2oz/¼ cup butter, melted

green salad, to serve

FROM THE STORECUPBOARD

salt and ground black pepper, to taste

Energy 307kcal/1286kJ; Protein 24.8g; Carbohydrate 23.1g, of which sugars 4g; Fat 13g, of which saturates 8.1g; Cholesterol 78mg; Calcium 99mg; Fibre 1g; Sodium 199mg

Turkey Patties ✳

Minced turkey is very good value for money and makes deliciously light patties, which are ideal for summer meals and are especially popular with children. The recipe is a flavourful variation on a classic burger.

SERVES SIX

675g/1¹/₂lb minced (ground) turkey

1 small red onion, finely chopped

grated rind and juice of 1 lime

small handful of fresh thyme leaves

FROM THE STORECUPBOARD

15–30ml/1–2 tbsp olive oil

salt and ground black pepper, to taste

• During the summer, when fresh herbs are at their best, try using fresh oregano, parsley or basil in place of thyme.

• Use minced chicken in place of the turkey.

VARIATIONS

1 Mix together the minced turkey, chopped onion, lime rind and juice, thyme and seasoning in a large bowl.

2 Cover the bowl with clear film (plastic wrap) and chill for up to 4 hours to allow the flavours to infuse, then divide the mixture into six equal portions and shape into round patties.

3 Preheat a griddle pan. Brush the patties with oil, then place them on the pan and cook for 10–12 minutes.

4 Turn the patties over, brush with more olive oil and cook for 10–12 minutes on the second side, or until cooked through.

5 Serve the patties immediately with bread rolls, salad and chips (French fries), if you like.

Energy 141kcal/592kJ; Protein 27.7g; Carbohydrate 1.2g, of which sugars 0.6g; Fat 2.8g, of which saturates 0.6g; Cholesterol 64mg; Calcium 23mg; Fibre 0.1g; Sodium 57mg

Marvellous Meat

THERE IS A HUGE RANGE OF DIFFERENT TYPES
AND CUTS OF MEAT, ALL OF WHICH VARY IN PRICE AND
IN THEIR COOKING REQUIREMENTS. BY CHOOSING
GOOD-VALUE CUTS, COMBINING THEM WITH CHEAPER
INGREDIENTS AND COOKING IN AN APPROPRIATE
MANNER, MOST TYPES OF MEAT BECOME AFFORDABLE.
SO ADD A LITTLE SPICE TO YOUR LIFE WITH CHILLI CON
CARNE, TUCK INTO A SUCCULENT LAMB POT-ROAST OR
FOR A SUPER-HEALTHY AND VERY CHEAP MEAL ENJOY
LAMB'S LIVER AND BACON CASSEROLE.

Beef Patties with Onions and Peppers ✳✳

This is a firm family favourite. It is easy to make, delicious and good value for money. Try adding other vegetables, such as sliced red peppers, broccoli or mushrooms, and serve with salad and bread.

SERVES FOUR

1 Place the minced beef, chopped onion and 15ml/1 tbsp garlic-flavoured oil in a bowl and combine. Season well and form into four large or eight small patties.

2 Heat the remaining oil in a large non-stick pan, then add the patties and cook on both sides until browned. Sprinkle over 15ml/1 tbsp water and add a little seasoning.

3 Cover the patties with the sliced onions and peppers. Sprinkle in another 15ml/1 tbsp water and a little seasoning, then cover the pan. Reduce the heat to low and braise for 20–30 minutes.

4 When the onions are turning golden brown, remove the pan from the heat. Serve the patties with onions and peppers, and a side salad and some bread or potatoes, if you like.

500g/1¹/₂lb lean minced (ground) beef

4 onions, 1 finely chopped and 3 sliced

2–3 green (bell) peppers, seeded and sliced lengthways into strips

FROM THE STORECUPBOARD

30ml/2 tbsp garlic-flavoured olive oil

salt and ground black pepper, to taste

Energy 431kcal/1789kJ; Protein 27.9g; Carbohydrate 21.1g, of which sugars 17.2g; Fat 26.6g, of which saturates 9.6g; Cholesterol 75mg; Calcium 60mg; Fibre 4.4g; Sodium 110mg

Spaghetti with Meatballs ✳✳

For a great introduction to the charm of chillies, this simple pasta dish is hard to beat. Children love the gentle heat of the sweet and spicy tomato sauce.

SERVES FOUR

1 Put the beef in a bowl. Add the egg, with half the parsley and half the crushed chillies. Season with plenty of salt and pepper.

2 Tear the bread into pieces and place in a bowl. Moisten with the milk. Leave to soak for a few minutes, then squeeze out the excess milk and crumble the bread over the meat mixture. Mix everything together with a wooden spoon, then use your hands to knead the mixture so that it becomes smooth and quite sticky.

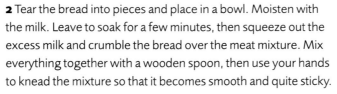

3 Wash your hands, rinse them under the cold tap, then pick up small pieces of the mixture and roll them to make about 20–30 small balls. Place on a tray and chill for 30 minutes.

4 Heat the oil in a large non-stick frying pan. Cook the meatballs in batches until browned on all sides.

COOK'S TIP *This is an ideal dish to make ahead and freeze. Leave to cool at the end of step 5, then freeze.*

5 Meanwhile, pour the passata and stock into a pan. Heat gently, then add the remaining chillies and the sugar, and season. Add the meatballs and simmer for 20 minutes.

6 Cook the pasta until it is just tender, following the instructions on the packet. Drain and tip it into a large heated bowl. Pour over the sauce and toss gently. Sprinkle with the remaining parsley and shavings of Parmesan cheese. Serve immediately.

350g/12oz minced (ground) beef

1 egg

60ml/4 tbsp roughly chopped fresh flat leaf parsley

2.5ml/^{1}/$_2$ tsp crushed dried red chillies

1 thick slice white bread, crusts removed

30ml/2 tbsp milk

shavings of Parmesan cheese, to serve

FROM THE STORECUPBOARD

salt and ground black pepper, to taste

about 30ml/2 tbsp olive oil

400ml/14fl oz/1^2/$_3$ cups vegetable stock

300ml/^{1}/$_2$ pint/1^1/$_4$ cups passata (bottled strained tomatoes)

5ml/1 tsp sugar

350–450g/12oz–1lb dried spaghetti

Energy 598kcal/2517kJ; Protein 30.7g; Carbohydrate 71.8g, of which sugars 6.7g; Fat 22.9g, of which saturates 7.5g; Cholesterol 101mg; Calcium 61mg; Fibre 3.1g; Sodium 301mg

COOK'S TIP

Red kidney beans are traditionally used in chilli con carne, but in this recipe black beans are used instead. They are the same shape and size as red kidney beans but have a shiny black skin. They are also known as Mexican or Spanish black beans and are available from most supermarkets.

500g/1¼lb braising steak

2 onions, chopped

1 garlic clove, crushed

1 fresh green chilli, seeded and finely chopped

1 dried red chilli, crumbled

5ml/1 tsp hot pepper sauce

1 fresh red (bell) pepper, seeded and chopped

fresh coriander (cilantro), to garnish

FROM THE STORECUPBOARD

225g/8oz/1¼ cups dried black beans

30ml/2 tbsp vegetable oil

15ml/1 tbsp paprika

10ml/2 tsp ground cumin

10ml/2 tsp ground coriander

400g/14oz can chopped tomatoes

300ml/½ pint/1¼ cups beef stock

salt and ground black pepper, to taste

boiled rice, to serve

Chilli Con Carne **✳✳**

Fresh green and dried red chillies add plenty of fire to this classic Tex-Mex dish of tender beef cooked in a spicy tomato sauce.

SERVES SIX

VARIATION

You could use minced (ground) beef in place of the diced braising steak, if you want to.

1 Put the beans in a large pan. Add enough cold water to cover, bring to the boil and boil vigorously for 10 minutes. Drain, tip into a bowl, cover with cold water and soak for 8 hours.

2 Preheat the oven to 150°C/300°F/Gas 2. Cut the braising steak into small dice. Heat the vegetable oil in a large, flameproof casserole. Add the onion, garlic and green chilli and cook gently for 5 minutes, then transfer the mixture to a plate.

3 Increase the heat to high, add the meat to the casserole and brown on all sides, then stir in the paprika, ground cumin and ground coriander.

4 Add the tomatoes, beef stock, dried chilli and hot pepper sauce. Drain the beans and add them to the casserole, with enough water to cover. Bring to simmering point, cover and cook in the oven for 2 hours. Stir occasionally and add extra water, if necessary.

5 Season the casserole to taste and add the chopped red pepper. Replace the lid, return the casserole to the oven and cook for 30 minutes more, or until the meat and beans are tender. Sprinkle over the fresh coriander and serve with rice.

Energy 331kcal/1387kJ; Protein 29.1g; Carbohydrate 26.6g, of which sugars 8.5g; Fat 12.7g, of which saturates 3.9g; Cholesterol 48mg; Calcium 70mg; Fibre 8g; Sodium 70mg

1 onion, chopped

2 garlic cloves, crushed

1 fresh red chilli, seeded and sliced

350g/12oz braising steak, cut into small cubes

3 large wheat tortillas

FOR THE SALSA PICANTE

2 garlic cloves, halved

1 onion, quartered

1–2 fresh red chillies, seeded and roughly chopped

5ml/1 tsp chopped fresh oregano

water, if required

FOR THE CHEESE SAUCE

50g/2oz/¼ cup butter

600ml/1 pint/ 2½ cups milk

115g/4oz/1 cup grated Cheddar cheese

FROM THE STORECUPBOARD

2 x 400g/14oz cans chopped tomatoes

5ml/1 tsp ground cumin

2.5–5ml/½–1 tsp cayenne pepper

50g/2oz/½ cup plain (all-purpose) flour

15ml/1 tbsp oil

225g/8oz/2 cups cooked long grain rice

beef stock, to moisten

salt and ground black pepper, to taste

Mexican Spicy Beef Tortilla ✳✳✳

This dish is not unlike a lasagne, except that the spicy meat is mixed with rice and is layered between Mexican tortillas with a hot salsa sauce.

SERVES FOUR

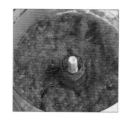

1 Make the salsa picante. Place the tomatoes, garlic, onion and chillies in a blender or food processor and process until smooth. Pour into a pan, add the spices and oregano, and season with salt. Bring to the boil, stirring occasionally.

2 Boil for 1–2 minutes, then lower the heat, cover and simmer for 15 minutes. The sauce should be thick, but of a pouring consistency. If it is too thick, dilute it with a little water. Preheat the oven to 180°C/350°F/Gas 4.

3 Make the cheese sauce. Melt the butter in a pan and stir in the flour. Cook for 1 minute. Add the milk, stirring all the time until the sauce boils and thickens. Stir in all but 30ml/2 tbsp of the cheese and season. Set aside.

4 Put the onion, garlic and chilli in a large bowl. Mix in the meat. Heat the oil in a pan and fry the meat until it has browned. Stir in the rice and stock to moisten. Season to taste.

5 Pour about one-quarter of the cheese sauce into the base of a round ovenproof dish. Add a tortilla and then spread over half the salsa followed by half the meat mixture. Repeat these layers, then add half the remaining cheese sauce and the final tortilla. Pour over the remaining cheese sauce and sprinkle the reserved cheese. Bake in the oven for 15–20 minutes until golden on top.

Energy 907kcal/3802kJ; Protein 43.8g; Carbohydrate 106.5g, of which sugars 15.1g; Fat 34.8g, of which saturates 18.3g; Cholesterol 114mg; Calcium 514mg; Fibre 4.1g; Sodium 598mg

Madras Beef Curry with Spicy Rice ✳✳✳

Chillies are an indispensable ingredient of a hot and spicy Madras curry. After long, gentle simmering, they merge with the other flavourings to give a delectable result that goes perfectly with the spicy rice.

SERVES FOUR

1 Heat half the vegetable oil with half the butter in a large, shallow pan. When it is hot, fry the meat, in batches if necessary, until it is browned on all sides. Transfer to a plate and set aside.

2 Heat the remaining vegetable oil and butter and fry the onion for about 3–4 minutes until it is softened and lightly browned.

3 Add the cardamom pods and fry for 1 minute, then stir in the chillies, ginger and garlic, and fry for 2 minutes more.

4 Stir in the curry paste, 5ml/1 tsp each of ground cumin and coriander, then return the meat to the pan.

5 Stir in the stock. Season with salt, bring to the boil, then reduce the heat and simmer very gently for 1–1¹/₂ hours, until the meat is tender.

6 When the curry is almost ready, prepare the spicy rice. Put the basmati in a bowl and pour over enough boiling water to cover.

7 Set aside for 10 minutes, then drain, rinse under cold water and drain again. The rice will still be uncooked but should have lost its brittle texture.

8 Heat the sunflower oil and butter in a flameproof casserole and fry the onion and garlic gently for 3–4 minutes until softened and lightly browned.

9 Stir in the remaining ground cumin and coriander, the green cardamom pods and the cinnamon stick. Fry for 1 minute, then add the diced peppers.

10 Add the rice, stirring well to coat the grains thoroughly in the spice mixture, and pour in the chicken stock.

11 Bring to the boil, then reduce the heat, cover the pan tightly and simmer for about 8–10 minutes, or until the rice is tender and the stock has been absorbed.

12 Spoon the spicy rice into a bowl and serve immediately with the curry. You can also serve this with a generous dollop of natural (plain) yogurt and some naan bread.

25g/1oz/2 tbsp butter

675g/1¹/₂lb stewing beef, cut into bitesize cubes

1 onion, chopped

3 green cardamom pods

2 fresh green chillies, seeded and finely chopped

2.5cm/1in piece of fresh root ginger, grated

2 garlic cloves, crushed

15ml/1 tbsp Madras curry paste

FOR THE RICE

25g/1oz/2 tbsp butter

1 onion, finely chopped

1 garlic clove, crushed

4 green cardamom pods

1 small red (bell) pepper, seeded and diced

1 small green (bell) pepper, seeded and diced

FROM THE STORECUPBOARD

30ml/2 tbsp vegetable oil

10ml/2 tsp ground cumin

7.5ml/1¹/₂ tsp ground coriander

150ml/¹/₄ pint/²/₃ cup beef stock

salt

225g/8oz/generous 1 cup basmati rice

15ml/1 tbsp sunflower oil

1 cinnamon stick

300ml/¹/₂ pint/1¹/₄ cups beef stock

Energy 717kcal/2984kJ; Protein 44.2g; Carbohydrate 53.8g, of which sugars 7.1g; Fat 36g, of which saturates 14.2g; Cholesterol 125mg; Calcium 41mg; Fibre 1.8g; Sodium 189mg

Slow Baked Beef with Potato Crust ✻✻✻

This recipe makes the best of braising beef by marinating it in red wine and topping it with a cheese-flavoured grated potato crust that bakes to a golden, crunchy consistency. For a change, instead of grating the potatoes, slice them thinly and layer over the top of the beef with onion rings and crushed garlic.

SERVES FOUR

1 Place the diced beef in a non-metallic bowl. Add the red wine and orange peel and season with black pepper. Mix the ingredients together and then cover and marinate in the refrigerator for at least 4 hours or overnight if possible.

2 Preheat the oven to 160°C/325°F/Gas 3. Drain the beef, reserving the marinade.

3 Heat 30ml/2 tbsp of the oil in a large flameproof casserole and cook the meat, in batches, for 5 minutes to seal. Add the onions, carrots and garlic and cook for 5 minutes. Stir in the mushrooms, red wine marinade and beef stock. Simmer.

4 Mix the cornflour with water to make a smooth paste. Stir into the pan. Season, cover and cook for 1¹/₂ hours.

5 Make the crust 30 minutes before the end of the cooking time for the beef. Start by blanching the grated potatoes in boiling water for 5 minutes. Drain well and then squeeze out all the extra liquid.

6 Stir in the remaining oil, the horseradish and the cheese, then sprinkle evenly over the surface of the beef.

7 Increase the oven temperature to 200°C/400°F/Gas 6 and cook the dish for a further 30 minutes so that the top is crispy and slightly browned.

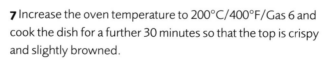

COOK'S TIPS

• Use a large grater on the food processor for the potatoes. They will hold their shape better than if you use a finer blade.

• It is worth remembering that the better the quality of the wine you use when cooking, the better the dish will taste. It is a mistake to use a nasty-tasting wine that you wouldn't be prepared to drink on the grounds that it will do for cooking. There are plenty of inexpensive good quality wines available. In fact, a good rule of thumb is to use the same wine for cooking that you plan to serve with the dish.

• Shin (shank), leg, chuck and blade (rib) are all good cuts to use for this dish. While economical, they have an excellent flavour and both marinating and long, slow cooking will produce a melt-in-the-mouth tenderness that is hard to beat.

675g/1¹/₂lb stewing beef, diced

300ml/¹/₂ pint/1¹/₄ cups red wine

slice of orange peel

2 onions, cut into chunks

2 carrots, cut into chunks

1 garlic clove, crushed

225g/8oz/3 cups button (white) mushrooms

FOR THE CRUST

450g/1lb potatoes, grated

30ml/2 tbsp creamed horseradish

50g/2oz/¹/₂ cup grated mature (sharp) Cheddar cheese

FROM THE STORECUPBOARD

30ml/2 tbsp olive oil

150ml/¹/₄ pint/²/₃ cup beef stock

45ml/3 tbsp cornflour (cornstarch)

salt and ground black pepper, to taste

Energy 630kcal/2632kJ; Protein 45.9g; Carbohydrate 40.1g, of which sugars 10.8g; Fat 26.9g, of which saturates 10.2g; Cholesterol 111mg; Calcium 152mg; Fibre 4.2g; Sodium 308mg

COOK'S TIPS

• If there is any lamb gravy left over from a roast dinner, mix a little in with the raw ingredients: it will add flavour and make the pies juicier.

• It is important that you trim all of the fat and gristle from the mutton and cut into very small pieces, or the pie will be spoilt by large lumps of tough meat and gristle, and the meat won't cook properly.

Lamb and Potato Pies **

These tasty pies originate from Ireland, where they are often called "dingle pies". They are made using mutton, which is packed with flavour and normally much better value for money than lamb. Serve the pies hot with steamed vegetables, or cold as a delicious packed lunch.

SERVES FOUR

1 To make the pastry, sieve the flour into a large bowl and add the butter. Rub the butter into the flour with the fingertips until it resembles coarse breadcrumbs. Add the chilled water. Mix with a knife until the mixture clings together. Turn on to a floured worktop and knead once or twice until smooth. Wrap in baking parchment and chill for 20 minutes before using.

2 Trim any fat or gristle from the meat and cut it up into very small pieces. Place in a large bowl and add the diced onion, carrots, potato and celery. Mix well and season to taste.

3 Preheat the oven to 180°C/350°F/Gas 4. Cut a third off the ball of pastry and reserve to make the lids of the pies. Roll out the rest and cut out six circles. Divide the meat mixture between the circles, piling it in the middle of each.

4 Roll out the remaining pastry and cut out six smaller circles, about 10cm/4in across. Lay these on top. Dampen the edges of the pastry bases, bring the pastry up around the meat, pleat it to fit the lid and pinch the edges together.

5 Make a small hole in the top of each pie, brush with beaten egg and slide the pies on to baking sheets. Bake for an hour, then serve hot or cold.

450g/1lb boneless mutton

1 large onion, diced

2 carrots, diced

1 potato, diced

2 celery sticks, diced

1 egg, beaten

FOR THE
SHORTCRUST PASTRY

250g/9oz/generous 1 cup butter

120ml/4fl oz/¹/₂ cup very cold water

FROM THE STORECUPBOARD

500g/1¹/₄lb/5 cups plain (all-purpose) flour

salt and ground black pepper, to taste

Energy 784Kcal/3275kJ; Protein 25.1g; Carbohydrate 74.6g, of which sugars 5.2g; Fat 44.9g, of which saturates 26.1g; Cholesterol 178mg; Calcium 155mg; Fibre 4g; Sodium 345mg

Lamb Pot-roast ✳✳

This slow-braised dish of lamb and tomatoes, spiced with cinnamon and stewed with green beans, has a Greek influence. It is good served with warm crusty bread to mop up the delicious juices.

SERVES EIGHT

1kg/2¼lb lamb on the bone

8 garlic cloves, chopped

juice of 1 lemon

2 onions, thinly sliced

400g/14oz/scant 3 cups runner (green) beans, cut into 2.5cm/1in lengths

chopped fresh parsley, to garnish

FROM THE STORECUPBOARD

2.5–5ml/½–1 tsp ground cumin

45ml/3 tbsp olive oil

salt and ground black pepper, to taste

about 500ml/17fl oz/ 2¼ cups lamb, beef or vegetable stock

75–90ml/5–6 tbsp tomato purée (paste)

1 cinnamon stick

2–3 large pinches of ground allspice or ground cloves

15–30ml/1–2 tbsp sugar

VARIATION *You could substitute sliced courgettes for the green beans if you prefer. They will take less time to cook than the beans, so check them often during the cooking time.*

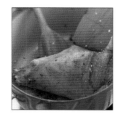

1 Preheat the oven to 160°C/325°F/Gas 3. Coat the joint of lamb with the garlic, cumin, olive oil, lemon juice, salt and pepper.

2 Heat a flameproof casserole. Sear the lamb on all sides. Add the onions and pour the stock over the meat to cover. Stir in the tomato purée, spices and sugar. Cover and cook in the oven for 2–3 hours.

3 Remove the casserole from the oven and pour the stock into a pan. Move the onions to the side of the dish and return to the oven, uncovered, for 20 minutes.

4 Meanwhile, add the beans to the stock and cook until tender. Slice the meat and serve with the pan juices, onions and beans. Garnish with parsley and serve immediately.

Energy 307kcal/1279kJ; Protein 28.4g; Carbohydrate 9.8g, of which sugars 8.5g; Fat 17.4g, of which saturates 6.8g; Cholesterol 103mg; Calcium 39mg; Fibre 1.9g; Sodium 83mg

North African Lamb ✳✳✳

This dish is full of contrasting flavours that create a rich, spicy and fruity main course. For best results, use lamb that still retains some fat, as this will help keep the meat moist and succulent during roasting. Serve the lamb with couscous and steamed seasonal green vegetables.

SERVES FOUR

1 Preheat the oven to 200°C/400°F/Gas 6. Season the lamb with salt and pepper. Heat a frying pan, preferably non-stick, and cook the lamb on all sides until beginning to brown. Transfer to a roasting pan, reserving any fat in the frying pan.

2 Peel the onions and cut each into six wedges. Toss with the lamb and roast for about 30–40 minutes, until the lamb is cooked through and the onions are deep golden brown.

3 Tip the cooked lamb and onions back into the frying pan. Mix the harissa with 250ml/8fl oz/1 cup boiling water and add to the roasting pan. Scrape up any residue left in the in the pan and pour the mixture over the lamb and onions.

4 Stir in the prunes and heat until just simmering. Cover and simmer for 5 minutes, then serve.

675g/1¹⁄₂lb lamb fillet or shoulder steaks, cut into chunky pieces

5 small onions

7.5ml/1¹⁄₂ tsp harissa

115g/4oz ready-to-eat pitted prunes, halved

FROM THE STORECUPBOARD

salt and ground black pepper, to taste

Energy 379kcal/1585kJ; Protein 35g; Carbohydrate 17.7g, of which sugars 15.4g; Fat 19.2g, of which saturates 8.8g; Cholesterol 128mg; Calcium 48mg; Fibre 3.1g; Sodium 151mg

Lamb and Carrot Casserole with Barley ✳✳

Barley and carrots make natural partners for lamb and mutton. In this convenient casserole the barley bulks out the meat and adds to the flavour and texture as well as thickening the sauce. The dish is comfort food at its best. Serve with boiled or baked potatoes and steamed green vegetables.

SERVES SIX

675g/1¹/₂lb stewing lamb

2 onions, sliced

675g/1¹/₂lb carrots, sliced

4–6 celery sticks, sliced

45ml/3 tbsp pearl barley, rinsed

FROM THE STORECUPBOARD

15ml/1 tbsp oil

stock or water

salt and ground black pepper, to taste

1 Trim the lamb of any fat or gristle and cut it into bitesize pieces. Heat the oil in a flameproof casserole, add the lamb and toss until the lamb is browned all over.

2 Add the vegetables to the casserole and fry them briefly with the meat. Add the barley and enough stock or water to cover, and season to taste.

3 Cover the casserole and simmer gently or cook in a slow oven, 150°C/300°F/Gas 2 for 1–1¹/₂ hours until the meat is tender. Add extra stock or water during cooking if necessary. Serve immediately with potatoes and vegetables.

4 Alternatively, allow the casserole to cool, then refrigerate or freeze until needed. This will allow the flavours to mature. Thaw, if necessary, and reheat until piping hot before serving.

Energy 304Kcal/1263kJ; Protein 23.2g; Carbohydrate 13g, of which sugars 11.3g; Fat 18g, of which saturates 7.5g; Cholesterol 84mg; Calcium 53mg; Fibre 3.6g; Sodium 110mg

Roast Loin of Pork with Stuffing ✱✱✱

Sage and onion make a classic stuffing for roast pork, duck and turkey, with the sage counteracting the fattiness of the rich meats. Serve with apple sauce, roast potatoes and boiled or steamed vegetables.

SERVES EIGHT

1 Preheat the oven to 220°C/425°F/Gas 7. To make the stuffing, melt the butter in a pan and cook the bacon until it begins to brown, then add the onions and cook until softened. Mix with the breadcrumbs, sage, thyme, lemon rind and egg, then season.

2 Cut the rind off the pork in one piece and score it with a knife. Place the pork fat side down, and season. Add a layer of stuffing, then roll up and tie neatly. Lay the rind over the pork and rub in 5ml/1 tsp salt. Roast for 2–2¹⁄₂ hours, basting with the pork fat. Reduce the temperature to 190°C/375°F/Gas 5 after 20 minutes. Shape the remaining stuffing into balls and add to the pan for the last 30 minutes.

3 Remove the rind from the top of the pork. Increase the oven temperature to 220°C/425°F/Gas 7 and roast the rind for a further 25 minutes, until crisp. Mix the breadcrumbs and sage and press into the fat in the pan. Cook the pork for a further 10 minutes, then cover and set aside for 15–20 minutes.

4 Remove all but 30–45ml/2–3 tbsp of the fat from the roasting pan and place the pan on the hob (stovetop). Stir in the flour, followed by the cider and water. Bring to the boil, then simmer for 10 minutes. Strain into a clean pan, add the crab apple or redcurrant jelly, and cook for another 5 minutes.

5 Serve the pork cut into thick slices and the crisp crackling cut into strips with the cider gravy, garnished with thyme.

1.3–1.6kg/3–3¹⁄₂lb boneless loin of pork

60ml/4 tbsp fine, dry breadcrumbs

10ml/2 tsp chopped fresh sage

300ml/¹⁄₂ pint/1¹⁄₄ cups (hard) cider

150ml/¹⁄₄ pint/²⁄₃ cup water

5–10ml/1–2 tsp crab apple or redcurrant jelly

fresh thyme sprigs, to garnish

FOR THE STUFFING

25g/1oz/2 tbsp butter

50g/2oz bacon, chopped

2 large onions, finely chopped

75g/3oz/1¹⁄₂ cups fresh white breadcrumbs

30ml/2 tbsp chopped fresh sage

5ml/1 tsp chopped fresh thyme

10ml/2 tsp finely grated lemon rind

1 small (US medium) egg, beaten

FROM THE STORECUPBOARD

25ml/1¹⁄₂ tbsp plain (all-purpose) flour

salt and ground black pepper, to taste

Energy 446Kcal/1872kJ; Protein 53.6g; Carbohydrate 21.1g, of which sugars 5g; Fat 15.8g, of which saturates 6.1g; Cholesterol 161mg; Calcium 66mg; Fibre 1.2g; Sodium 356mg

Dublin Coddle ✳✳

This simple dish combines bacon and sausages, and is best accompanied by a crisp green vegetable, such as lightly cooked Brussels sprouts, purple sprouting broccoli or cabbage.

SERVES SIX

6 x 8mm/⅓in thick ham or dry-cured bacon slices

6 best-quality lean pork sausages

4 large onions, sliced

900g/2lb potatoes, peeled and sliced

90ml/6 tbsp chopped fresh parsley

FROM THE STORECUPBOARD

salt and ground black pepper, to taste

1 Cut the ham or bacon into chunks and cook with the sausages in a large pan containing 1.2 litres/2 pints/5 cups boiling water for 5 minutes. Drain, but reserve the cooking liquor.

2 Put the meat into a large pan with the sliced onions, potatoes and the parsley. Season, and add just enough of the reserved cooking liquor to cover completely.

3 Lay a piece of buttered foil or baking parchment on top of the mixture in the pan, then cover with a tight-fitting lid.

4 Simmer gently over a low heat for about 1 hour, or until the liquid is reduced by half and all the ingredients are cooked but not mushy.

5 Serve the coddle immediately with the Brussels sprouts or broccoli, or any other vegetable of your choice.

Energy 336kcal/1409kJ; Protein 12.7g; Carbohydrate 39.3g, of which sugars 9g; Fat 15.4g, of which saturates 6.2g; Cholesterol 33mg; Calcium 80mg; Fibre 3.6g; Sodium 695mg

Potato and Sausage Bake ✳✳✳

This easy-to-make bake combines top-quality sausages, bacon, onions, garlic and potatoes to create a warming and sustaining dish that is perfect for a cold winter's day. Serve with seasonal cabbage or broccoli.

SERVES SIX

1 Preheat the oven to 180°C/350°F/Gas 4. Grease a large ovenproof dish and set aside.

2 Heat the oil in a frying pan. Add the bacon to the pan and cook for 2 minutes, then add the onions and cook for 5–6 minutes, until golden. Add the garlic and cook for 1 minute, then remove the mixture from the pan and set aside. Add the sausages to the pan and cook for 5–6 minutes, until golden.

3 Arrange the potatoes in the base of the prepared dish. Spoon the bacon and onion mixture on top. Season with the salt and pepper and sprinkle with the fresh sage.

4 Pour on the stock and top with the sausages. Cover and bake for 1 hour. Serve hot with soda bread if you like.

15ml/1 tbsp vegetable oil

4 bacon rashers (strips), cut into 2.5cm/1in pieces

2 large onions, chopped

2 garlic cloves, crushed

8 large pork sausages

4 large baking potatoes, thinly sliced

1.5ml/¹/₄ tsp fresh sage

FROM THE STORECUPBOARD

300ml/¹/₂ pint/1¹/₄ cups vegetable stock

salt and ground black pepper, to taste

Energy 451kcal/1879kJ; Protein 14g; Carbohydrate 35.2g, of which sugars 7.5g; Fat 29.2g, of which saturates 10.5g; Cholesterol 44mg; Calcium 61mg; Fibre 2.9g; Sodium 844mg

Toad in the Hole ✳✳✳

This is one of those dishes that is classic comfort food – perfect for lifting the spirits on cold days. Use only the best sausages for this grown-up version, which includes chives.

SERVES FOUR TO SIX

1 Preheat the oven to 220°C/425°F/Gas 7. Sift the flour into a bowl with a pinch of salt and pepper. Make a well in the centre of the flour.

2 Whisk the chives, if using, with the eggs and milk, then pour into the flour. Whisk the flour into the liquid to make a smooth batter. Cover and leave for at least 30 minutes.

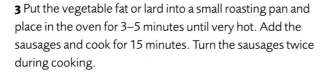

3 Put the vegetable fat or lard into a small roasting pan and place in the oven for 3–5 minutes until very hot. Add the sausages and cook for 15 minutes. Turn the sausages twice during cooking.

4 Pour the batter over the sausages and cook for about 20 minutes, or until the batter is risen and golden. Serve immediately with vegetables.

30ml/2 tbsp chopped fresh chives (optional)

2 eggs

300ml/$^1/_2$ pint/$1^1/_4$ cups milk

50g/2oz/$^1/_3$ cup white vegetable fat or lard

450g/1lb Cumberland sausages or good-quality pork sausages

FROM THE STORECUPBOARD

175g/6oz/$1^1/_2$ cups plain (all-purpose) flour

salt and ground black pepper, to taste

VARIATION *To make small individual toad-in-the-holes, cook small cocktail sausages in patty tins (muffin pans) until golden. Add the batter and cook for 10–15 minutes, or until puffed and golden brown.*

Energy 497kcal/2070kJ; Protein 14.5g; Carbohydrate 32.1g, of which sugars 3.8g; Fat 35.4g, of which saturates 13.6g; Cholesterol 109mg; Calcium 141mg; Fibre 1.3g; Sodium 616mg

225g/8oz rindless unsmoked back (lean) bacon rashers (strips), cut into pieces

2 onions, halved and sliced

175g/6oz/2¹/₃ cups chestnut mushrooms, wiped clean and halved

450g/1lb lamb's liver, trimmed and sliced

25g/1oz/2 tbsp butter

FROM THE STORECUPBOARD

30ml/2 tbsp sunflower oil

15ml/1 tbsp soy sauce

30ml/2 tbsp plain (all-purpose) flour

150ml/¹/₄ pint/²/₃ cup chicken stock

salt and ground black pepper, to taste

Lamb's Liver and Bacon Casserole ✳✳

Boiled new potatoes tossed in butter go well with this simple casserole. The trick when cooking liver is to seal it quickly, then simmer it gently and briefly. Prolonged and/or fierce cooking makes liver hard and grainy.

SERVES FOUR

COOK'S TIP *Liver is packed with minerals and iron and is extremely good value for money.*

1 Heat the oil in a frying pan and cook the bacon until crisp. Add the onions to the pan and cook for about 10 minutes, stirring frequently, or until softened. Add the mushrooms to the pan and cook for a further 1 minute.

2 Use a slotted spoon to remove the bacon and vegetables from the pan and set aside. Add the liver to the pan and cook over a high heat for 3–4 minutes, turning once to seal the slices on both sides. Remove the liver from the pan and keep warm.

3 Melt the butter in the pan, add the soy sauce and flour and blend together. Stir in the stock and bring to the boil, stirring until thickened. Return the liver and vegetables to the pan and heat through for 1 minute. Season with salt and pepper to taste, and serve with new potatoes and lightly cooked green beans.

Energy 440kcal/1832kJ; Protein 35g; Carbohydrate 14.3g, of which sugars 6.1g; Fat 27.4g, of which saturates 9.4g; Cholesterol 527mg; Calcium 50mg; Fibre 2.1g; Sodium 1259mg

4–6 lamb's kidneys

butter, for frying

250ml/8fl oz/1 cup white wine

5ml/1 tsp chopped fresh mixed herbs, such as rosemary, thyme, parsley and chives

1 small garlic clove, crushed

about 30ml/2 tbsp single (light) cream

fresh parsley, to garnish

FROM THE STORECUPBOARD

Dijon mustard or other mild mustard, to taste

salt and ground black pepper, to taste

Lamb's Kidneys with Creamy Mustard Sauce ✳✳

This piquant recipe is simple and flexible, so the exact amounts of any one ingredient are unimportant. It would be suitable as a supper dish for two, in which case rice and green salad makes a good accompaniment.

SERVES FOUR

1 Skin the kidneys and slice them horizontally. Remove the cores with scissors, and then wash them thoroughly in plenty of cold water. Drain and dry off with kitchen paper.

2 Heat a little butter in a heavy frying pan and gently cook the kidneys in it until cooked as you like them, but be careful not to overcook. Remove the kidneys from the pan and keep warm.

3 Add a spoonful of mustard to the pan with the wine, herbs and garlic. Simmer to reduce by about half, then add enough cream to make a smooth sauce.

4 Return the kidneys to their sauce and reheat gently, without cooking any further, or the kidneys will be tough. Serve garnished with parsley, and with rice or a green salad.

Energy 138Kcal/578kJ; Protein 15.6g; Carbohydrate 0.6g, of which sugars 0.6g; Fat 3.8g, of which saturates 1.7g; Cholesterol 288mg; Calcium 20mg; Fibre 0g; Sodium 140mg

Versatile Vegetarian Dishes

Vegetarian dishes are healthy, economical and extremely adaptable. Try using different combinations of vegetables, depending on your personal preferences and the season. From quick-and-easy dishes such as Cheese and Tomato Soufflés or Tofu, Roasted Peanut and Pepper Kebabs to slow-cooked Vegetable Hot-pot or Hot and Spicy Parsnips with Chickpeas, there is a delicious dish for everyone, whether you are vegetarian or not.

Potato Gnocchi with Parmesan Cheese and Basil *

Gnocchi make a substantial and tasty alternative to pasta. Serve with a green side salad for a simple yet delicious light meal.

SERVES SIX

1 Cook the potatoes in their skins in a large pan of boiling water until tender but not falling apart. Drain and peel while warm.

2 Spread a layer of flour on a work surface. Pass the hot potatoes through a food mill, dropping them directly on to the flour. Sprinkle with half of the remaining flour and mix in very lightly. Break the egg into the mixture. Add the nutmeg and knead, adding more flour if the mixture is too loose. When the dough is no longer moist, it is ready to be rolled.

3 Divide the dough into four pieces. On a lightly floured surface, form each into a roll about 2cm/³⁄₄ in in diameter. Cut the rolls crossways into pieces about 2cm/³⁄₄ in long. One by one, press and roll the gnocchi lightly along the prongs of a fork towards the points, making ridges on one side, and a depression from your thumb on the other.

4 Bring a large pan of water to a fast boil, then drop in half the gnocchi. When they rise to the surface, they are done. Drain well, and place in a warmed serving bowl. Dot with butter. Cover to keep warm while cooking the remainder. As soon as they are cooked, toss the gnocchi with the butter, garnish with Parmesan shavings and basil leaves, and serve immediately.

1kg/2¹⁄₄lb waxy potatoes

1 egg

25g/1oz/2 tbsp butter

Parmesan cheese cut in shavings, to garnish

fresh basil leaves, to garnish

FROM THE STORECUPBOARD

250–300g/9–11oz/ 2¹⁄₄–2³⁄₄ cups plain (all-purpose) flour, plus more if necessary

pinch of freshly grated nutmeg

salt

Energy 302kcal/1279kJ; Protein 7.8g; Carbohydrate 59.2g, of which sugars 2.8g; Fat 5.4g, of which saturates 2.7g; Cholesterol 41mg; Calcium 74mg; Fibre 3g; Sodium 57mg

Baked Cheese Polenta with Tomato Sauce ✳

Polenta, or cornmeal, is very cheap. It is prepared like a sort of oatmeal, and eaten soft, or left to set, cut into shapes, then cooked.

SERVES FOUR

1 Preheat the oven to 200°C/400°F/ Gas 6. Line a 28 x 18cm/11 x 7in tin (pan) with clear film (plastic wrap). Boil 1 litre/1³/₄ pints/4 cups water in a large pan.

2 Add the salt and pour in the polenta in a steady stream and cook, stirring constantly, for 5 minutes. Beat in the paprika and nutmeg. Pour into the tin and smooth the surface. Leave to cool.

3 Heat the oil in a pan and cook the onion and garlic until soft. Add the tomatoes, tomato purée and sugar. Season. Simmer for 20 minutes.

4 Cut the polenta into 5cm/2in squares. Layer the polenta and tomato sauce in an ovenproof dish. Sprinkle with the cheese and bake for 25 minutes, until golden. Serve immediately.

1 large onion, finely chopped

2 garlic cloves, crushed

75g/3oz Gruyère cheese or other mild cheese, grated

FROM THE STORECUPBOARD

5ml/1 tsp salt

250g/9oz/1¹/₂ cups quick-cook polenta

5ml/1 tsp paprika

2.5ml/¹/₂ tsp ground nutmeg

30ml/2 tbsp extra virgin olive oil

2 x 400g/14oz cans chopped tomatoes, or 450g/1lb fresh tomatoes

15ml/1 tbsp tomato purée (paste)

5ml/1 tsp sugar

salt and ground black pepper, to taste

Energy 425kcal/1777kJ; Protein 13.1g; Carbohydrate 59.4g, of which sugars 12g; Fat 14.5g, of which saturates 5.1g; Cholesterol 18mg; Calcium 175mg; Fibre 4.5g; Sodium 165mg

Vegetable Hot-pot ✳✳✳

Make this healthy one-dish meal in the summer, when the vegetables are in season, and serve with Italian bread, such as foccacia.

SERVES FOUR

1 large onion, chopped

2 small or medium aubergines (eggplants), cut into small cubes

4 courgettes (zucchini), cut into small chunks

2 red, yellow or green (bell) peppers, seeded and chopped

115g/4oz/1 cup frozen peas

115g/4oz green beans

450g/1lb new or salad potatoes, peeled and cubed

4–5 tomatoes, peeled

30ml/2 tbsp chopped fresh parsley

3–4 garlic cloves, crushed

black olives and fresh parsley, to garnish

FROM THE STORECUPBOARD

60ml/4 tbsp extra virgin olive oil

200g/7oz can flageolet (small cannellini) beans, rinsed and drained

2.5ml/$\frac{1}{2}$ tsp ground cinnamon

2.5ml/$\frac{1}{2}$ tsp ground cumin

5ml/1 tsp paprika

400g/14oz can chopped tomatoes

350ml/12fl oz/1$\frac{1}{2}$ cups vegetable stock

salt and ground black pepper, to taste

1 Preheat the oven to 190°C/375°F/ Gas 5. Heat 45ml/3 tbsp of the oil in a heavy pan, and cook the onion until golden.

2 Add the aubergines, sauté for 3 minutes, then add the courgettes, peppers, peas, beans and potatoes, and stir in the spices and seasoning. Cook for 3 minutes, stirring constantly.

3 Cut the tomatoes in half and scoop out the seeds. Chop the tomatoes finely and place them in a bowl.

4 Stir in the canned tomatoes with the chopped fresh parsley, crushed garlic and the remaining olive oil.

5 Spoon the aubergine mixture into a shallow ovenproof dish and level the surface.

6 Pour the stock over the aubergine mixture and then spoon over the prepared tomato mixture.

7 Cover the dish with foil and bake for 30–45 minutes, until the vegetables are tender. Serve hot, garnished with black olives and parsley.

Energy 386kcal/1618kJ; Protein 15.4g; Carbohydrate 51.7g, of which sugars 22.6g; Fat 14.5g, of which saturates 2.5g; Cholesterol 0mg; Calcium 142mg; Fibre 14.3g; Sodium 234mg

Hot and Spicy Parsnips and Chickpeas ✳✳

The sweet flavour of parsnips goes very well with the aromatic spices in this hearty and healthy Indian-style vegetable stew. Offer Indian breads such as naan to mop up the delicious sauce.

SERVES FOUR

7 garlic cloves, finely chopped

1 small onion, chopped

5cm/2in piece fresh root ginger, chopped

2 green chillies, seeded and finely chopped

450ml/³/₄ pint/scant 2 cups plus 75ml/5 tbsp water

50g/2oz cashew nuts, toasted and ground

250g/9oz tomatoes, peeled and chopped

900g/2lb parsnips, cut into chunks

juice of 1 lime, to taste

fresh coriander (cilantro) leaves, to garnish

cashew nuts, toasted, to garnish

FROM THE STORECUPBOARD

200g/7oz dried chickpeas, soaked overnight in cold water, then drained

60ml/4 tbsp vegetable oil

5ml/1 tsp cumin seeds

10ml/2 tsp ground coriander seeds

5ml/1 tsp ground turmeric

2.5–5ml/¹/₂–1 tsp chilli powder or mild paprika

5ml/1 tsp ground roasted cumin seeds

salt and ground black pepper, to taste

1 Put the soaked chickpeas in a pan, cover with cold water and bring to the boil. Boil vigorously for 10 minutes, then reduce the heat so that the water boils steadily, and cook for 1–1¹/₂ hours until the chickpeas are tender. Drain well.

2 Set 10ml/2 tsp of the garlic aside, then place the remainder in a food processor or blender with the onion, ginger and half the chillies. Add the 75ml/5 tbsp water and process to make a smooth paste.

3 Heat the oil in a large, deep, frying pan and cook the cumin seeds for 30 seconds. Stir in the coriander seeds, turmeric, chilli powder or paprika and the ground cashew nuts. Add the ginger and chilli paste and cook, stirring frequently, until the water begins to evaporate. Add the tomatoes and stir-fry until the mixture begins to turn red-brown in colour.

4 Mix in the chickpeas and parsnips with the rest of the water, the lime juice, 5ml/1 tsp salt and black pepper. Bring to the boil, stir, then simmer, uncovered, for 15–20 minutes, until the parsnips are completely tender.

5 Reduce the liquid until the sauce is thick. Add the ground roasted cumin. Stir in the reserved garlic and green chilli, and cook for a further 1–2 minutes. Sprinkle the coriander leaves and toasted cashew nuts over and serve immediately.

Energy 506kcal/2124kJ; Protein 18.4g; Carbohydrate 60.1g, of which sugars 18.2g; Fat 23.1g, of which saturates 3.4g; Cholesterol 0mg; Calcium 192mg; Fibre 17.1g; Sodium 86mg

Leek, Squash and Tomato Gratin ✳✳

You can use virtually any kind of squash for this colourful and succulent gratin, from patty pans and acorn squash to pumpkins, depending on what is in season and your personal preference.

SERVES SIX

1 Steam the prepared squash in a steamer set over boiling salted water for 10 minutes.

2 Heat half the oil in a frying pan and cook the leeks gently for 5–6 minutes, until lightly coloured. Try to keep the slices intact. Preheat the oven to 190°C/375°F/Gas 5.

3 Layer all the squash, leeks and tomatoes in a 2 litre/ 3¹/₂ pint/8 cup gratin dish, arranging them in rows. Season with salt, pepper and cumin.

4 Pour the cream into a small pan and add the chilli and garlic. Bring to the boil over a low heat, then stir in the mint. Pour the mixture evenly over the layered vegetables, using a rubber spatula to scrape all the sauce out of the pan.

5 Cook for 50–55 minutes, or until the gratin is bubbling and tinged brown. Sprinkle the parsley and breadcrumbs on top and drizzle over the remaining oil. Bake for another 15–20 minutes until the breadcrumbs are browned and crisp. Serve immediately.

450g/1lb peeled and seeded squash, cut into 1cm/¹/₂in slices

450g/1lb leeks, cut into thick, diagonal slices

675g/1¹/₂lb tomatoes, peeled and thickly sliced

300ml/¹/₂ pint/1¹/₄ cups single (light) cream

1 fresh red chilli, seeded and sliced

1 garlic clove, finely chopped

15ml/1 tbsp chopped fresh mint

30ml/2 tbsp chopped fresh parsley

60ml/4 tbsp fine white breadcrumbs

FROM THE STORECUPBOARD

60ml/4 tbsp olive oil

2.5ml/¹/₂ tsp ground toasted cumin seeds

salt and ground black pepper, to taste

VARIATIONS

• *For a curried version of this dish, use ground coriander as well as cumin seeds, and coconut milk instead of cream. Use fresh coriander (cilantro) instead of mint and parsley.*

• *You can remove or add more fresh chilli, with or without the seeds, depending on how spicy you like it.*

Energy 248kcal/1032kJ; Protein 5.7g; Carbohydrate 16.7g, of which sugars 7.8g; Fat 18g, of which saturates 7.4g; Cholesterol 28mg; Calcium 126mg; Fibre 3.8g; Sodium 104mg

675g/1¹/₂lb courgettes (zucchini)

450g/1lb potatoes, peeled and cut into chunks

1 onion, finely sliced

3 garlic cloves, chopped

1 large red (bell) pepper, seeded and cubed

150ml/¹/₄ pint/²/₃ cup hot water

45ml/3 tbsp chopped fresh flat leaf parsley, plus a few extra sprigs, to garnish

FROM THE STORECUPBOARD

400g/14oz can chopped tomatoes

150ml/¹/₄ pint/²/₃ cup extra virgin olive oil

5ml/1 tsp dried oregano

salt and ground black pepper, to taste

Courgette and Potato Bake ✳

Cook this delicious dish in early autumn, and the aromas spilling from the kitchen will recall the rich summer tastes and colours just past.

SERVES FOUR

1 Preheat the oven to 190°C/375°F/Gas 5. Scrape the courgettes lightly under running water to dislodge any grit and then slice them into thin rounds.

2 Put the courgettes in a large baking dish and add the chopped potatoes, onion, garlic, red pepper and tomatoes. Mix well, then stir in the olive oil, hot water and dried oregano.

3 Spread the mixture evenly, then season with salt and ground black pepper. Bake for 30 minutes in the centre of the preheated oven, then stir in the parsley and a little more water.

4 Return the baking dish to the oven and cook for 1 hour, increasing the temperature to 200°C/400°F/Gas 6 for the final 10–15 minutes, so that the potatoes brown.

5 Serve immediately, garnished with the remaining parsley. You could also serve this as an accompaniment to grilled (broiled) meats, such as sausages, pork chops or steak.

Energy 374Kcal/1,554kJ; Protein 6.6g; Carbohydrate 28.6g, of which sugars 11.2g; Fat 26.7g, of which saturates 4g; Cholesterol 0mg; Calcium 86mg; Fibre 5.1g; Sodium 29mg

Peppers Filled with Spiced Vegetables ✳✳

Indian spices season the potato and aubergine stuffing in these colourful baked peppers. They are good with plain rice and a lentil dhal. Alternatively, serve them with a crisp green salad, Indian breads and a cucumber or mint and yogurt raita.

SERVES SIX

1 Cut the tops off the red or yellow peppers then remove and discard the seeds. Cut a thin slice off the base of the peppers, if necessary, to make them stand upright.

2 Bring a large pan of lightly salted water to the boil. Add the peppers and cook for 5–6 minutes. Drain well and leave the peppers upside down in a colander to drain completely.

3 Cook the potatoes in large pan of lightly salted, boiling water for 10–12 minutes, until just tender. Drain, cool and peel, then cut into 1cm/$^1\!/_2$in dice.

4 Put the onion, garlic, ginger and green chillies in a food processor or blender with 60ml/4 tbsp of the water and process to a purée.

5 Heat 45ml/3 tbsp of the oil in a large, deep frying pan and cook the aubergine, stirring occasionally, until browned on all sides. Remove from the pan and set aside. Add another 30ml/2 tbsp of the oil to the pan and cook the potatoes until lightly browned. Remove from the pan and set aside.

6 If necessary, add another 15ml/1 tbsp oil to the pan, then add the cumin and *kalonji* seeds. Cook briefly until they darken, then add the turmeric, coriander and ground cumin. Cook for 15 seconds. Stir in the onion and garlic purée and cook, scraping the pan, until it begins to brown.

7 Return the potatoes and aubergines to the pan, season with salt, pepper and 1–2 pinches of cayenne. Add the remaining water and 15ml/1 tbsp lemon juice and then cook, stirring, until the liquid evaporates. Preheat the oven to 190°C/375°F/Gas 5.

8 Fill the peppers with the potato mixture and place on a lightly greased baking sheet. Brush the peppers with a little oil and bake for 30–35 minutes, until the peppers are cooked. Leave to cool a little, then sprinkle with a little more lemon juice, garnish with the coriander and serve.

6 large red or yellow (bell) peppers

500g/1$^1\!/_4$lb waxy potatoes

1 small onion, chopped

4–5 garlic cloves, chopped

5cm/2in piece fresh root ginger, chopped

1–2 fresh green chillies, seeded and chopped

105ml/7 tbsp water

1 aubergine (eggplant), cut into 1cm/$^1\!/_2$in dice

5ml/1 tsp *kalonji* seeds

about 30ml/2 tbsp lemon juice

30ml/2 tbsp chopped fresh coriander (cilantro), to garnish

FROM THE STORECUPBOARD

90–105ml/6–7 tbsp groundnut (peanut) oil

10ml/2 tsp cumin seeds

2.5ml/$^1\!/_2$ tsp ground turmeric

5ml/1 tsp ground coriander

5ml/1 tsp ground toasted cumin seeds

pinch of cayenne pepper

salt and ground black pepper, to taste

COOK'S TIP Kalonji, *or nigella as it is sometimes known, is a tiny black seed. It is widely used in Indian cookery, especially sprinkled over breads or in potato dishes, and is available from large supermarkets. It has a mild, slightly nutty flavour and is best toasted for a few seconds in a dry frying pan over a medium heat. This helps to bring out its flavour.*

Energy 234kcal/976kJ; Protein 4.2g; Carbohydrate 28.1g, of which sugars 14.8g; Fat 12.4g, of which saturates 2.4g; Cholesterol 0mg; Calcium 45mg; Fibre 5.5g; Sodium 21mg

Roasted Aubergines Stuffed with Feta Cheese and Fresh Coriander ✳✳✳

Aubergines take on a lovely smoky flavour when grilled on a barbecue. Choose a good-quality Greek feta cheese for the best flavour.

SERVES SIX

1 Prepare a barbecue. Cook the aubergines for 20 minutes on the barbecue, turning occasionally, until they are slightly charred and soft. Remove and cut in half lengthways.

2 Carefully scoop the aubergine flesh into a bowl, reserving the skins. Mash the flesh roughly with a fork.

3 Crumble the feta cheese, and then stir it into the mashed aubergine with the chopped coriander and olive oil. Season with salt and ground black pepper to taste.

4 Spoon the feta mixture back into the skins and return to the barbecue for 5 minutes to warm through.

5 Serve immediately with a fresh green salad coated with fruity extra virgin olive oil, garnished with sprigs of fresh coriander.

3 medium to large aubergines (eggplant)

400g/14oz feta cheese

a small bunch of fresh coriander (cilantro), roughly chopped, plus extra sprigs to garnish

FROM THE STORECUPBOARD

60ml/4 tbsp extra virgin olive oil

salt and freshly ground black pepper

Energy 257Kcal/1,066kJ; Protein 12g; Carbohydrate 4.2g, of which sugars 3.9g; Fat 21.5g, of which saturates 10.3g; Cholesterol 47mg; Calcium 286mg; Fibre 3.3g; Sodium 968mg.

4 large onions

150g/5oz goat's cheese, crumbled or cubed

50g/2oz/1 cup fresh breadcrumbs

8 sun-dried tomatoes in oil, drained and chopped

1–2 garlic cloves, chopped

2.5ml/¹/₂ tsp chopped fresh thyme

30ml/2 tbsp chopped fresh parsley

1 small (US medium) egg, beaten

45ml/3 tbsp pine nuts, toasted

30ml/2 tbsp oil from the sun-dried tomatoes

FROM THE STORECUPBOARD

salt and ground black pepper, to taste

VARIATIONS

• *Use feta cheese in place of the goat's cheese and substitute mint, currants and pitted black olives for the other flavourings.*

• *Stuff the onions with wilted spinach and cooked long grain rice mixed with smoked mozzarella cheese and toasted flaked almonds.*

• *Substitute 175g/6oz Roquefort or Gorgonzola for the goat's cheese, omit the sun-dried tomatoes and pine nuts, and add 75g/3oz chopped walnuts and 115g/4oz chopped celery, cooked until soft with the chopped onion in 25ml/ 1¹/₂ tbsp olive oil.*

Onions Stuffed with Goat's Cheese and Sun-dried Tomatoes ✳✳

Roasted onions and tangy cheese are a winning combination. They make an excellent main course when served with rice.

SERVES FOUR

1 Bring a large pan of lightly salted water to the boil. Add the whole onions in their skins and boil for 10 minutes. Drain and cool, then cut each onion in half horizontally and peel.

2 Using a teaspoon, remove the centre of each onion, leaving a thick shell around the outside. Reserve the flesh and place the shells in an oiled ovenproof dish. Preheat the oven to 190°C/375°F/Gas 5.

3 Chop the scooped-out onion flesh and place in a bowl. Add the goat's cheese, breadcrumbs, sun-dried tomatoes, garlic, thyme, parsley and egg. Mix well, then season with salt and pepper and add the toasted pine nuts.

4 Divide the stuffing among the onions and cover with foil. Bake for about 25 minutes.

5 Uncover the onions, drizzle with the oil and cook for another 30–40 minutes, until bubbling and well cooked. Baste occasionally during cooking.

Energy 402kcal/1669kJ; Protein 14.8g; Carbohydrate 25.1g, of which sugars 11.7g; Fat 27.7g, of which saturates 8.8g; Cholesterol 82mg; Calcium 120mg; Fibre 3.2g; Sodium 346mg

Bubble and Squeak ✳

Whether you have leftovers or cook this old-fashioned classic from fresh, be sure to give it a really good "squeak" in the pan so it turns a rich honey brown. Serve with warm bread for a quick vegetarian supper, or as an accompaniment to grilled pork chops or fried eggs.

SERVES FOUR

1 medium onion, chopped

450g/1lb floury potatoes, cooked and mashed

225g/8oz cooked cabbage or Brussels sprouts, finely chopped

FROM THE STORECUPBOARD

60ml/4 tbsp vegetable oil

salt and ground black pepper, to taste

VARIATIONS
• Add any left-over gravy from a roast dinner for a really delicious flavour.

• Use bacon fat in place of the oil for a non-vegetarian version.

1 Heat 30ml/2 tbsp of the oil in a heavy frying pan. Add the onion and cook over a medium heat, stirring frequently, until softened but not browned.

2 In a large bowl, mix together the potatoes and cooked cabbage or Brussels sprouts and season with salt and plenty of ground black pepper to taste.

3 Add the vegetables to the pan with the cooked onions, stir well, then press the vegetable mixture into a large, even cake.

4 Cook over a medium heat for about 15 minutes, until the cake has browned underneath.

5 Invert a large plate over the pan and, holding it tightly against the pan, turn them both over together.

6 Lift off the frying pan, return it to the heat and add the remaining oil. When hot, slide the cake back into the pan, browned side uppermost.

7 Cook over a medium heat for 10 minutes, or until the underside is golden brown. Serve hot, in wedges.

Energy 205Kcal/857kJ; Protein 3.5g; Carbohydrate 23.3g, of which sugars 4.2g; Fat 11.5g, of which saturates 1.2g; Cholesterol 0mg; Calcium 34mg; Fibre 3g; Sodium 15mg

Peanut and Tofu Cutlets ✳✳

These delicious, high-protein patties make a filling and satisfying vegetarian midweek meal served with lightly steamed green vegetables or a crisp salad, and a tangy salsa or ketchup. They make an ideal alternative to beef or turkey patties when served in bread rolls.

SERVES FOUR

1 Cook the rice according to the instructions on the packet until tender, then drain. Heat the vegetable oil in a large, heavy frying pan and cook the onion and garlic over a low heat, stirring occasionally, for about 5 minutes, until softened and golden.

2 Meanwhile, spread out the peanuts on a baking sheet and toast under the grill (broiler) for a few minutes, until browned. Place the peanuts, onion, garlic, rice, tofu, coriander or parsley, if using, and soy sauce in a blender or food processor and process until the mixture comes together in a thick paste.

3 Divide the paste into eight equal-size mounds and form each mound into a cutlet shape or square.

4 Heat the olive oil for shallow frying in a large, heavy frying pan. Add the cutlets, in two batches if necessary, and cook for 5–10 minutes on each side, until golden and heated through.

5 Remove from the pan with a fish slice or metal spatula and drain on kitchen paper. Keep warm while you cook the remaining batch, then serve immediately.

1 onion, finely chopped

1 garlic clove, crushed

200g/7oz/1³/₄ cups unsalted peanuts

small bunch of fresh coriander (cilantro) or parsley, chopped (optional)

250g/9oz firm tofu, drained and crumbled

FROM THE STORECUPBOARD

90g/3¹/₂oz/¹/₂ cup brown rice

15ml/1 tbsp vegetable oil

30ml/2 tbsp soy sauce

30ml/2 tbsp olive oil, for shallow frying

Energy 495kcal/2059kJ; Protein 20.2g; Carbohydrate 27.1g, of which sugars 5.3g; Fat 34.7g, of which saturates 5.9g; Cholesterol 0mg; Calcium 381mg; Fibre 4.4g; Sodium 543mg

Tofu and Green Bean Thai Red Curry ✱✱✱

This is one of those versatile recipes that should be in every cook's repertoire. This version uses green beans, but other types of vegetable work equally well, depending on what is available. The tofu takes on the flavour of the spice paste and also boosts the nutritional value.

SERVES FOUR

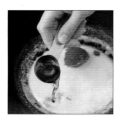

1 Pour about one-third of the coconut milk into a wok or large frying pan. Cook gently until it starts to separate and an oily sheen appears on the surface.

2 Add the red curry paste, fish sauce and sugar to the coconut milk. Mix thoroughly, then add the mushrooms. Stir and cook for 1 minute.

3 Stir in the remaining coconut milk. Bring back to the boil, then add the green beans and tofu cubes. Simmer gently for 4–5 minutes more.

4 Stir in the kaffir lime leaves and sliced red chillies. Spoon the curry into a serving dish, garnish with the coriander leaves and serve immediately.

600ml/1 pint/2¹/₂ cups canned coconut milk

15ml/1 tbsp Thai red curry paste

225g/8oz/3¹/₄ cups button (white) mushrooms

115g/4oz/scant 1 cup green beans, trimmed

175g/6oz firm tofu, rinsed, drained and cut in 2cm/³/₄in cubes

4 kaffir lime leaves, torn

2 fresh red chillies, seeded and sliced

fresh coriander (cilantro) leaves, to garnish

FROM THE STORECUPBOARD

45ml/3 tbsp Thai fish sauce (*nam pla*)

10ml/2 tsp light muscovado (brown) sugar

Energy 59kcal/250kJ; Protein 3.8g; Carbohydrate 7.5g, of which sugars 7.1g; Fat 1.8g, of which saturates 0.4g; Cholesterol 0mg; Calcium 188mg; Fibre 0.8g; Sodium 291mg

Tofu, Roasted Peanut and Pepper Kebabs ✳✳✳

A coating of ground, dry-roasted peanuts pressed on to cubed tofu provides plenty of flavour along with the peppers. Use metal or bamboo skewers for the kebabs – if you use bamboo, then soak them in cold water for 30 minutes before using, to prevent scorching.

SERVES FOUR

250g/9oz firm tofu, drained

50g/2oz/¹/₂ cup dry-roasted peanuts

2 red and 2 green (bell) peppers, halved and seeded

60ml/4 tbsp sweet chilli dipping sauce

1 Pat the tofu dry on kitchen paper, then cut it into small cubes. Finely grind the peanuts in a blender or food processor and transfer to a plate. Coat the tofu in the ground nuts.

2 Preheat the grill (broiler) to moderate. Cut the halved and seeded peppers into large chunks. Thread the chunks of pepper on to four large skewers with the tofu cubes and place on a foil-lined grill rack.

3 Grill (broil) the kebabs, turning them frequently, for 10–12 minutes, or until the peppers and peanuts are beginning to brown. Transfer the kebabs to plates and serve with the dipping sauce.

Energy 175kcal/730kJ; Protein 10g; Carbohydrate 12.9g, of which sugars 11.4g; Fat 9.6g, of which saturates 1.6g; Cholesterol 0mg; Calcium 339mg; Fibre 3.6g; Sodium 108mg

Vegetable Pancakes with Tomato Salsa ✳

Spinach and egg pancakes are tasty, inexpensive and nutritious. Serve with flavoursome sun-dried tomato salsa and bread for a light snack, or with boiled new potatoes for a more sustaining main meal.

MAKES TEN

225g/8oz spinach

1 small leek

a few sprigs of fresh coriander (cilantro) or parsley

3 large (US extra large) eggs

25g/1oz/¹⁄₃ cup freshly grated Parmesan cheese

FOR THE SALSA

2 tomatoes, peeled and chopped

¹⁄₄ fresh red chilli, chopped

2 pieces sun-dried tomato in oil, drained and chopped

1 small red onion, chopped

1 garlic clove, crushed

30ml/2 tbsp sherry

FROM THE STORECUPBOARD

60ml/4 tbsp olive oil

2.5ml/¹⁄₂ tsp soft light brown sugar

50g/2oz/¹⁄₂ cup plain (all-purpose) flour, sifted

vegetable oil, for frying

salt, ground black pepper and freshly grated nutmeg

1 Prepare the tomato salsa: place the tomatoes, chilli, sun-dried tomatoes, onion, garlic, olive oil, sherry and brown sugar in a bowl and toss together to combine. Cover and leave to stand in a cool place for 2–3 hours.

2 To make the pancakes, finely chop the spinach, leek and coriander or parsley, then place in a bowl and beat in the eggs and seasoning. Blend in the flour and 30–45ml/2–3 tbsp water and leave to stand for 20 minutes.

3 Drop spoonfuls of the batter into a lightly oiled frying pan and cook until golden underneath. Using a fish slice (metal spatula), turn the pancakes over and cook on the other side.

4 Lift the pancakes out of the pan, drain on kitchen paper and keep warm while you cook the remaining mixture. Sprinkle with Parmesan cheese and serve with the salsa.

COOK'S TIP *Try to find sun-ripened tomatoes for the salsa, as these have the best flavour and are superior to those ripened under glass.*

Energy 153kcal/634kJ; Protein 4.6g; Carbohydrate 6.2g, of which sugars 2.1g; Fat 11.8g, of which saturates 2.2g; Cholesterol 63mg; Calcium 92mg; Fibre 1.3g; Sodium 84mg

25g/1oz/1 cup chopped fresh herbs

120ml/4fl oz/¹/₂ cup milk

3 eggs

FOR THE SAUCE

1 small onion, chopped

2 garlic cloves, crushed

FOR THE FILLING

450g/1lb fresh spinach, cooked and drained

175g/6oz/³/₄ cup ricotta cheese

25g/1oz/¹/₄ cup pine nuts, toasted

5 sun-dried tomato halves in olive oil, drained and chopped

30ml/2 tbsp shredded fresh basil

4 egg whites

FROM THE STORECUPBOARD

15ml/1 tbsp sunflower oil, plus extra for frying and greasing

25g/1oz/¹/₄ cup plain (all-purpose) flour

pinch of salt

30ml/2 tbsp olive oil

400g/14oz can chopped tomatoes

pinch of soft light brown sugar

grated nutmeg and ground black pepper

Baked Herb Crêpes with Spinach and Ricotta ✳✳✳

Turn light herb crêpes into something special. Fill with a spinach, cheese and pine nut filling, then bake and serve with a delicious tomato sauce.

SERVES FOUR

1 To make the crêpes, place the herbs and sunflower oil in a food processor and process until smooth. Add the milk, eggs, flour and salt and process again. Leave to rest for 30 minutes.

2 Heat a small non-stick frying pan and add a small amount of sunflower oil. Pour in a ladleful of the batter. Swirl around until the batter covers the base evenly. Cook for 2 minutes, turn over and cook for a further 1–2 minutes. Make seven more crêpes.

3 To make the sauce, heat the olive oil in a pan, add the onion and garlic, and cook for 5 minutes. Stir in the tomatoes and sugar, and cook for 10 minutes until thickened. Process in a blender, then sieve (strain). Preheat the oven to 190°C/375°F/ Gas 5.

4 To make the filling, mix together the spinach and the ricotta, pine nuts, tomatoes, basil, nutmeg and pepper. Whisk the egg whites until they are stiff. Stir one-third into the spinach mixture, then gently fold in the rest.

5 Place one crêpe at a time on a lightly oiled baking sheet, add a spoonful of filling and fold into quarters. Bake for 12 minutes. Meanwhile, pour the tomato sauce into a small pan and reheat it gently, stirring occasionally. Serve the sauce with the hot crêpes.

Energy 434Kcal/1800kJ; Protein 14.9g; Carbohydrate 15.1g, of which sugars 9.8g; Fat 35.4g, of which saturates 8.3g; Cholesterol 161mg; Calcium 251mg; Fibre 5g; Sodium 229mg

Frittata with Sun-dried Tomatoes ✳✳

This Italian omelette, made with tangy Parmesan cheese, can be eaten warm or cold. It is perfect as a light vegetarian meal when served with a large mixed salad.

SERVES FOUR

6 sun-dried tomatoes

1 small onion, finely chopped

pinch of fresh thyme leaves

6 eggs

25g/1oz/¹/₃ cup freshly grated Parmesan cheese, plus shavings to serve

thyme sprigs, to garnish

FROM THE STORECUPBOARD

60ml/4 tbsp olive oil

salt and ground black pepper, to taste

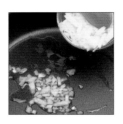

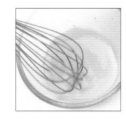

1 Place the tomatoes in a bowl and pour over hot water to cover. Leave to soak for 15 minutes, then pat dry on kitchen paper. Reserve the soaking water. Cut the tomatoes into strips.

2 Heat the olive oil in a large non-stick frying pan. Cook the onion for 5–6 minutes. Add the thyme and tomatoes and cook for a further 2–3 minutes.

3 Break the eggs into a bowl and beat lightly. Stir in 45ml/3 tbsp of the tomato soaking water and the Parmesan and season to taste. Raise the heat under the pan. When the oil is sizzling, add the eggs. Mix quickly into the other ingredients, then stop stirring. Lower the heat to medium and cook for 4–5 minutes, or until the base is golden and the top puffed.

4 Take a large plate, invert it over the pan and, holding it firmly with oven gloves, turn the pan and the frittata over on to it. Slide the frittata back into the pan, and continue cooking for 3–4 minutes until golden brown on the second side. Remove the pan from the heat. Cut the frittata into wedges, garnish with thyme sprigs and parmesan, and serve immediately.

Energy 170Kcal/705kJ; Protein 5.7g; Carbohydrate 3g, of which sugars 2.6g; Fat 15.2g, of which saturates 4.1g; Cholesterol 13mg; Calcium 158mg; Fibre 0.6g; Sodium 167mg

Cheese and Tomato Soufflés **

Guests are always impressed by a home-made soufflé and this recipe for little individual ones is the ultimate in effortless entertaining. Serve with a green salad and some warm bread.

SERVES SIX

25g/1oz/2 tbsp butter

350ml/¹/₂ pint/1¹/₄ cups full-fat (whole) milk

115g/4oz/1 cup grated Cheddar cheese

50g/2oz sun-dried tomatoes in olive oil, drained, plus 10ml/ 2 tsp of the oil

130g/4¹/₂ oz/1¹/₂ cups grated Parmesan cheese

4 large (US extra large) eggs, separated

FROM THE STORECUPBOARD

25g/1oz/2 tbsp plain (all-purpose) flour

salt and ground black pepper, to taste

1 Melt the butter in a pan, then stir in the flour to form a paste and cook for 1 minute. Pour in the milk and stir until smooth, then bring to the boil, stirring continuously. Stir in the Cheddar and mix until the cheese has melted and the sauce is smooth.

2 Preheat the oven to 200°C/400°F/Gas 6. Tip the cheese sauce into a bowl. Thinly slice the sun-dried tomatoes and add them to the sauce with 90g/3¹/₂oz/generous 1 cup of the Parmesan cheese and the egg yolks. Season well and stir.

3 Brush the base and sides of six 200ml/7fl oz/scant 1 cup ramekins or individual soufflé dishes with the oil, then coat the insides with half of the remaining cheese, tilting them until evenly covered. Tip out any excess cheese and set aside.

4 Whisk the egg whites in a clean, grease-free bowl until stiff. Use a large metal spoon to stir one-quarter of the egg whites into the sauce, then fold in the remaining egg whites.

5 Spoon the mixture into the ramekins or soufflé dishes and sprinkle with the reserved cheese. Place on a baking sheet and bake for about 15–18 minutes, or until the soufflé is well risen and golden. Serve immediately with a mixed green salad.

Energy 328kcal/1364kJ; Protein 20g; Carbohydrate 6.2g, of which sugars 3g; Fat 24.7g, of which saturates 13.6g; Cholesterol 184mg; Calcium 497mg; Fibre 0.2g; Sodium 473mg

Substantial Salads

WHETHER YOU WANT A LIGHT SALAD FOR A SUMMER LUNCH OR QUICK MEAL, OR A TASTY DISH FOR A HEALTHY SUPPER, THERE IS A SALAD HERE TO SUIT YOU. CHOOSE FROM SIMPLE SUMMER SALADS SUCH AS SALAD NIÇOISE OR COUNTRY PASTA SALAD, WHICH MAKE THE MOST OF SEASONAL INGREDIENTS, OR WHY NOT TRY SOMETHING MORE UNUSUAL, SUCH AS LENTIL AND SPINACH SALAD WITH ONIONS, CUMIN AND GARLIC, GADO GADO SALAD, OR RICE SALAD WITH CHICKEN, ORANGE AND CASHEW NUTS?

Warm Salad with Poached Eggs ✳✳

Soft poached eggs, chilli oil, hot croûtons and cool, crisp salad leaves make a lively and unusual combination. This delicious salad will provide a sustaining lunch or supper, served with bread.

SERVES TWO

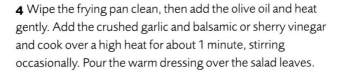

1 Heat the chilli oil in a large, heavy frying pan. Add the cubes of bread and cook for 5 minutes, tossing the cubes occasionally, until they are crisp and golden. Remove from the pan and drain on a sheet of kitchen paper.

2 Bring a large pan of water to a gentle boil. Break each egg into a jug (pitcher) and slide it carefully into the water. Poach for 3–4 minutes.

3 Meanwhile, divide the salad leaves equally between two small serving plates. Scatter the croûtons over the mixed salad leaves.

4 Wipe the frying pan clean, then add the olive oil and heat gently. Add the crushed garlic and balsamic or sherry vinegar and cook over a high heat for about 1 minute, stirring occasionally. Pour the warm dressing over the salad leaves.

5 Remove the poached eggs from the pan with a slotted spoon, and pat them dry on kitchen paper. Place one egg on top of each plate of salad, then top with shavings of fresh Parmesan cheese and season with black pepper. Serve immediately.

1 slice wholegrain bread, crusts removed and cubed

2 eggs

115g/4oz mixed salad leaves

2 garlic cloves, crushed

50g/2oz Parmesan cheese, shaved

FROM THE STORECUPBOARD

25ml/1¹⁄₂ tbsp chilli oil

45ml/3 tbsp extra virgin olive oil

15ml/1 tbsp balsamic or sherry vinegar

ground black pepper

Energy 697kcal/2907kJ; Protein 25.9g; Carbohydrate 41.3g, of which sugars 2.8g; Fat 49g, of which saturates 11.5g; Cholesterol 215mg; Calcium 408mg; Fibre 6.3g; Sodium 914mg

225g/8oz new potatoes, scrubbed and halved

2 carrots, cut into sticks

115g/4oz green beans

$^1/_2$ small cauliflower, broken into florets

$^1/_4$ firm white cabbage, shredded

200g/7oz bean or lentil sprouts

4 eggs, hard-boiled and quartered

bunch of watercress (optional)

FOR THE SAUCE

90ml/6 tbsp crunchy peanut butter

300ml/$^1/_2$ pint/1$^1/_4$ cups cold water

1 garlic clove, crushed

15ml/1 tbsp dry sherry

15ml/1 tbsp fresh lemon juice

5ml/1 tsp anchovy essence (extract)

FROM THE STORECUPBOARD

30ml/2 tbsp dark soy sauce

10ml/2 tsp caster (superfine) sugar

COOK'S TIP
There is a range of nut butters available in health-food stores and supermarkets. Alternatively, you can make your own peanut butter by blending 225g/8oz/2 cups peanuts with 120ml/ 4fl oz/$^1/_2$ cup oil in a food processor.

Gado Gado Salad ✳✳

This Indonesian salad combines lightly steamed vegetables and hard-boiled eggs with a richly flavoured peanut and soy sauce dressing.

SERVES SIX

1 Place the halved potatoes in a metal colander or steamer and set over a pan of gently boiling water. Cover the pan or steamer with a lid and cook the potatoes for 10 minutes.

2 Add the rest of the vegetables to the steamer and steam for a further 10 minutes, until tender.

3 Cool and arrange on a platter with the egg quarters and the watercress, if using.

4 Beat together the peanut butter, water, garlic, sherry, lemon juice, anchovy essence, soy sauce and sugar in a large mixing bowl until smooth. Drizzle a little sauce over each portion then pour the rest into a small bowl and serve separately.

Energy 235kcal/979kJ; Protein 12.7g; Carbohydrate 18.3g, of which sugars 10.6g; Fat 12.5g, of which saturates 3.2g; Cholesterol 127mg; Calcium 91mg; Fibre 4.8g; Sodium 494mg

Spiced Aubergine Salad with Yogurt and Parsley **

The delicate flavours of aubergine, tomatoes and cucumber are lightly spiced with cumin and coriander in this fresh-tasting salad. Make it in the summer, when the vegetables are at their best, and serve with bread.

SERVES FOUR

1 Preheat the grill (broiler). Lightly brush the aubergine slices with olive oil and cook them under a high heat, turning once, until they are golden and tender. Alternatively, cook them on a griddle pan.

2 When they are done, remove the aubergine slices to a chopping board and cut them into quarters.

3 Mix together the remaining oil, the vinegar, garlic, lemon juice, cumin and coriander. Season with salt and pepper to taste and mix thoroughly.

4 Add the warm aubergines to the bowl, stir well and chill for at least 2 hours. Add the cucumber and tomatoes.

5 Transfer to a serving dish and spoon the yogurt on top. Sprinkle with parsley and serve with warm crusty bread.

2 small aubergines (eggplants), sliced

2 garlic cloves, crushed

15ml/1 tbsp lemon juice

$1/2$ cucumber, thinly sliced

2 well-flavoured tomatoes, thinly sliced

30ml/2 tbsp natural (plain) yogurt

chopped fresh flat leaf parsley, to garnish

FROM THE STORECUPBOARD

75ml/5 tbsp extra virgin olive oil

50ml/2fl oz/$1/4$ cup red wine vinegar

2.5ml/$1/2$ tsp ground cumin

2.5ml/$1/2$ tsp ground coriander

salt and ground black pepper, to taste

Energy 155Kcal/642kJ; Protein 1.9g; Carbohydrate 4.9g, of which sugars 4.7g; Fat 14.4g, of which saturates 2.2g; Cholesterol 0mg; Calcium 35mg; Fibre 2.7g; Sodium 14mg

Grilled Aubergine, Mint and Couscous Salad ✳✳

Packets of flavoured couscous are available in most supermarkets – you can use whichever you like, but garlic and coriander is particularly good for this recipe. Serve with a crisp green salad.

SERVES TWO

1 large aubergine (eggplant)

110g/4oz packet flavoured couscous

30ml/2 tbsp chopped fresh mint

FROM THE STORECUPBOARD

30ml/2 tbsp olive oil

salt and ground black pepper, to taste

1 Preheat the grill (broiler) to high. Cut the aubergine into large chunky pieces and toss them with the olive oil.

2 Season with salt and pepper to taste and spread the aubergine pieces on a non-stick baking sheet.

3 Grill the aubergine pieces for 5–6 minutes, turning occasionally, until they are golden brown.

4 Meanwhile, prepare the couscous according to the instructions on the packet.

5 Stir the grilled aubergine and chopped mint into the couscous, toss thoroughly and serve immediately with a crisp green salad.

Energy 251kcal/1044kJ; Protein 4.8g; Carbohydrate 32.5g, of which sugars 2g; Fat 12.1g, of which saturates 1.7g; Cholesterol 0mg; Calcium 53mg; Fibre 2g; Sodium 5mg

Warm Black-eyed Bean Salad with Rocket and Black Olives ✳✳

This is an easy dish, as black-eyed beans do not need to be soaked overnight. By adding spring onions and dill, it is transformed into a refreshing and healthy meal. It can be served hot or cold.

SERVES FOUR

1 Thoroughly rinse the beans and drain them well. Tip into a pan and pour in cold water to just about cover them. Slowly bring to the boil over a low heat. As soon as the water is boiling, remove from the heat and drain the water off immediately.

2 Put the beans back in the pan with fresh cold water to cover and add a pinch of salt – this will make their skins harder and stop them from disintegrating when they are cooked.

3 Bring the beans to the boil over a medium heat, then lower the heat and cook them until they are soft but not mushy. They will take 20–30 minutes only, so keep an eye on them.

4 Drain the beans, reserving 75–90ml/5–6 tbsp of the cooking liquid. Tip the beans into a large salad bowl. Immediately add the remaining ingredients, including the reserved liquid, and mix well. Serve immediately, piled on the lettuce leaves, or leave to cool slightly and serve later.

5 spring onions (scallions), sliced into rounds

a large handful of fresh rocket (arugula) leaves, chopped if large

45–60ml/3–4 tbsp chopped fresh dill

juice of 1 lemon, or to taste

10–12 black olives

small cos or romaine lettuce leaves, to serve

FROM THE STORECUPBOARD

275g/10oz/1¹/₂ cups black-eyed beans (peas)

150ml/¹/₄ pint/²/₃ cup extra virgin olive oil

salt and ground black pepper, to taste

Energy 434Kcal/1,811kJ; Protein 16.6g; Carbohydrate 31.4g, of which sugars 2.7g; Fat 27.8g, of which saturates 4g; Cholesterol 0mg; Calcium 149mg; Fibre 12.5g; Sodium 334mg.

1 celery stick

fresh thyme sprig

1 onion or 3–4 shallots, finely chopped

400g/14oz young spinach

30–45ml/2–3 tbsp chopped fresh parsley

toasted French bread, to serve

FOR THE DRESSING

1 small garlic clove, finely chopped

2.5ml/½ tsp finely grated lemon rind

FROM THE STORECUPBOARD

225g/8oz/1 cup Puy lentils

1 fresh bay leaf

105ml/7 tbsp olive oil

5ml/1 tsp Dijon mustard

15–25ml/1–1½ tbsp red wine vinegar

salt and ground black pepper, to taste

10ml/2 tsp crushed toasted cumin seeds

Lentil and Spinach Salad with Onion, Cumin and Garlic ✳✳

This earthy and sustaining salad combines Puy lentils with onions, bay, thyme, parsley and cumin in a mustard, garlic and lemon dressing.

SERVES SIX

1 Rinse the lentils and place them in a large pan. Add enough water to cover. Tie the bay leaf, celery and thyme into a bundle and add to the pan, then bring to the boil. Reduce the heat and cook the lentils for 30–45 minutes, or until just tender.

2 Meanwhile, to make the dressing, mix 75ml/5 tbsp of the olive oil, the mustard and 15ml/1 tbsp vinegar with the garlic and lemon rind, and season well with salt and pepper.

3 Thoroughly drain the lentils and turn them into a bowl. Add most of the dressing and toss well, then set the lentils aside.

4 Heat the remaining olive oil in a deep frying pan and sauté the chopped onion or shallots over a low heat for 4–5 minutes, then add the cumin and cook for a further 1 minute.

5 Add the spinach and season to taste with salt and pepper, then cover and cook until wilted. Stir the spinach into the lentils and leave to cool.

6 Stir in the remaining dressing and chopped parsley. Adjust the seasoning, and add extra red wine vinegar, if necessary. Turn on to a serving dish and serve with toasted French bread.

Energy 248kcal/1037kJ; Protein 11.2g; Carbohydrate 20.3g, of which sugars 2.1g; Fat 14.1g, of which saturates 2g; Cholesterol 0mg; Calcium 150mg; Fibre 5.1g; Sodium 102mg

Summer Salad ✴

Ripe tomatoes, creamy mozzarella and juicy olives make a good base for a fresh pasta salad that is perfect for a light summer lunch.

SERVES FOUR

1 Cook the pasta for 10–12 minutes, or according to the instructions on the packet. Tip it into a colander and rinse briefly under cold running water, then shake the colander to remove as much water as possible and leave to drain.

2 Make the dressing. Whisk the olive oil and balsamic vinegar or lemon juice in a jug (pitcher) with a little salt and pepper to taste.

3 Place the pasta, mozzarella, tomatoes, olives and spring onion in a large bowl, pour the dressing over and toss together well. Taste for seasoning before serving, sprinkled with basil leaves.

150g/5oz packet buffalo mozzarella, drained and diced

3 ripe tomatoes, diced

10 pitted black olives, sliced

10 pitted green olives, sliced

1 spring onion (scallion), thinly sliced on the diagonal

1 handful fresh basil leaves

FOR THE DRESSING

15ml/1 tbsp balsamic vinegar or lemon juice

FROM THE STORECUPBOARD

350g/12oz/3 cups dried penne

90ml/6 tbsp olive oil

salt and ground black pepper, to taste

Country Pasta Salad ✴✴

Colourful, tasty and nutritious, this is the ideal pasta salad for a summer picnic or an *al fresco* lunch. Serve with plenty of bread and butter.

SERVES SIX

1 Cook the pasta according to the instructions on the packet. Drain it into a colander, rinse under cold running water until cold, then shake the colander to remove as much water as possible. Leave to drain and dry.

2 Trim the beans and cut them into 5cm/2in lengths, and dice the potato. Put the beans and the potato in a pan of boiling water for 5–6 minutes or steam for 8–10 minutes. Drain and leave to cool.

3 To make the dressing, put the olive oil, balsamic vinegar and parsley in a large bowl with a little salt and ground black pepper to taste and whisk well to mix.

4 Halve the tomatoes, finely chop the spring onions, and add to the dressing with the grano padano, olive rings and capers. Stir in the cold pasta, beans and potato. Toss well to mix. Cover and leave to stand for about 30 minutes. Taste for seasoning before serving.

150g/5oz fine green beans

1 potato

200g/7oz cherry tomatoes

2 spring onions (scallions)

90g/3$\frac{1}{2}$oz/scant 1$\frac{1}{4}$ cups grano padano cheese, shaved

6–8 pitted black olives, cut into rings

15–30ml/1–2 tbsp capers

FOR THE DRESSING

15ml/1 tbsp chopped fresh flat leaf parsley

FROM THE STORECUPBOARD

300g/11oz/2$\frac{3}{4}$ cups dried fusilli

90ml/6 tbsp extra virgin olive oil

15ml/1 tbsp balsamic vinegar

salt and ground black pepper, to taste

Top: Energy 577kcal/2420kJ; Protein 18.2g; Carbohydrate 67.2g, of which sugars 5.3g; Fat 28g, of which saturates 8.1g; Cholesterol 22mg; Calcium 175mg; Fibre 3.9g; Sodium 580mg

Above: Energy 381kcal/1600kJ; Protein 13.3g; Carbohydrate 44.4g, of which sugars 3.8g; Fat 18g, of which saturates 5g; Cholesterol 15mg; Calcium 212mg; Fibre 2.9g; Sodium 341mg

Bean Salad with Tuna and Red Onion ✳✳

This makes a great main meal dish if served with a green salad, some garlic mayonnaise and plenty of warm, crusty bread. Using good-quality canned tuna brings the overall cost of the dish right down, making it affordable as well as healthy and absolutely delicious.

SERVES FOUR

1 Drain the dried beans and bring them to the boil in fresh water with the bay leaf added. Boil rapidly for 10 minutes, then reduce the heat and boil steadily for 1–1¹/₂ hours, until tender. Drain well. Discard the bay leaf.

2 Meanwhile, place the olive oil, tarragon vinegar and mustard, and garlic in a jug (pitcher) and whisk until mixed. Season to taste with salt, pepper, lemon juice and a pinch of caster sugar, if you like. Leave to stand.

3 Blanch the green beans in boiling water for 3–4 minutes. Drain, refresh under cold water and drain thoroughly again.

4 Place both types of beans in a bowl. Add half the dressing and toss to mix. Stir in the onion and half the chopped parsley, then season to taste with salt and pepper.

5 Flake the tuna into large chunks with a knife and toss it into the beans with the tomato halves.

6 Arrange the salad on four individual plates. Drizzle the remaining dressing over the salad and sprinkle the remaining chopped parsley on top. Garnish with a few onion rings and serve immediately, at room temperature.

200–250g/7–9oz fine green beans, trimmed

1 large red onion, sliced

45ml/3 tbsp chopped fresh flat leaf parsley

200–250g/7–9oz good-quality canned tuna in olive oil, drained

200g/7oz cherry tomatoes, halved

a few onion rings, to garnish

FOR THE DRESSING

1 garlic clove, finely chopped

5ml/1 tsp finely grated lemon rind

a little lemon juice

FROM THE STORECUPBOARD

250g/9oz/1¹/₃ cups dried haricot (navy) or cannellini beans, soaked overnight in cold water

1 bay leaf

90ml/6 tbsp olive oil

15ml/1 tbsp tarragon vinegar

5ml/1 tsp tarragon mustard

pinch of caster (superfine) sugar (optional)

salt and ground black pepper, to taste

Energy 461kcal/1929kJ; Protein 29.9g; Carbohydrate 37g, of which sugars 8.7g; Fat 22.6g, of which saturates 3.3g; Cholesterol 25mg; Calcium 131mg; Fibre 13g; Sodium 167mg

115g/4oz green beans, trimmed and cut in half

115g/4oz mixed salad leaves

1/2 small cucumber, thinly sliced

4 ripe tomatoes, quartered

50g/2oz can anchovies, drained

4 eggs, hard-boiled

1 tuna steak, about 175g/6oz

1/2 bunch of small radishes, trimmed

50g/2oz/1/2 cup small black olives

FOR THE DRESSING

2 garlic cloves, crushed

FROM THE STORECUPBOARD

90ml/6 tbsp extra virgin olive oil, plus extra for brushing

15ml/1 tbsp white wine vinegar

salt and ground black pepper, to taste

VARIATION

• Opinions vary on whether Salad Niçoise should include potatoes or not, but, if you like, include a handful of small cooked new potatoes for a more substantial salad.

• Fresh tuna can be expensive, so buy it when it is on special offer. Alternatively, you could use a 250g/9oz can of tuna instead. Simply drain the canned fish in a sieve (strainer) and flake the flesh with a fork.

Salad Niçoise ✳✳✳

Made with the freshest of seasonal ingredients, this classic Provençal salad makes a simple yet unbeatable summer dish. Serve with warm country-style bread for a nutritious and sustaining main meal.

SERVES FOUR

1 To make the dressing, whisk together 90ml/6 tbsp of the olive oil, the garlic and the vinegar in a bowl and season to taste with salt and pepper. Alternatively, shake together in a screw-top jar. Set aside.

2 Cook the green beans in a pan of boiling water for 2 minutes, until just tender, then drain.

3 Mix together the salad leaves, sliced cucumber, tomatoes and green beans in a large, shallow bowl. Halve the anchovies lengthways and shell and quarter the eggs.

4 Preheat the grill (broiler). Brush the tuna with olive oil and sprinkle with salt and black pepper. Grill (broil) for 3–4 minutes on each side until cooked through. Cool, then flake with a fork.

5 Sprinkle the flaked tuna, sliced anchovies, quartered eggs, radishes and olives over the salad. Pour over the dressing and toss together lightly to combine. Serve immediately.

Energy 351kcal/1457kJ; Protein 21.7g; Carbohydrate 5.3g, of which sugars 5g; Fat 27.3g, of which saturates 5g; Cholesterol 210mg; Calcium 114mg; Fibre 2.6g; Sodium 876mg

Chicken and Tomato Salad with Hazelnut Dressing ✳✳✳

This simple, warm salad combines pan-fried chicken and spinach with a light, nutty dressing. Serve it with bread for a sustaining main meal.

SERVES FOUR

30ml/2 tbsp hazelnut oil

1 garlic clove, crushed

15ml/1 tbsp chopped fresh mixed herbs

225g/8oz baby spinach leaves

250g/9oz cherry tomatoes, halved

1 bunch of spring onions (scallions), chopped

2 skinless, chicken breast fillets, cut into thin strips

FROM THE STORECUPBOARD

45ml/3 tbsp olive oil

15ml/1 tbsp white wine vinegar

salt and ground black pepper, to taste

1 First make the dressing: place 30ml/ 2 tbsp of the olive oil, the hazelnut oil, vinegar, garlic and chopped herbs in a small bowl or jug (pitcher) and whisk together until mixed. Set aside.

2 Trim any long stalks from the spinach leaves, then place in a large serving bowl with the tomatoes and spring onions, and toss together to mix.

3 Heat the remaining olive oil in a frying pan, and stir-fry the chicken over a high heat for 7–10 minutes, until it is cooked, tender and lightly browned.

4 Arrange the cooked chicken pieces over the salad. Give the dressing a quick whisk to blend, then drizzle it over the salad. Add salt and pepper to taste, toss lightly and serve immediately.

Energy 247kcal/1029kJ; Protein 23.5g; Carbohydrate 3.6g, of which sugars 3.5g; Fat 15.5g, of which saturates 2.1g; Cholesterol 61mg; Calcium 114mg; Fibre 2.2g; Sodium 139mg

Rice Salad with Chicken, Orange and Cashew Nuts ✳✳✳

With their tangy flavour, orange segments are the perfect partner for tender chicken in this tasty and wholesome rice salad.

SERVES FOUR

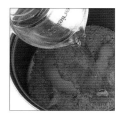

COOK'S TIP *To make a simple vinaigrette, whisk 45ml/ 3 tbsp wine vinegar with 90ml/6 tbsp olive oil. Add 60ml/4 tbsp extra virgin olive oil and season well.*

1 Pare one of the oranges thinly, removing only the rind, not the white pith. Put the pieces of rind in a pan and add the rice.

2 Pour in 475ml/16fl oz/2 cups water and bring to the boil. Cover and cook over a very low heat for about 15 minutes, or until the rice is tender and all the water has been absorbed.

3 Meanwhile, peel the oranges, removing all the white pith. Working over a plate to catch the juices, separate them into segments. Tip the juices into a small bowl and add the vinaigrette with the mustard and sugar, whisking to combine.

4 When the rice is cooked, remove it from the heat and discard the pieces of orange rind. Spoon into a bowl, let it cool slightly, then add half the dressing. Toss well, then set aside to cool.

5 Add the chicken, chives, toasted nuts and orange segments to the cooled rice. Pour over the remaining dressing and toss gently to combine. Serve on a bed of mixed salad leaves.

3 large seedless oranges

450g/1lb cooked chicken, diced

45ml/3 tbsp chopped fresh chives

75g/3oz/$^3/_4$ cup almonds or cashew nuts, toasted

mixed salad leaves, to serve

FROM THE STORECUPBOARD

175g/6oz/scant 1 cup long grain rice

175ml/6fl oz/$^3/_4$ cup home-made vinaigrette (*see* Cook's Tip)

10ml/2 tsp strong Dijon mustard

2.5ml/1/2 tsp caster (superfine) sugar

salt and ground black pepper, to taste

Energy 668kcal/2785kJ; Protein 35.9g; Carbohydrate 47.8g, of which sugars 12.3g; Fat 37.2g, of which saturates 4.8g; Cholesterol 79mg; Calcium 141mg; Fibre 4.1g; Sodium 80mg

Scrumptious Side Dishes

Side dishes not only add nutritional value to main courses, but they also help more expensive dishes to stretch further, and provide extra flavours, colours and textures. This section contains some simple ideas for using seasonal vegetables, such as Braised Red Cabbage, or Baked Winter Squash with Tomatoes, as well as year-round family favourites such as Roasted Potatoes with Peppers and Shallots, or Carrot and Parsnip Purée.

Steamed Cauliflower and Broccoli with Breadcrumbs and Eggs ✳

Steamed vegetables are a delicious and extremely healthy accompaniment for any main meal. Here they are given a tasty twist with the addition of an egg and breadcrumb topping.

SERVES SIX

1 Trim the cauliflower and broccoli and break into medium-sized florets, then place in a steamer over a pan of boiling water and steam for about 12 minutes, or until tender. Alternatively, if you prefer, you can boil the vegetables in a large pan of salted water for 5–7 minutes, until just tender.

2 Drain the vegetables well in a colander (strainer) and transfer to a warmed serving dish.

3 While the vegetables are cooking, make the topping. In a bowl, combine the lemon rind, garlic and breadcrumbs.

4 Finely chop the eggs, add to the bowl and mix into the breadcrumb mixture.

5 Season the mixture with salt and black pepper to taste, then sprinkle the chopped egg mixture over the cooked vegetables and serve immediately.

500g/1¼lb cauliflower and broccoli

finely grated rind of ½ lemon

1 garlic clove, crushed

25g/1oz/½ cup wholegrain breadcrumbs, lightly baked or grilled (broiled) until crisp

2 eggs, hard-boiled and shelled

FROM THE STORECUPBOARD

salt and ground black pepper, to taste

Energy 67kcal/280kJ; Protein 6.2g; Carbohydrate 4.7g, of which sugars 1.4g; Fat 2.7g, of which saturates 0.7g; Cholesterol 63mg; Calcium 62mg; Fibre 2.3g; Sodium 62mg

50g/2oz/¹/₄ cup butter

4 Little Gem (Bibb) lettuces, halved lengthways

2 bunches spring onions (scallions), trimmed and cut into 5cm/2in lengths

400g/14oz shelled peas (about 1kg/2¹/₂lb in pods), or frozen peas, thawed

4 fresh mint sprigs

120ml/4fl oz/¹/₂ cup chicken or vegetable stock

15ml/1 tbsp chopped fresh mint

FROM THE STORECUPBOARD

5ml/1 tsp caster (superfine) sugar

salt and ground black pepper, to taste

Braised Lettuce and Peas with Spring Onions and Mint **

This simple recipe is delicious served with steamed or baked fish, or roast duck. You can use fresh or frozen peas, depending on your preference.

SERVES FOUR

VARIATION
Fry 115g/4oz chopped pancetta or dry cured streaky (fatty) bacon with 1 small chopped onion in the butter.

COOK'S TIP
Frozen peas tend to be much cheaper than fresh peas, and since the peas are frozen very shortly after being picked, they are often fresher too.

1 Gently melt half the butter in a large pan over a low heat. Add the lettuces and spring onions.

2 Turn the vegetables in the butter, then sprinkle in the caster sugar, 2.5ml/¹/₂ tsp salt and plenty of black pepper. Cover and cook very gently for about 5 minutes, stirring once.

3 Add the peas and mint sprigs. Turn the peas in the buttery juices and pour in the stock, then cover and cook over a gentle heat for a further 5 minutes. Uncover and increase the heat to reduce the liquid to a few tablespoons.

4 Stir in the remaining butter and adjust the seasoning. Transfer to a warmed serving dish and sprinkle with the chopped mint. Serve immediately.

Energy 191kcal/790kJ; Protein 8g; Carbohydrate 13.3g, of which sugars 4.2g; Fat 12.3g, of which saturates 6.9g; Cholesterol 27mg; Calcium 52mg; Fibre 5.7g; Sodium 81mg

Braised Red Cabbage ✳

Cook this very economical, vibrantly coloured dish in the oven at the same time as a pork casserole or joint of meat for a simple, easy-to-prepare meal that is perfect for a cold winter day.

SERVES EIGHT

1 Cut the red cabbage into fine shreds, discarding any tough outer leaves and the core, and place in an ovenproof dish.

2 Thinly slice the onion, then fry in the olive oil in a frying pan until the onion is soft and golden.

3 Preheat the oven to 190°C/375°F/Gas 5. Peel, core and slice the apples, and peel and coarsley grate the beetroot.

4 Stir the apple slices, vegetable stock and red wine vinegar into the onions, then transfer to the ovenproof dish.

5 Season with salt and pepper to taste, and cover. Put the dish in the preheated oven and cook for 1 hour. Stir in the beetroot, re-cover the dish and cook for a further 20–30 minutes, or until the cabbage and beetroot are tender.

6 Serve immediately with a roasted joint of meat or a casserole, or on its own with plenty of creamy mashed potatoes.

675g/1¹/₂lb red cabbage

1 onion

2 tart eating apples

375g/13oz raw beetroot (beet)

FROM THE STORECUPBOARD

30ml/2 tbsp olive oil

300ml/¹/₂ pint/1¹/₄ cups vegetable stock

60ml/4 tbsp red wine vinegar

salt and ground black pepper, to taste

Energy 74kcal/309kJ; Protein 2.1g; Carbohydrate 10g, of which sugars 9.5g; Fat 3g, of which saturates 0.4g; Cholesterol 0mg; Calcium 53mg; Fibre 3.1g; Sodium 38mg

350g/12oz carrots

450g/1lb parsnips

15g/^{1}/₂oz/1 tbsp butter

about 15ml/1 tbsp single
(light) cream (optional)

1 small bunch parsley
leaves, chopped (optional),
plus extra to garnish

FROM THE STORECUPBOARD

pinch of grated nutmeg

salt and ground black
pepper, to taste

COOK'S TIP *Any leftover purée can be thinned to taste with good-quality chicken stock and heated to make a quick home-made soup.*

Carrot and Parsnip Purée ✳

Carrot and parsnips are good value, flavoursome and popular winter vegetables. The combination of the two works well together in this simple side dish, which is an ideal accompaniment to grilled (broiled) meats.

1 Peel the carrots and slice them fairly thinly. Peel the parsnips and cut into bitesize chunks (they are softer and will cook more quickly than the carrots). Boil the two vegetables, separately, in lightly salted water, until tender.

2 Drain them well and put them through a mouli-légumes (food mill) or food processor with the grated nutmeg, a good seasoning of salt and ground black pepper, and the butter. Purée together and taste for seasoning.

3 If you like, blend in some single cream to taste, and add chopped parsley for extra flavour.

4 Transfer the purée to a warmed serving bowl, sprinkle with freshly chopped parsley to garnish and serve immediately.

Energy 92Kcal/385kJ; Protein 1.8g; Carbohydrate 14.1g, of which sugars 8.7g; Fat 3.5g, of which saturates 1.8g; Cholesterol 7mg; Calcium 48mg; Fibre 4.9g; Sodium 38mg

Radicchio and Chicory Gratin ✳✳

Baking seasonal salad vegetables in a creamy sauce creates a dish that is wholesome, warming and sustaining. It is delicious served with grilled meat or fish, or with a bean or lentil casserole.

SERVES FOUR

1 Preheat the oven to 180°C/350°F/Gas 4. Grease a 1.2 litre/ 2 pint/5 cup ovenproof dish and arrange the radicchio and chicory in it.

2 Sprinkle over the sun-dried tomatoes and brush the vegetables with oil from the jar.

3 Season to taste and cover with foil. Bake for 15 minutes, then uncover and bake for a further 10 minutes.

4 To make the sauce, place the butter in a small pan and melt over a medium heat. When it is foaming, add the flour and cook for 1 minute, stirring.

5 Remove from the heat and gradually add the milk, whisking all the time until smooth.

6 Return to the heat and bring to the boil, then simmer for 3 minutes to thicken. Season to taste and add the nutmeg.

7 Pour the sauce over the vegetables and sprinkle with the cheese. Bake for about 20 minutes. Serve immediately.

2 heads radicchio, quartered lengthways

2 heads chicory (Belgian endive), quartered lengthways

25g/1oz/¹/₂ cup drained sun-dried tomatoes in oil, coarsely chopped

25g/1oz/2 tbsp butter

250ml/8fl oz/1 cup milk

50g/2oz/¹/₂ cup grated Emmenthal cheese

FROM THE STORECUPBOARD

15g/¹/₂oz/2 tbsp plain (all-purpose) flour

pinch of freshly grated nutmeg

salt and ground black pepper, to taste

VARIATION *You could use fennel in place of the radicchio and chicory. Par-boil the fennel before putting it in the ovenproof dish, then continue as in the recipe.*

Energy 159kcal/662kJ; Protein 6.3g; Carbohydrate 8g, of which sugars 4.4g; Fat 11.6g, of which saturates 6.9g; Cholesterol 29mg; Calcium 196mg; Fibre 1g; Sodium 158mg

Baked Winter Squash with Tomatoes ✳

Acorn, butternut or Hubbard squash can all be used in this simple recipe. Serve the squash as a light main course, with warm crusty bread, or as a side dish for grilled meat or poultry.

SERVES SIX

1 Preheat the oven to 160°C/325°F/Gas 3. Heat the oil in a large frying pan and cook the pumpkin or squash slices, in batches, until they are golden brown. Remove them from the pan and set them aside as they are cooked.

2 Add the tomatoes to the pan and cook over a medium-high heat for 10 minutes, or until the mixture is of a thick sauce consistency. Stir in the rosemary and season to taste with salt and ground black pepper.

3 Layer the pumpkin slices and tomatoes in an ovenproof dish, ending with a layer of tomatoes.

4 Bake for 35 minutes, or until the top is lightly glazed and beginning to turn golden brown, and the pumpkin is tender. Serve immediately.

1kg/2¼lb pumpkin or orange winter squash, peeled and sliced

2–3 fresh rosemary sprigs, stems removed and leaves chopped

FROM THE STORECUPBOARD

45ml/3 tbsp garlic-flavoured olive oil

2 x 400g/14oz cans chopped tomatoes

salt and ground black pepper, to taste

Energy 94kcal/392kJ; Protein 2.1g; Carbohydrate 7.8g, of which sugars 7g; Fat 6.2g, of which saturates 1.1g; Cholesterol 0mg; Calcium 58mg; Fibre 3g; Sodium 12mg

Potatoes and Parsnips Baked with Garlic and Cream ✳

This creamy, flavoursome baked dish is the ideal accompaniment to any number of main course dishes and is particularly good during the winter months. As the potatoes and parsnips cook, they gradually absorb the garlic-flavoured cream, while the cheese browns to a crispy finish.

3 large potatoes, total weight about 675g/1¹/₂lb

350g/12oz small–medium parsnips

200ml/7fl oz/scant 1 cup single (light) cream

105ml/7 tbsp milk

2 garlic cloves, crushed

butter or olive oil, for greasing

75g/3oz/³/₄ cup coarsely grated Cheddar cheese

FROM THE STORECUPBOARD

about 5ml/1 tsp freshly grated nutmeg

salt and ground black pepper, to taste

1 Peel the potatoes and parsnips and cut them into thin slices using a sharp knife. Place them in a steamer and cook for 5 minutes. Leave to cool slightly.

2 Meanwhile, pour the cream and milk into a heavy pan, add the crushed garlic and bring to the boil over a medium heat.

3 Remove the pan from the heat and leave to stand at room temperature for about 10 minutes to allow the flavour of the garlic to infuse into the cream and milk mixture.

4 Lightly grease a 25cm/10in long, shallow rectangular earthenware baking dish with butter or oil. Preheat the oven to 180°C/350°F/Gas 4.

5 Arrange the thinly sliced potatoes and parsnips in layers in the greased earthenware dish, sprinkling each layer of vegetables with a little freshly grated nutmeg, a little salt and plenty of ground black pepper.

6 Pour the cream and milk mixture into the dish and then press the sliced potatoes and parsnips down into the liquid. The liquid should come to just underneath the top layer of vegetables.

7 Cover the dish with a piece of lightly buttered foil or baking parchment and bake for 45 minutes.

8 Remove the dish from the oven and remove the foil or paper from the dish. Sprinkle the grated Cheddar cheese over the vegetables in an even layer.

9 Return the dish to the oven and bake uncovered for a further 20–30 minutes, or until the potatoes and parsnips are tender and the topping is golden brown.

VARIATION

You can use orange-fleshed sweet potatoes in place of some or all of the ordinary potatoes for a delicious and sustaining alternative. Other root vegetables such as Jerusalem artichokes, carrots, swede (rutabaga) or turnips would also work well in combination with the potato.

Energy 1443kcal/6055kJ; Protein 47g; Carbohydrate 161.8g, of which sugars 38.1g; Fat 70.4g, of which saturates 43.1g; Cholesterol 189mg; Calcium 1042mg; Fibre 22.8g; Sodium 755mg

Roasted Potatoes, Peppers and Shallots ✳✳

These potatoes soak up both the taste and wonderful aromas of the shallots and rosemary – just wait till you open the oven door.

SERVES FOUR

500g/1¼lb waxy potatoes

12 shallots

2 yellow (bell) peppers

2 rosemary sprigs

FROM THE STORECUPBOARD

olive oil, for drizzling

crushed black peppercorns, to garnish

salt and ground black pepper, to taste

1 Preheat the oven to 200°C/400°F/Gas 6. Par-boil the potatoes in their skins, then drain and leave to cool. Peel and cut in half. Peel the shallots, and cut each pepper lengthways into eight strips, discarding the seeds and pith.

2 Oil a shallow ovenproof dish. Arrange the potatoes and peppers in alternating rows and stud with the shallots.

3 Cut the rosemary sprigs into 5cm/2in lengths and tuck among the vegetables. Season, pour over the olive oil and roast, uncovered, for 30–40 minutes until all the vegetables are tender. Turn the vegetables occasionally to brown evenly. Serve hot or at room temperature, with crushed peppercorns.

Energy 192kcal/806kJ; Protein 3.9g; Carbohydrate 31.7g, of which sugars 11.2g; Fat 6.4g, of which saturates 1g; Cholesterol 0mg; Calcium 33mg; Fibre 3.7g; Sodium 20mg

Mashed Potatoes with Spring Onions ✳

Serve this variation on standard mashed potato as an accompaniment to beef or lamb stew, for a hearty winter meal.

SERVES FOUR

1kg/2¹/₄lb potatoes, cut into chunks

300ml/¹/₂ pint/1¹/₄ cups milk

1 bunch spring onions (scallions), thinly sliced, plus extra to garnish

115g/4oz/½ cup butter

FROM THE STORECUPBOARD

salt and ground black pepper, to taste

1 Boil the potatoes in a large pan of lightly salted water for 20–25 minutes, or until they are tender. Drain and mash the potatoes with a fork until smooth.

2 Place the milk, spring onions and half the butter in a small pan and set over a low heat until just simmering. Cook for 2–3 minutes, until the butter has melted and the spring onions have softened.

3 Beat the milk mixture into the mashed potato using a wooden spoon until the mixture is light and fluffy. Reheat gently, adding seasoning to taste.

4 Turn the potato into a warmed serving dish and make a well in the centre with a spoon. Place the remaining butter in the well and let it melt. Serve immediately, sprinkled with extra spring onion.

VARIATION
To make colcannon, an Irish speciality, follow the main recipe, using half the butter. Cook about 500g/1¹/₄lb shredded green cabbage or kale in a little water until tender, drain and then beat into the creamed potato. This is delicious served with sausages and grilled (broiled) ham or bacon. It may also be fried in butter then browned under the grill (broiler).

Energy 429kcal/1795kJ; Protein 7.5g; Carbohydrate 44.7g, of which sugars 7.7g; Fat 25.8g, of which saturates 16.1g; Cholesterol 66mg; Calcium 120mg; Fibre 2.9g; Sodium 236mg

Mixed Green Leaf and Fresh Herb Salad ✳

This flavourful salad makes an ideal side dish that goes well with meat and fish. You could turn it into a more substantial dish for a light lunch by adding some cooked asparagus tips and pitted green olives.

SERVES FOUR

1 Wash and dry the herbs and salad leaves in a salad spinner, or use two clean, dry dish towels to pat them dry.

2 To make the dressing, blend together the olive oil and cider vinegar in a small bowl and season with salt and ground black pepper to taste.

3 Place the prepared mixed herbs and salad leaves in a large salad bowl.

4 Just before serving, pour over the dressing and toss thoroughly to mix well, using your hands. Serve immediately.

15g/¹/₂oz/¹/₂ cup mixed fresh herbs, such as chervil, tarragon (use sparingly), dill, basil, marjoram (use sparingly), flat leaf parsley, mint, sorrel, fennel and coriander (cilantro)

350g/12oz mixed salad leaves, such as rocket (arugula), radicchio, chicory (Belgian endive), watercress, frisée, baby spinach, oakleaf lettuce and dandelion

FROM THE STORECUPBOARD

50ml/2fl oz/¹/₄ cup extra virgin olive oil

15ml/1 tbsp cider vinegar

salt and ground black pepper, to taste

Energy 92Kcal/377kJ; Protein 0.7g; Carbohydrate 1.6g, of which sugars 1.6g; Fat 9.2g, of which saturates 1.4g; Cholesterol 0mg; Calcium 26mg; Fibre 0.8g; Sodium 3mg

Baby Spinach and Roast Garlic Salad ✳✳

Tender young spinach leaves are packed with flavour and goodness. Here they are combined with sweet roasted garlic, crunchy pine nuts and zesty lemon juice to create a healthy and delicious side dish.

SERVES FOUR

1 Preheat the oven to 190°C/375°F/Gas 5. Place the unpeeled garlic cloves in a small roasting pan, drizzle over 30ml/2 tbsp of the olive oil and toss to coat. Bake the garlic cloves for about 15 minutes until the skins are slightly charred.

2 Place the garlic cloves, still in their skins, in a salad bowl. Add the spinach, pine nuts, lemon juice and remaining olive oil. Toss well to mix thoroughly, and season with plenty of salt and ground black pepper to taste.

3 Serve immediately, gently squeezing the softened garlic purée out of the skins to eat.

12 garlic cloves, unpeeled

450g/1lb baby spinach leaves

50g/2oz/$^1/_2$ cup pine nuts, lightly toasted

juice of $^1/_2$ lemon

FROM THE STORECUPBOARD

60ml/4 tbsp olive oil

salt and ground black pepper, to taste

Energy 238Kcal/980kJ; Protein 6.9g; Carbohydrate 6.4g, of which sugars 2.6g; Fat 20.6g, of which saturates 2.3g; Cholesterol 0mg; Calcium 198mg; Fibre 3.6g; Sodium 159mg

Turnip Salad in Sour Cream ✳

Usually served cooked, raw young tender turnips have a tangy, slightly peppery flavour and a crunchy texture. Serve this as an accompaniment for grilled poultry or meat. It is also delicious as an appetizer, garnished with parsley and paprika, and served with warmed flat breads such as pitta or naan. Garnish the salad with fresh flat leaf parsley and paprika, if you like.

SERVES FOUR

1 Thinly slice or coarsely grate the turnips. Alternatively, slice half the turnips and grate the remaining half. Put in a bowl.

2 Add the onion and vinegar and season to taste with salt and plenty of freshly ground black pepper. Toss together, then stir in the sour cream. Chill well before serving.

VARIATIONS

• *You can use large white radishes instead of turnips for a more peppery flavour. Simply peel, then thinly slice or coarsly grate the radishes.*

• *Crème fraîche or natural (plain) yogurt can be substituted for the sour cream, if you prefer.*

2–4 young, tender turnips, peeled

¹/₄–¹/₂ onion, finely chopped

60–90ml/4–6 tbsp sour cream

FROM THE STORECUPBOARD

2–3 drops white wine vinegar, or to taste

Energy 48kcal/198kJ; Protein 1.1g; Carbohydrate 4.1g, of which sugars 3.7g; Fat 3.2g, of which saturates 1.9g; Cholesterol 9mg; Calcium 42mg; Fibre 1.4g; Sodium 14mg

Potato and Olive Salad ✳

This delicious salad is simple and zesty – the perfect choice for lunch, as an accompaniment, or as an appetizer. Similar in appearance to flat leaf parsley, fresh coriander has a distinctive pungent, almost spicy flavour. It is widely used in India, the Middle and Far East and in eastern Mediterranean countries. If new potatoes are not in season, you can substitute another waxy variety, such as Charlotte potatoes.

SERVES FOUR

8 large new potatoes

**60–90ml/4–6 tbsp
chopped fresh herbs,
such as coriander (cilantro)
and chives**

10–15 black olives

FROM THE STORECUPBOARD

**45–60ml/3–4 tbsp
garlic oil (*see* page 31)**

1 Cut the new potatoes into chunks. Put them in a pan, pour in water to cover and add a pinch of salt.

2 Bring to the boil, then reduce the heat and cook gently for about 10 minutes, or until the potatoes are just tender.

3 Drain the potatoes well and leave in a colander to dry thoroughly and cool slightly.

4 When they are cool enough to handle, chop the potatoes and put them in a large serving bowl.

5 Drizzle the garlic oil over the potatoes. Toss well and sprinkle with the chopped fresh herbs, and black olives. Chill in the refrigerator for at least 1 hour before serving.

Energy 238kcal/998kJ; Protein 4g; Carbohydrate 32.6g, of which sugars 2.9g; Fat 11.1g, of which saturates 1.7g; Cholesterol 0mg; Calcium 49mg; Fibre 3.2g; Sodium 448mg

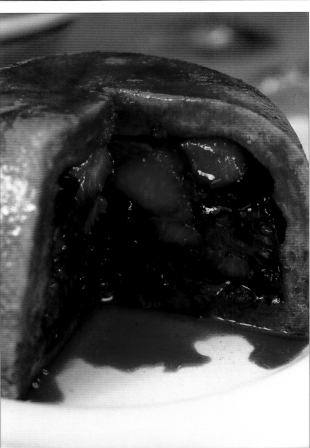

Delectable Desserts, Cakes and Bakes

NOTHING BEATS HOME-MADE DESSERTS, CAKES AND
BAKES. AS WELL AS HAVING A SUPERIOR TASTE TO
STORE-BOUGHT VARIETIES, THEY ARE ALSO A LOT
CHEAPER, AND WILL FILL THE HOUSE WITH AN
IRRESISTIBLE AROMA THAT WILL MAKE YOUR MOUTH
WATER. SO GO ON, TREAT YOURSELF TO A SLICE OF
WARM APPLE PIE OR TREACLE TART TO ROUND OFF
A FAMILY MEAL, OR TRY MAKING CARROT CAKE OR
CHOCOLATE CHIP BROWNIES FOR A DELICIOUS SNACK
AT ANY TIME OF THE DAY.

Moroccan Rice Pudding ✳

This comforting dessert is simple and delicious alternative to traditional and much-loved rice pudding. In this recipe, the rice is cooked in almond-flavoured milk and flavoured with warming cinnamon.

SERVES SIX

1 Put the almonds in a food processor or blender with 60ml/ 4 tbsp of very hot water. Process until finely chopped, then push through a sieve (strainer) into a bowl. Return to the food processor or blender, add a further 60ml/4 tbsp hot water, and process again. Push through the sieve into a pan.

2 Add 300ml/^{1}/$_2$ pint/1^1/$_4$ cups water and bring the mixture to the boil. Add the rice, caster sugar, cinnamon stick, half the butter, the almond essence, half the milk and half the cream, and mix to combine thoroughly.

3 Bring to the boil, then simmer, covered, for about 30 minutes, adding more milk and cream as the rice mixture thickens. Continue to cook the rice, stirring, and adding the remaining milk and cream, until the pudding becomes thick and creamy.

4 At the end of the cooking time, taste the rice pudding for sweetness, adding a little extra sugar, if necessary.

5 Pour the rice pudding into a serving bowl and sprinkle with the toasted flaked almonds. Dot with the remaining butter and dust with a little ground cinnamon. Serve the pudding hot.

25g/1oz/^{1}/$_4$ cup almonds

50g/2oz/^{1}/$_4$ cup butter

1.5ml/^{1}/$_4$ tsp almond essence (extract)

175ml/6fl oz/^{3}/$_4$ cup milk

175ml/6fl oz/^{3}/$_4$ cup single (light) cream

toasted flaked (sliced) almonds and ground cinnamon, to decorate

FROM THE STORECUPBOARD

450g/1lb/2^1/$_4$ cups short grain rice

25g/1oz/^{1}/$_4$ cup caster (superfine) sugar

1 cinnamon stick

Energy 443kcal/1847kJ; Protein 8.5g; Carbohydrate 66.6g, of which sugars 6.6g; Fat 15.6g, of which saturates 8.4g; Cholesterol 36mg; Calcium 89mg; Fibre 0.3g; Sodium 72mg

Lemon Surpise Pudding ✳

This much-loved dessert is cheap and easy to make, and is perfect for all the family on a cold day. The surprise is the unexpected, rich, tangy sauce that is concealed beneath the delectable light sponge.

SERVES FOUR

1 Preheat the oven to 190°C/375°F/Gas 5. Use a little butter to grease a 1.2 litre/2 pint/5 cup baking dish.

2 Beat the lemon rind, remaining butter and caster sugar in a bowl until pale and fluffy. Add the egg yolks and flour and beat together well. Gradually whisk in the lemon juice and milk (the mixture will curdle, but this is supposed to happen).

3 Fold the egg whites lightly into the lemon mixture using a metal spoon, then pour into the prepared baking dish.

4 Place the dish in a roasting pan and pour in hot water to come halfway up the side of the dish. Bake for 45 minutes until golden. Serve immediately.

50g/2oz/¹/₄ cup butter, plus extra for greasing

grated rind and juice of 2 lemons

2 eggs, separated

300ml/¹/₂ pint/1¹/₄ cups milk

FROM THE STORECUPBOARD

115g/4oz/¹/₂ cup caster (superfine) sugar

50g/2oz/¹/₂ cup self-raising (self-rising) flour

COOK'S TIP *Lemons are often waxed, so you should either buy unwaxed lemons or scrub the peel thoroughly under hot water to remove the wax before grating.*

Energy 320kcal/1346kJ; Protein 7.1g; Carbohydrate 43.4g, of which sugars 33.8g; Fat 14.5g, of which saturates 8.1g; Cholesterol 126mg; Calcium 139mg; Fibre 0.4g; Sodium 145mg

Hot Chocolate Pudding with Rum Custard *

These delicious chocolate puddings are sure to be a hit. The rum custard turns them into a more adult pudding; for a family dessert, flavour the custard with vanilla or orange rind instead, if you like.

SERVES SIX

1 Lightly grease a 1.2 litre/2 pint/5 cup heatproof bowl or six individual dariole moulds. Cream the butter and sugar until pale and creamy. Gently blend in the eggs and the vanilla essence.

2 Sift together the cocoa powder and flour, and fold gently into the egg mixture with the chopped chocolate and sufficient milk to give a soft dropping consistency.

3 Spoon the mixture into the basin or moulds, cover with buttered greaseproof paper and tie down. Fill a pan with 2.5–5cm/1–2in water, place the puddings in the pan, cover with a lid and bring to the boil. Steam the large pudding for 1^1/2–2 hours and the individual puddings for 45–50 minutes, topping up the pan with water if necessary. When firm, turn out on to warm plates.

4 To make the rum custard, bring the milk and sugar to the boil. Whisk together the egg yolks and cornflour, then pour on the hot milk, whisking constantly. Return the mixture to the pan and stir continuously while it slowly comes back to the boil. Allow the sauce to simmer gently as it thickens, stirring all the time. Remove from the heat and stir in the rum.

115g/4oz/^{1}/2 cup butter, plus extra for greasing

2 eggs, beaten

drops of vanilla essence (extract)

45ml/3 tbsp unsweetened cocoa powder, sifted

75g/3oz bitter (semisweet) chocolate, chopped

a little milk, warmed

FOR THE RUM CUSTARD

250ml/8fl oz/1 cup milk

2 egg yolks

30–45ml/2–3 tbsp rum

FROM THE STORECUPBOARD

115g/4oz/^{1}/2 cup soft light brown sugar

115g/4oz/1 cup self-raising (self-rising) flour

15ml/1 tbsp caster (superfine) sugar

10ml/2 tsp cornflour (cornstarch)

Energy 458Kcal/1915kJ; Protein 8.3g; Carbohydrate 49g, of which sugars 31.5g; Fat 25.6g, of which saturates 14.5g; Cholesterol 186mg; Calcium 145mg; Fibre 1.8g; Sodium 302mg

Bread and Butter Pudding with Whiskey Sauce ✳

This traditional dessert is a great way of using up stale white bread. The whiskey sauce is heavenly, but the pudding can also be served with chilled cream or vanilla ice cream, if you prefer.

SERVES SIX

8 slices of white bread, buttered

115–150g/4–5oz/²/₃–³/₄ cup sultanas (golden raisins), or mixed dried fruit

2 large (US extra large) eggs

300ml/¹/₂ pint/1¹/₄ cups single (light) cream

450ml/3/4 pint/scant 2 cups milk

5ml/1 tsp of vanilla essence (extract)

FOR THE WHISKEY SAUCE

150g/5oz/10 tbsp butter

1 egg

45ml/3 tbsp Irish whiskey

FROM THE STORECUPBOARD

2.5ml/¹/₂ tsp grated nutmeg

260g/9¹/₂oz/1¹/₄ cups caster (superfine) sugar

light muscovado (brown) sugar, for sprinkling (optional)

1 Preheat the oven to 180°C/350°F/Gas 4. Remove the crusts from the bread and put four slices, buttered side down, in the base of an ovenproof dish. Sprinkle with the sultanas or mixed dried fruit, some of the nutmeg and 15ml/1 tbsp sugar.

2 Place the remaining four slices of bread on top, buttered side down, and sprinkle again with nutmeg and 15ml/1 tbsp sugar.

3 Beat the eggs, add the cream, milk, vanilla essence and 115g/4oz/generous ¹/₂ cup caster sugar, and mix well to make a custard. Pour over the bread, and sprinkle light muscovado sugar over the top, if you like to have a crispy crust. Bake for 1 hour, or until the pudding has risen and is brown.

4 Meanwhile, make the whiskey sauce: melt the butter in a heavy pan, add the remaining caster sugar and dissolve over a gentle heat. Remove from the heat and add the egg, whisking vigorously, and then add the whiskey. Serve the pudding on hot serving plates, with the whiskey sauce poured over the top.

Energy 757Kcal/3168kJ; Protein 11.7g; Carbohydrate 82g, of which sugars 65.2g; Fat 40.8g, of which saturates 24.3g; Cholesterol 207mg; Calcium 232mg; Fibre 0.9g; Sodium 472mg

Baked Bananas with Toffee Sauce ✳

Bananas make one of the cheapest and easiest of all hot desserts, and they are just as welcome as a comforting winter treat as they are to follow a barbecue. For an extra sweet finishing touch, grate some plain (semisweet) chocolate on the bananas, over the sauce, just before serving. If you are baking them on a barbecue, turn the bananas occasionally to ensure even cooking.

SERVES FOUR

4 large bananas

75ml/5 tbsp double (heavy) cream

4 scoops good-quality vanilla ice cream

FROM THE STORECUPBOARD

75g/3oz/scant ¹/₂ cup light muscovado (brown) sugar

1 Preheat the oven to 180°C/350°F/Gas 4. Put the unpeeled bananas in an ovenproof dish and bake for 15–20 minutes, until the skins are very dark and the flesh feels soft when squeezed.

2 Meanwhile, heat the light muscovado sugar in a small, heavy pan with 75ml/5 tbsp water until dissolved. Bring to the boil and add the double cream. Cook for 5 minutes, until the sauce has thickened and is toffee coloured. Remove from the heat.

3 Transfer the baked bananas in their skins to serving plates and split them lengthways to reveal the flesh. Pour some of the sauce over the bananas and top with scoops of vanilla ice cream. Serve any remaining sauce separately.

Energy 368kcal/1546kJ; Protein 3.8g; Carbohydrate 55g, of which sugars 52g; Fat 15.5g, of which saturates 10g; Cholesterol 40mg; Calcium 85mg; Fibre 1.1g; Sodium 42mg

Treacle Tart ✳

It is worth taking the time to make your own pastry for this old-fashioned favourite, with its sticky filling and twisted lattice topping. Smooth creamy custard is the classic accompaniment, but it is also delicious served with cream or vanilla ice cream. For a more textured filling, use wholemeal (whole-wheat) breadcrumbs or crushed cornflakes instead of the white breadcrumbs.

SERVES FOUR TO SIX

1 On a lightly floured surface, roll out three-quarters of the pastry to a thickness of 3mm/^{1}/8in. Transfer to a 20cm/8in fluted flan tin (pan) and trim off the overhang. Chill the pastry case (pie shell) for 20 minutes. Reserve the trimmings.

2 Put a baking sheet in the oven and preheat to 200°C/400°F/Gas 6. To make the filling, warm the syrup in a pan until it melts. Grate the lemon rind and squeeze the juice.

3 Remove the syrup from the heat and stir in the breadcrumbs and lemon rind. Leave to stand for 10 minutes, then add more crumbs if the mixture is too thin and moist. Stir in 30ml/2 tbsp of the lemon juice, then spread the mixture evenly in the pastry case.

4 Roll out the reserved pastry and cut into 10–12 thin strips. Twist the strips into spirals, then lay half of them on the filling. Arrange the remaining strips at right angles to form a lattice. Press the ends on to the rim.

5 Place the tart on the hot baking sheet and bake for 10 minutes. Lower the oven temperature to 190°C/375°F/Gas 5. Bake for 15 minutes more, until golden. Serve warm.

350g/12oz (unsweetened) shortcrust pastry (*see* Cook's Tip)

260g/9^1/2oz/generous ^{3}/4 cup golden (light corn) syrup

1 lemon

75g/3oz/1^1/2 cups fresh white breadcrumbs

COOK'S TIP *To make the pastry: place 225g/8oz/2cups plain (all-purpose) flour into a bowl. Rub in 115g/4oz/^{1}/2 cup cold butter, until the mixture resembles breadcrumbs. Sprinkle over 45–60ml/3–4 tbsp water, and gently knead to bind. Wrap and chill for 30 minutes.*

Energy 437kcal/1837kJ; Protein 4.9g; Carbohydrate 71.2g, of which sugars 35.1g; Fat 16.6g, of which saturates 5.1g; Cholesterol 8mg; Calcium 73mg; Fibre 1.4g; Sodium 445mg

Apple Pie ✳

There are many variations on this classic all-time-favourite recipe, and it is a great way of enjoying seasonal apples. For a slightly different twist, you could add ground cinnamon or dried cranberries to the filling, if you like. Bake in a traditional metal pie plate so that the pastry base will be perfectly cooked. Serve warm or cold with chilled whipped cream, or vanilla ice cream.

SERVES SIX

130g/4¹/₂oz/generous ¹/₂ cup butter, or mixed butter and white vegetable fat (shortening)

45ml/3 tbsp very cold milk or water

FOR THE FILLING

675g/1¹/₂lb cooking apples

75g/3oz/¹/₂ cup sultanas (golden raisins) (optional)

a little grated lemon rind (optional)

a knob (pat) of butter or 15ml/1 tbsp of water

a little milk, to glaze

icing (confectioners') sugar and whipped cream, to serve

FROM THE STORECUPBOARD

225g/8oz/2 cups plain (all-purpose) flour

100g/4oz/8 tbsp caster (superfine) sugar

1 Sift the flour into a large mixing bowl, add the butter and cut it into small pieces.

2 Rub the butter, or butter and fat, into the flour with the fingertips, or using a pastry (cookie) cutter, lifting the mixture as much as possible to aerate, which will make the pastry lighter.

3 Mix 25g/1oz/2 tbsp caster sugar with the chilled milk or water, add to the bowl and mix with a knife or fork until the mixture clings together.

4 Turn the pastry on to a floured worktop and knead lightly once or twice until smooth.

5 Wrap in baking parchment or foil and leave in the refrigerator to relax for 20 minutes before using. Meanwhile, preheat the oven to 200°C/400°F/Gas 6.

6 Roll out one-third of the pastry and use to line a 23cm/9in pie plate. Use any trimmings to make a rim of pastry around the top edge of the pie plate.

7 To make the filling, peel, core and slice the apples and arrange half of them on the pastry base, then sprinkle over the sultanas and lemon rind, if using. Top with the caster sugar, the remaining apples and butter or water.

8 Roll out the remainder of the pastry to make a circle about 2.5cm/1in larger than the pie plate.

9 Dampen the pastry edging on the rim and lay the top over the apples, draping it gently over any lumps to avoid straining the pastry. Press the rim well to seal. Pinch the edges with your fingers to make a fluted edge.

10 Brush the pastry lightly with milk and bake the pie in the preheated oven for about 30 minutes, or until the pastry has browned and is crisp, and the fruit is cooked.

11 To serve, dust the pastry with icing sugar and serve hot, warm or cold, but not straight from the refrigerator. The pie is delicious with vanilla ice cream or whipped cream.

Energy 393Kcal/1650kJ; Protein 4.1g; Carbohydrate 56.3g, of which sugars 27.7g; Fat 18.4g, of which saturates 11.4g; Cholesterol 46mg; Calcium 68mg; Fibre 2.5g; Sodium 136mg

Autumn Crumble ✳

Autumn heralds the harvest of apples and succulent soft fruits, and it is the perfect season to go foraging among the hedgerows. The pinhead oatmeal in the topping makes this traditional hot dessert especially crunchy and flavoursome. Serve hot with crème fraîche or ice cream.

SERVES EIGHT

1 Preheat the oven to 200°C/400°F/Gas 6. To make the crumble topping, rub the butter into the flour, and then add the oatmeal and brown sugar and continue to rub in until the mixture begins to stick together, forming large crumbs. Mix in the grated lemon rind, if using.

2 Peel and core the cooking apples, then slice into wedges. Put the apples, blackberries, lemon juice (if using), 30ml/2 tbsp water and the sugar into a shallow ovenproof dish, about 2 litres/3½ pints/9 cups capacity.

3 Cover the fruit with the crumble topping and sprinkle with a little cold water. Bake for 15 minutes, then reduce the heat to 190°C/375°F/Gas 5 and cook for another 15–20 minutes until crunchy and brown on top.

4 Serve hot with custard, crème fraîche or vanilla ice cream.

900g/2lb cooking apples

450g/1lb/4 cups blackberries

juice of ½ lemon (optional)

FOR THE TOPPING

115g/4oz/½ cup butter

50g/2oz/½ cup fine or medium pinhead oatmeal

grated lemon rind (optional)

FROM THE STORECUPBOARD

115g/4oz/1 cup wholemeal (whole-wheat) flour

50g/2oz/½ cup soft light brown sugar

175g/6oz/scant 1 cup sugar

VARIATION *You can use almost any combination of fruit in a crumble, including rhubarb, blackcurrants and gooseberries.*

Energy 470Kcal/1974kJ; Protein 5.1g; Carbohydrate 78.2g, of which sugars 60.3g; Fat 17.2g, of which saturates 10g; Cholesterol 41mg; Calcium 71mg; Fibre 7g; Sodium 128mg

Autumn Pudding ✳

Although summer pudding is made more often, this pudding is equally easy to make, using autumnal fruit instead of the soft fruits of summer. This juicy dessert is very simple to make, but it looks superb. Serve with lightly whipped chilled cream, or crème fraîche.

SERVES EIGHT

1 loaf white bread, 2 or 3 days old

675g/1¹/₂lb/6 cups mixed soft fruit, such as blackberries, autumn raspberries, late strawberries, and peeled and chopped eating apples

FROM THE STORECUPBOARD

115g/4oz/generous ¹/₂ cup caster (superfine) sugar

1 Remove the crusts from the loaf and slice the bread thinly. Use several slices to line the base and sides of a 900ml–1.2 litres/1¹/₂–2 pints/3³/₄–5 cup pudding bowl or soufflé dish, cutting them so that the pieces fit closely together.

2 Put all the fruit into a wide, heavy pan, sprinkle the sugar over and bring very gently to the boil. Cook for 2–3 minutes, or until the sugar has dissolved and the juices run.

3 Remove the pan from the heat and set aside 30–45ml/2–3 tbsp of the juices. Spoon the fruit and the remaining juices into the prepared bread-lined dish and cover the top closely with the remaining slices of bread. Put a plate that fits neatly inside the top of the dish on top of the pudding and weigh it down with a heavy can or jar. Leave in the refrigerator for at least 8 hours, or overnight.

4 Before serving the dish, remove the weight and plate, cover the bowl with a serving plate and turn upside down to unmould the pudding.

5 Use the reserved fruit juice to pour over any patches of the bread that have not been completely soaked and coloured by the fruit juices. Serve cold, cut into wedges with lightly whipped chilled cream or crème fraîche.

Energy 261Kcal/1112kJ; Protein 7.7g; Carbohydrate 57.5g, of which sugars 27.1g; Fat 1.7g, of which saturates 0.4g; Cholesterol 0mg; Calcium 153mg; Fibre 4.2g; Sodium 398mg

Meringue Layer Cake with Raspberries

This delicious dessert is made with a basic meringue mixture, and is the perfect way to enjoy raspberries, or any other soft fruit, depending on availability and personal preference.

SERVES TEN

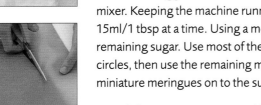

1 Preheat the oven to 150°C/300°F/Gas 2. Line two baking sheets with non-stick baking parchment and draw two circles: one 23cm/9in in diameter and the other 20cm/8in. Fit a piping (icing) bag with a 1cm/^{1}/$_2$in star nozzle.

2 Whisk the egg whites until stiff peaks form, using an electric mixer. Keeping the machine running, add half of the sugar, 15ml/1 tbsp at a time. Using a metal spoon, carefully fold in the remaining sugar. Use most of the mixture to pipe inside the circles, then use the remaining meringue mixture to pipe nine miniature meringues on to the surrounding baking parchment.

3 Cook for 50–60 minutes, until lightly coloured and dry (the small ones will take less time). Peel off the parchment, cool on wire racks and, when cold, store in airtight containers.

4 Whip the cream until soft peaks form, sweeten with sugar and flavour with a few drops of vanilla essence or liqueur.

5 Lay the larger meringue on a serving dish. Spread with three-quarters of the cream and raspberries. Add the smaller meringue, spread with the remaining cream, and arrange the small meringues around the edge. Decorate the top with the remaining fruit and dust lightly with icing sugar.

4 egg whites

FOR THE FILLING

300ml/^{1}/$_2$ pint/1^1/$_4$ cups whipping cream

3–4 drops of good quality vanilla essence (extract) or 2.5ml/^{1}/$_2$ tsp liqueur, such as Kirsch or Crème de Framboise

about 450g/1lb/2^3/$_4$ cups raspberries

FROM THE STORECUPBOARD

225g/8oz/generous 1 cup caster (superfine) sugar, plus extra, to taste

icing (confectioners') sugar, for dusting

COOK'S TIPS

• Don't leave cooked meringues exposed to the air, as they will absorb moisture from the air, soften and "weep".

• Don't assemble the dessert too far ahead of serving, as the meringue will become soggy.

• If stored carefully in an airtight container, the meringues will keep well for several days.

• Making meringues is a great way of using up eggs that are not absolutely fresh.

Energy 298Kcal/1252kJ; Protein 3.2g; Carbohydrate 39.5g, of which sugars 39.5g; Fat 15.3g, of which saturates 9.5g; Cholesterol 39mg; Calcium 55mg; Fibre 1.4g; Sodium 44mg

1 x 15–18cm/6–7in sponge cake (*see* p227)

225g/8oz raspberry jam

150ml/¹⁄₄ pint/²⁄₃ cup whiskey

450g/1lb ripe fruit, such as pears and bananas

300ml/¹⁄₂ pint/1¹⁄₄ cups whipping cream

blanched almonds, glacé (candied) cherries and angelica, to decorate (optional)

FOR THE CUSTARD

450ml/³⁄₄ pint/scant 2 cups full-fat (whole) milk

1 vanilla pod (bean) or a few drops of vanilla essence (extract)

3 eggs

FROM THE STORECUPBOARD

25g/1oz/2 tbsp caster (superfine) sugar

Irish Whiskey Trifle ✳✳

This rich trifle is made with real sponge cake, fresh fruit and rich egg custard, but with Irish whiskey rather than the usual sherry flavouring. For family occasions you could use good-quality tinned fruit.

SERVES EIGHT

1 To make the custard, put the milk into a pan with the vanilla pod, if using, and bring almost to the boil. Remove from the heat. Whisk the eggs and sugar together lightly. Remove the vanilla pod from the milk. Gradually whisk the milk into the egg mixture.

2 Rinse out the pan, return the mixture to it and stir over low heat until it thickens; do not allow it to boil. Turn into a bowl and add the vanilla essence, if using. Cover with clear film (plastic wrap).

3 Halve the sponge cake horizontally, spread with the raspberry jam and make a sandwich. Cut into slices and use them to line the bottom and lower sides of a large serving bowl. Sprinkle with whiskey.

4 Peel and slice the fruit, then spread it out over the sponge. Pour the custard on top, cover with clear film to prevent a skin forming, and leave to cool. Chill until required. Before serving, whip the cream and spread it over the set custard. Decorate with the almonds, glacé cherries and angelica, if you like.

Energy 710Kcal/2959kJ; Protein 12.1g; Carbohydrate 58g, of which sugars 42.6g; Fat 43.2g, of which saturates 14.4g; Cholesterol 171mg; Calcium 194mg; Fibre 2.3g; Sodium 336mg

Blackcurrant Fool ✳✳

The strong flavour and deep colour of this easily grown fruit makes it especially suitable for fools and ices, although this is an adaptable recipe which can be made using other soft fruits too. The fool can also be used to make an easy no-stir ice cream, if you prefer.

SERVES SIX

1 Put the blackcurrants into a small pan with 45ml/3 tbsp water, and cook over a low heat until soft. Remove from the heat, add the sugar according to taste, and stir until dissolved.

2 Leave to cool, then liquidize (blend) or sieve (strain) to make a purée. Set aside and cool. Add the lemon juice and stir well.

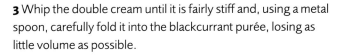

3 Whip the double cream until it is fairly stiff and, using a metal spoon, carefully fold it into the blackcurrant purée, losing as little volume as possible.

4 Turn the mixture into a single large serving dish or six individual serving glasses and leave to set. Chill in the refrigerator until ready to serve.

350g/12oz/3 cups blackcurrants

5ml/1 tsp lemon juice

300ml/¹/₂ pint/1¹/₄ cups double (heavy) cream

FROM THE STORECUPBOARD

about 175g/6oz/scant 1 cup caster (superfine) sugar

VARIATION To make blackcurrant ice cream, turn the completed fool into a freezerproof container. Cover and freeze (preferably at the lowest setting). Transfer from the freezer to the refrigerator 10–15 minutes before serving to allow the ice cream to soften. Serve with whipped cream and cookies, if you like.

COOK'S TIP Fools are a very good way of using up a glut of seasonal fruit, especially if it has gone past its best and is a bit soft, since it is pulped up and combined with cream. Other fruits that work well include strawberries, raspberries, mangoes, gooseberries, peaches and rhubarb.

Energy 379Kcal/1581kJ; Protein 1.5g; Carbohydrate 35.2g, of which sugars 35.2g; Fat 26.9g, of which saturates 16.7g; Cholesterol 69mg; Calcium 75mg; Fibre 2.1g; Sodium 15mg

Lemon Sorbet ✳

This is probably the most classic sorbet of all. Refreshingly tangy and yet deliciously smooth, it quite literally melts in the mouth. Try to buy unwaxed lemons for recipes such as this one where the lemon rind is used. The wax coating can adversely affect the flavour of the rind.

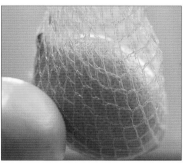

SERVES SIX

1 Put the sugar in a pan and pour in 300ml/$\frac{1}{2}$ pint/1$\frac{1}{4}$ cups water. Bring to the boil, stirring occasionally until the sugar has just dissolved.

2 Using a swivel vegetable peeler, pare the rind thinly from two of the lemons and put in a pan. Simmer for 2 minutes, then take the pan off the heat. Leave to cool, then chill.

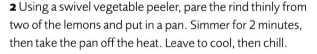

3 Squeeze the juice from all the lemons and add it to the syrup. Strain the syrup into a shallow freezerproof container, reserving the rind. Freeze for 4 hours, until it is mushy.

4 Process the sorbet in a food processor until it is smooth. Lightly whisk the egg white with a fork until it is just frothy. Replace the sorbet in the container, beat in the egg white and return to the freezer for 4 hours, or until it is firm.

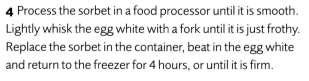
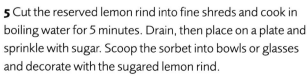

5 Cut the reserved lemon rind into fine shreds and cook in boiling water for 5 minutes. Drain, then place on a plate and sprinkle with sugar. Scoop the sorbet into bowls or glasses and decorate with the sugared lemon rind.

4 lemons, well scrubbed

1 egg white

FROM THE STORECUPBOARD

200g/7oz/1 cup caster (superfine) sugar, plus extra for coating rind to decorate

COOK'S TIP *Sorbets are especially delicious during the summer months, as they are refreshing and tangy without being too sweet. Lemon sorbet is great for cleansing the palate, and makes the ideal dessert after a spicy main meal. It is also extremely cheap and reasonably easy to make.*

Energy 134kcal/570kJ; Protein 0.7g; Carbohydrate 34.9g, of which sugars 34.9g; Fat 0g, of which saturates 0g; Cholesterol 0mg; Calcium 18mg; Fibre 0g; Sodium 12mg

Oranges in Syrup ✳

This recipe works well with most citrus fruits – for example, try pink grapefruit or sweet, perfumed clementines, which have been peeled but left whole. Serve the oranges with 300ml/½ pint/1¼ cups whipped cream flavoured with 5ml/1 tsp ground cinnamon, or 5ml/1 tsp ground nutmeg or with Greek (US strained plain) yogurt for an elegant summer dessert.

SERVES SIX

6 medium oranges

100ml/3½fl oz/ scant ½ cup fresh strong brewed coffee

50g/2oz/½ cup pistachio nuts, chopped (optional)

FROM THE STORECUPBOARD

200g/7oz/1 cup sugar

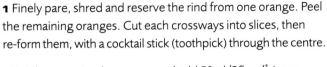
1 Finely pare, shred and reserve the rind from one orange. Peel the remaining oranges. Cut each crossways into slices, then re-form them, with a cocktail stick (toothpick) through the centre.

2 Put the sugar in a heavy pan and add 50ml/2fl oz/¼ cup water. Heat gently until the sugar dissolves, then bring to the boil and cook until the syrup turns pale gold.

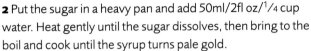
3 Remove from the heat and carefully pour 100ml/3½fl oz/ scant ½ cup freshly boiling water into the pan. Return to the heat until the syrup has dissolved in the water. Stir in the coffee.

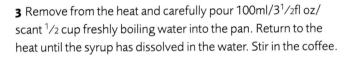
4 Add the oranges and the rind to the coffee syrup. Simmer for 15–20 minutes, turning the oranges once during cooking. Leave to cool, then chill. Serve sprinkled with pistachio nuts, if using.

Fresh Fig Compote ✳✳✳

A vanilla and coffee syrup brings out the wonderful flavour of figs. Serve Greek (US strained plain) yogurt or vanilla ice cream with the poached fruit. A good selection of different honeys is available – the aroma and flavour will be subtly scented by the plants surrounding the hives. Orange blossom honey works particularly well in this recipe, although any clear variety is suitable.

SERVES SIX

400ml/14fl oz/ 1²/₃ cups fresh brewed coffee

115g/4oz/½ cup clear honey

1 vanilla pod (bean)

12 slightly under-ripe fresh figs

1 Choose a frying pan with a lid, large enough to hold the figs in a single layer. Pour in the coffee and add the honey.

2 Split the vanilla pod lengthways and scrape the seeds into the pan. Add the vanilla pod, then bring to a rapid boil and cook until reduced to about 175ml/6fl oz/³/₄ cup.

3 Wash the figs and pierce the skins several times with a sharp skewer. Cut in half and add to the syrup. Reduce the heat, cover and simmer for 5 minutes. Remove the figs from the syrup with a slotted spoon and set aside to cool.

4 Strain the syrup over the figs. Allow to stand at room temperature for 1 hour before serving.

COOK'S TIP *Figs come in three main varieties – red, white and black – and all three are suitable for cooking. They are sweet and succulent, and complement the stronger, more pervasive flavours of coffee and vanilla very well.*

Top: Energy 191kcal/815kJ; Protein 2g; Carbohydrate 48.5g, of which sugars 48.5g; Fat 0.2g, of which saturates 0g; Cholesterol 0mg; Calcium 93mg; Fibre 2.7g; Sodium 10mg

Above: Energy 147kcal/628kJ; Protein 1.7g; Carbohydrate 36g, of which sugars 35.8g; Fat 0.6g, of which saturates 0g; Cholesterol 0mg; Calcium 103mg; Fibre 3g; Sodium 27mg

Quick and Easy Teabread ✳

This succulent, fruity teabread can be served just as it is, or spread with a little butter. The loaf can be stored, tightly wrapped in foil or in an airtight container, for up to five days. A great way to get children to eat some fruit, this teabread is ideal for packed lunches or picnics.

SERVES EIGHT

1 Put the fruit in a bowl. Add 150ml/^{1}/$_4$ pint/^{2}/$_3$ cup boiling water and leave to stand for 30 minutes.

2 Preheat the oven to 180°C/350°F/Gas 4. Grease and line the base and long sides of a 450g/1lb loaf tin (pan).

3 Beat the main quantity of sugar and the egg into the fruit. Sift the flour into the bowl and stir until combined. Turn into the prepared tin and level the surface. Sprinkle with the remaining sugar.

4 Bake the teabread for about 50 minutes, until risen and firm to the touch. When the bread is cooked, a skewer inserted into the centre will come out clean. Leave in the tin for 10 minutes before turning out on to a wire rack to cool.

350g/12oz/2 cups luxury mixed dried fruit

1 large (US extra large) egg

FROM THE STORECUPBOARD

75g/3oz/scant ^{1}/$_3$ cup demerara (raw) sugar, plus 15ml/1 tbsp

175g/6oz/1^1/$_3$ cups self-raising (self-rising) flour

Energy 236kcal/1004kJ; Protein 3.8g; Carbohydrate 56.1g, of which sugars 39.9g; Fat 1.1g, of which saturates 0.2g; Cholesterol 24mg; Calcium 117mg; Fibre 1.6g; Sodium 109mg

175g/6oz/³/₄ cup soft butter

3 eggs beaten

60ml/4 tbsp raspberry or strawberry jam (jelly)

150ml/¹/₄ pint/²/₃ cup whipped cream or crème fraîche

FROM THE STORECUPBOARD

175g/6oz/³/₄ cup caster (superfine) sugar

175g/6oz/1¹/₂ cups self-raising (self-rising) flour, sifted

15–30ml/1–2 tbsp icing (confectioners') sugar, for dusting

Victoria Sandwich Cake ✳

Serve this richly flavoured sponge cake sandwiched together with your favourite jam or preserve. For special occasions, fill the cake with prepared fresh fruit, such as raspberries, strawberries or sliced peaches, as well as jam and whipped cream or chilled crème fraîche.

MAKES ONE 18CM/7IN CAKE

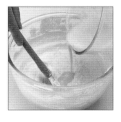

1 Preheat the oven to 180°C/350°F/Gas 4. Lightly grease and line the bottom of two 18cm/7in shallow round cake tins (pans) with baking (parchment) paper.

2 Place the butter and caster sugar in a bowl and cream together until pale and fluffy. This can be done by hand using a mixing spoon or with a hand-held electric mixer, if you have one, which is far quicker and easier.

3 Add the eggs, a little at a time, beating well after each addition. Fold in half the flour, using a metal spoon, then gently fold in the rest and mix to combine.

4 Divide the cake mixture between the two prepared cake tins and level the surfaces with the back of a spoon.

5 Bake for 25–30 minutes, until the cakes have risen, feel just firm to the touch and are golden brown. Turn out and cool on a wire rack.

6 When the cakes are cool, sandwich them with the jam and whipped cream or crème fraîche. Dust the top of the cake with sifted icing sugar and serve cut into slices. Store the cake in the refrigerator in an airtight container or wrapped in foil.

Energy 3577kcal/14948kJ; Protein 39.7g; Carbohydrate 377.4g, of which sugars 247.3g; Fat 223.1g, of which saturates 134g; Cholesterol 1101mg; Calcium 924mg; Fibre 5.4g; Sodium 1967mg

Carrot Cake ✳

Universally loved, this is one of the most irresistible cakes there is. Everyone has their own version; here poppyseeds add colour and crunch, and pineapple gives it extra moistness, while orange provides a tangy touch.

MAKES ONE LARGE LOAF

1 Preheat the oven to 180°C/350°F/Gas 4. Line the base of a 1.5 litre/2¹/₂ pint/6¹/₄ cup loaf tin (pan) with baking parchment. Grease the sides of the pan and dust with flour.

2 Sift together the flour, baking powder, bicarbonate of soda, salt and cinnamon into a bowl. Stir in the poppyseeds.

3 Mix together the brown sugar, eggs and orange rind in a separate bowl. Lightly squeeze the excess moisture from the grated carrots and stir the carrots into the egg mixture with the pineapple and walnut pieces. Gradually stir the sifted flour mixture into the egg mixture until well combined, then gently fold in the butter.

4 Spoon the mixture into the prepared pan, level the top and bake for about 1–1¹/₄ hours until risen and golden brown. (To check if the cake really is cooked in the centre, push a thin metal skewer right down into the middle of the cake. Pull it out immediately and feel if there is any sticky mixture clinging to the skewer. If it comes out clean the cake is done, if not, put it back for a further 10 minutes and test again.)

5 Remove the cake from the loaf tin and allow to cool on a wire rack. Remove the baking parchment when completely cold.

6 To make the icing, beat the mascarpone with the icing sugar and orange rind. Cover and chill until needed. When ready to serve, beat well, then spread thickly over the top of the cake. Cut into slices and eat.

45ml/3 tbsp poppyseeds

3 eggs, beaten

finely grated rind of
1 orange

225g/8oz raw carrots,
grated 75g/3oz/¹/₂ cup
fresh or canned pineapple,
drained and finely chopped

75g/3oz/³/₄ cup
walnut pieces

115g/4oz/¹/₂ cup butter,
melted and cooled

FOR THE ICING

150g/5oz/scant 1 cup
mascarpone

finely grated rind of
1 orange

FROM THE STORECUPBOARD

250g/9oz/2¹/₄ cups plain
(all-purpose) flour

10ml/2 tsp baking powder

5ml/1 tsp bicarbonate of
soda (baking soda)

2.5ml/¹/₂ tsp salt

5ml/1 tsp ground
cinnamon

225g/8oz/1¹/₃ cups soft
light brown sugar

30ml/2 tbsp icing
(confectioners')
sugar, sifted

Energy 3971kcal/16641kJ; Protein 76.3g; Carbohydrate 491.9g, of which sugars 294.7g; Fat 202.5g, of which saturates 84.5g; Cholesterol 879mg; Calcium 751mg; Fibre 17.6g; Sodium 992mg

Apple and Cinnamon Muffins

These fruity, spicy muffins are quick and easy to make and are perfect for serving for breakfast or tea, or for adding to a lunchbox for a tasty snack. The appetizing aroma as they bake is out of this world.

MAKES SIX

1 Preheat the oven to 200°C/400°F/Gas 6. Line a large muffin tin (pan) with six paper cases.

2 Put the egg, sugar, milk and melted butter in a large bowl, and beat with a spoon until thoroughly combined.

3 Sift in the flour, baking powder, salt and 2.5ml/$^{1}/_{4}$ tsp ground cinnamon. Add the chopped apple and mix roughly. Spoon the mixture into the prepared muffin cases.

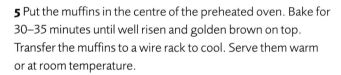

4 To make the topping, mix the crushed sugar cubes with the remaining cinnamon. Sprinkle over the uncooked muffins.

5 Put the muffins in the centre of the preheated oven. Bake for 30–35 minutes until well risen and golden brown on top. Transfer the muffins to a wire rack to cool. Serve them warm or at room temperature.

---

1 egg, beaten

120ml/4fl oz/$^{1}/_{2}$ cup milk

50g/2oz/$^{1}/_{4}$ cup butter, melted

2 small eating apples, peeled, cored and finely chopped

FOR THE TOPPING

12 brown sugar cubes, coarsely crushed

FROM THE STORECUPBOARD

40g/1$^{1}/_{2}$oz/3 tbsp caster (superfine) sugar

150g/5oz/1$^{1}/_{4}$ cups plain (all-purpose) flour

7.5ml/1$^{1}/_{2}$ tsp baking powder

pinch of salt

7.5ml/1$^{1}/_{4}$ tsp ground cinnamon

Energy 236kcal/995kJ; Protein 4.3g; Carbohydrate 38.2g, of which sugars 19.1g; Fat 8.5g, of which saturates 4.9g; Cholesterol 51mg; Calcium 74mg; Fibre 1.2g; Sodium 73mg

Chocolate Chip Brownies ✳

These chunky chocolate brownies are moist, dark and deeply satisfying. They are delicious with a morning cup of coffee or as a dessert.

SERVES SIX

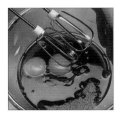

1 Preheat the oven to 180°C/350°F/Gas 4. Lightly grease a shallow 19cm/7¹/₂in square cake tin (pan). Melt the plain chocolate in a heatproof bowl over a pan of simmering water.

2 Beat together the oil, sugar, eggs and vanilla essence. Stir in the melted chocolate, then beat well until evenly mixed.

3 Sift the flour and cocoa powder into the bowl and fold in thoroughly. Stir in the chopped nuts and milk chocolate chips, then tip the mixture into the prepared tin and spread evenly to the edges.

4 Bake for about 30–35 minutes, until the top is firm and crusty. Cool in the tin before cutting into squares.

150g/5oz plain (semisweet) chocolate, chopped

2 eggs

5ml/1 tsp vanilla essence (extract)

60ml/4 tbsp (unsweetened) cocoa powder

75g/3oz/³/₄ cup chopped walnuts

60ml/4 tbsp milk chocolate chips

FROM THE STORECUPBOARD

120ml/4fl oz/¹/₂ cup sunflower oil

215g/7¹/₂ oz/scant 1 cup light muscovado (brown) sugar

65g/2¹/₂ oz/scant ²/₃ cup self-raising (self-rising) flour

COOK'S TIP
These brownies freeze well and can be stored in the freezer for up to 3 months in an airtight container or wrapped thoroughly in foil.

VARIATIONS
• To make white chocolate brownies, substitute white chocolate for the milk chocolate, and substitute additional flour for the (unsweetened) cocoa powder.

• You could also use dark (bittersweet) chocolate in place of the milk chocolate, if you prefer.

• Try replacing the walnuts with chopped pecan nuts.

Energy 611kcal/2559kJ; Protein 8.7g; Carbohydrate 69.7g, of which sugars 59.9g; Fat 35g, of which saturates 9.9g; Cholesterol 66mg; Calcium 80mg; Fibre 2.9g; Sodium 124mg

115g/4oz/$^{1}/_{2}$ cup butter, plus extra for greasing

2 eggs, lightly beaten

45–60ml/3–4 tbsp milk

5ml/1 tsp vanilla essence (extract)

115g/4oz/generous 1 cup rolled oats

175g/6oz plain (semisweet) chocolate chips

115g/4oz/1 cup pecan nuts, chopped

FROM THE STORECUPBOARD

115g/4oz/$^{1}/_{2}$ cup soft dark brown sugar

150g/5oz/1$^{1}/_{4}$ cups plain (all-purpose) flour

5ml/1 tsp baking powder

pinch of salt

Oat Chocolate Chip Cookies ✳

These crunchy cookies are easy enough for children to make and are sure to disappear as soon as they are baked. They make an ideal quick, easy and cheap dessert when served with ice cream.

MAKES ABOUT TWENTY

1 Cream the butter and sugar in a large bowl until pale and fluffy. Add the beaten eggs, milk and vanilla essence, and beat thoroughly.

2 Sift in the flour, baking powder and salt, and stir in until well mixed. Fold in the rolled oats, chocolate chips and chopped pecan nuts.

3 Chill the mixture in the refrigerator for at least 1 hour. Preheat the oven to 180°C/350°F/Gas 4. Grease two large baking trays.

4 Using two teaspoons, place mounds of the mixture well apart on the trays and flatten with a spoon or fork.

5 Bake the cookies for 10–12 minutes in the preheated oven until the edges are just colouring, then cool on wire racks.

Energy 207kcal/864kJ; Protein 3.2g; Carbohydrate 22.1g, of which sugars 12g; Fat 12.4g, of which saturates 5g; Cholesterol 32mg; Calcium 30mg; Fibre 1.1g; Sodium 46mg

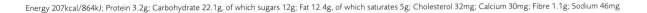

115g/4oz/¹/₂ cup unsalted (sweet) butter

90g/3¹/₂oz/generous ¹/₄ cup golden (light corn) syrup

1 large (US extra large) egg, beaten

150g/5oz preserved stem ginger in syrup, drained and coarsely chopped

FROM THE STORECUPBOARD

350g/12oz/3 cups self-raising (self-rising) flour

pinch of salt

200g/7oz/1 cup golden caster (superfine) sugar

15ml/1 tbsp ground ginger

5ml/1 tsp bicarbonate of soda (baking soda)

Ginger Cookies ✳

These are a supreme treat for ginger lovers – richly spiced cookies packed with chunks of succulent preserved stem ginger. They are sure to give a boost when your energy starts to flag.

MAKES THIRTY SMALL OR TWENTY LARGE COOKIES

1 Preheat the oven to 160°C/325°F/Gas 3. Line three baking sheets with baking parchment or lightly greased greaseproof (waxed) paper.

2 Sift the flour into a large mixing bowl, add the salt, caster sugar, ground ginger and bicarbonate of soda and stir to combine.

3 Dice the butter and put it in a small, heavy pan with the syrup. Heat gently, stirring, until the butter has melted. Remove from the heat and set aside to cool until just warm.

4 Pour the butter mixture over the dry ingredients, then add the egg and two-thirds of the ginger. Mix thoroughly, then use your hands to bring the dough together.

5 Shape the dough into 20 large or 30 small balls, depending on the size you require. Place them, spaced well apart, on the baking sheets and gently flatten the balls.

6 Press a few pieces of the remaining preserved stem ginger into the top of each of the cookies. Bake for about 12–15 minutes, depending on the size of your cookies, until light golden in colour.

7 Remove from the oven and leave to cool for 1 minute on the baking sheets to firm up. Using a metal spatula, transfer the cookies to a wire rack to cool completely.

Energy 108kcal/454kJ; Protein 1.4g; Carbohydrate 18.9g, of which sugars 10g; Fat 3.5g, of which saturates 2.1g; Cholesterol 15mg; Calcium 24mg; Fibre 0.4g; Sodium 38mg

Shortbread Rounds ✳

There should always be a supply of shortbread in the cookie jar – it is so moreish. It should melt in the mouth and taste buttery but never greasy.

MAKES ABOUT TWENTY FOUR

1 Place the butter and sugar in a bowl and cream together until light, pale and fluffy. Sift together the flour, ground rice, or rice flour, and salt, and stir into the butter and sugar with a wooden spoon, until the mixture resembles fine breadcrumbs.

2 Working quickly, gather the dough together with your hand, then put it on a clean work surface. Knead lightly until it forms a ball. Lightly roll into a sausage shape, about 7.5cm/3in thick. Wrap in clear film (plastic wrap) and chill until firm.

3 Preheat the oven to 190°C/375°F/Gas 5. Grease two large baking sheets and line with baking parchment.

4 Pour the demerara sugar on to a sheet of baking parchment. Unwrap the dough and roll it in the sugar until evenly coated. Using a large knife, slice the roll into discs about 1cm/¹⁄₂in thick. Place the discs on to the prepared baking sheets, spacing them well apart. Bake for 20–25 minutes until very pale gold in colour.

5 Remove from the oven and sprinkle with golden caster sugar. Leave to cool on the baking sheet for 10 minutes before transferring to a wire rack to cool completely.

450g/1lb/2 cups butter

225g/8oz/scant 1¹⁄₂ cups ground rice or rice flour

FROM THE STORECUPBOARD

225g/8oz/generous 1 cup caster (superfine) sugar

450g/1lb/4 cups plain (all-purpose) flour

5ml/1 tsp salt

demerara (raw) sugar, to decorate

golden caster (superfine) sugar, for dusting

COOK'S TIP *The rice flour adds a toothsome grittiness and shortness to the dough, which is the quality that distinguishes home-made shortbread from the store-bought variety.*

Energy 275kcal/1147kJ; Protein 2.5g; Carbohydrate 32g, of which sugars 10.2g; Fat 15.7g, of which saturates 9.8g; Cholesterol 40mg; Calcium 37mg; Fibre 0.8g; Sodium 115mg

Scones with Jam and Cream ✳

Scones, often known as biscuits in the US, are thought to originate from Scotland where they are still a popular part of afternoon tea served with jams, jellies and thick cream.

MAKES ABOUT EIGHT

1 Preheat the oven to 230°C/450°F/Gas 8. Sift the flour, baking powder, if using, and salt into a clean, dry mixing bowl. Add the diced butter and rub it into the flour with your fingertips until the mixture resembles fine, evenly textured breadcrumbs.

2 Whisk the lemon juice into the milk and leave for about 1 minute to thicken slightly, then pour into the flour mixture and mix to form a soft but pliable dough. The wetter the mixture, the lighter the resulting scone will be, but if they are too wet they will spread during baking and lose their shape.

3 Knead the dough lightly to form a ball, then roll it out on a floured surface to a thickness of at least 2.5cm/1in. Using a 5cm/2in pastry (cookie) cutter, and dipping it into flour each time, stamp out 12 scones. Place on a floured baking sheet. Re-roll any trimmings and cut out more scones if you can.

4 Brush the tops of the scones lightly with a little milk, then bake in the preheated oven for about 20 minutes, or until they have risen and are golden brown. Remove from the oven and wrap in a clean dish towel to keep them warm and soft until ready to serve. Eat with fruit jam and cream.

50g/2oz/¹/₄ cup butter, chilled and diced

15ml/1 tbsp lemon juice

about 400ml/14fl oz/ 1²/₃ cups milk, plus extra to glaze

fruit jam and clotted cream or whipped double (heavy) cream, to serve

FROM THE STORECUPBOARD

450g/1lb/4 cups self-raising (self-rising) flour, or 450g/1lb/4 cups plain (all-purpose) flour and 10ml/2 tsp baking powder

5ml/1 tsp salt

VARIATION
To make cheese scones, add 115g/4oz/1 cup of grated Cheddar cheese to the dough and knead it in well before rolling out on a lightly floured surface and cutting rounds.

Energy 170kcal/720kJ; Protein 4.5g; Carbohydrate 29.9g, of which sugars 2.1g; Fat 4.4g, of which saturates 2.6g; Cholesterol 11mg; Calcium 172mg; Fibre 1.2g; Sodium 338mg

Scotch Pancakes ✳

Variously known as girdlecakes, griddlecakes and Scotch pancakes, these make a quick and easy breakfast, or teatime snack served with butter and drizzled with honey.

MAKES EIGHT TO TEN

1 Lightly grease a griddle pan or heavy frying pan, then preheat it. Sift the flour, bicarbonate of soda and cream of tartar together into a mixing bowl. Add the diced butter and rub it into the flour with your fingertips until the mixture resembles fine, evenly textured breadcrumbs.

2 Make a well in the centre of the flour mixture, then stir in the egg. Add the milk a little at a time, stirring it in to check consistency. Add enough milk to give a thick consistency.

3 Cook the pancakes in batches. Drop 3 or 4 evenly sized spoonfuls of the mixture, spaced slightly apart, on the griddle or frying pan. Cook over a medium heat for 2–3 minutes, until bubbles rise to the surface and burst.

4 Turn the pancakes over and cook for a further 2–3 minutes, until golden underneath. Place the cooked pancakes between the folds of a clean dish towel while cooking the remaining batter. Serve warm, with butter and honey.

25g/1oz/2 tbsp butter, diced

1 egg, beaten

about 150ml/¹/₄ pint/ ²/₃ cup milk

a knob (pat) of butter and heather honey, to serve

FROM THE STORECUPBOARD

115g/4oz/1 cup plain (all-purpose) flour

5ml/1 tsp bicarbonate of soda (baking soda)

5ml/1 tsp cream of tartar

Energy 90kcal/379kJ; Protein 2.8g; Carbohydrate 12.1g, of which sugars 1.1g; Fat 3.8g, of which saturates 2.1g; Cholesterol 32mg; Calcium 47mg; Fibre 0.5g; Sodium 36mg

Back to Basics

MAKING YOUR OWN STOCKS, GRAVIES, SWEET AND SAVOURY SAUCES AND PRESERVES, BREADS AND PASTRIES WILL NOT ONLY SAVE YOU MONEY, BUT IT WILL ALSO ENABLE YOU TO PRODUCE DELICIOUS ACCOMPANIMENTS THAT ARE EXACTLY TAILORED TO YOUR PERSONAL PREFERENCES. FROM ONION GRAVY, CHOCOLATE FUDGE SAUCE AND MANGO CHUTNEY TO PITTA BREAD AND CHOUX PASTRY, HERE YOU WILL FIND A BASIC RECIPE THAT WILL TAKE YOUR COOKING TO NEW HEIGHTS.

Basic Stocks and Gravies

A well-flavoured stock or gravy can really affect the final taste of a dish. Good-quality ready-made stocks and gravies – either cube, powders or liquid concentrate – are readily available, but stocks are easy and cheap to make. Always ask for the meat bones when buying from a butcher, and trimmings if you have fish prepared by the fishmonger, as these are perfect for making good stock. A chicken carcass from a roast makes excellent stock, particularly if you've packed it with herbs, onions, or other aromatics before roasting.

Beef Stock MAKES ABOUT 1 LITRE/1¾ PINTS/4 CUPS

900g/2lb beef bones

2 unpeeled onions, quartered

1 bouquet garni

2 large carrots, roughly chopped

COOK'S TIP *If you don't have time to make stock straight after eating fish or roasted meats, you can freeze the main ingredients – meat bones, fish trimmings or a cooked chicken carcass – until you are ready to make it at a later date.*

1 Preheat the oven to 220°C/425°F/Gas 7. Put the bones in a roasting pan and roast for about 45 minutes, or until well browned.

2 Transfer the roasted bones to a large, heavy pan. Add the onion quarters, leaving the skins on, the bouquet garni and chopped carrots. Add 5ml/1 tsp salt and 5ml/1 tsp black peppercorns. Pour over about 1.7 litres/3 pints/7¹/₂ cups cold water and bring just to the boil.

3 Using a slotted spoon, skim off any scum on the surface of the stock. Reduce the heat and partially cover the pan. Simmer the stock on the lowest heat for about 3 hours, then set aside to cool.

4 Strain the stock into a large bowl and leave to cool completely, then remove any fat from the surface. Store the stock in the refrigerator for up to 3 days or freeze for up to 6 months.

Chicken Stock MAKES ABOUT 1 LITRE/1¾ PINTS/4 CUPS

1 large roast chicken carcass

2 unpeeled onions, quartered

3 bay leaves

2 large carrots, roughly chopped

COOK'S TIP *Stock freezes very well. Once the stock has been strained and the fat removed, reduce the volume by boiling the stock uncovered. This concentrates its flavour and it can then be frozen in an ice-cube tray.*

1 Put the chicken carcass and any loose bones and roasting juices into a heavy pan in which they fit snugly. Add the onion quarters, bay leaves and chopped carrots.

2 Add 2.5ml/¹/₂ tsp salt and 5ml/1 tsp black peppercorns to the pan, and pour over 1.7 litres/3 pints/7¹/₂ cups cold water. Bring to the boil.

3 Reduce the heat, partially cover the pan and cook on the lowest setting for 1¹/₂ hours. Using a large spoon, carefully turn the chicken in the stock and crush the carcass occasionally.

4 Leave the stock to cool slightly, then strain into a large bowl and leave to cool completely. When cool, remove any fat from the surface. Store the stock in the refrigerator for up to 2 days or freeze for up to 6 months.

Fish Stock MAKES ABOUT 600ML/1 PINT/2½ CUPS

500g/1¼lb fish bones and trimmings, without heads and gills

1 bouquet garni

1 onion or 3–4 shallots, peeled and quartered

2 celery sticks, roughly chopped

1 Pack the fish bones and trimmings into a heavy pan and add the bouquet garni, quartered onion or shallots and celery. Add 2.5ml/½ tsp salt and 2.5ml/½ tsp peppercorns to the pan and pour over 1 litre/1¾ pints/4 cups water. Bring to the boil.

2 Reduce the heat, cover the pan and cook on the lowest setting for 30 minutes. Leave to cool, then strain into a bowl. Store in the refrigerator for up to 24 hours or freeze for up to 3 months.

Vegetable Stock MAKES ABOUT 1 LITRE/1¾ PINTS/4 CUPS

3 unpeeled onions, quartered

200g/7oz large open mushrooms

300–400g/11–14oz mixed vegetables, such as broccoli, carrots, celery, tomatoes and/or spring onions (scallions), roughly chopped

45ml/3 tbsp green or brown lentils

1 Place the onions in a heavy pan with the mushrooms, mixed vegetables and green or brown lentils.

2 Add 2.5ml/½ tsp salt, 10ml/2 tsp peppercorns and 1.7 litres/ 3 pints/7½ cups water to the pan. Bring to the boil, then reduce the heat and simmer, partially covered, for 50–60 minutes.

3 Leave the stock to cool slightly, then strain into a bowl and leave to cool. Store in the refrigerator for up to 24 hours or freeze for up to 6 months.

Thickened Gravy MAKES ABOUT 450ML/¾ PINT/2 CUPS

25g/1oz/¼ cup plain (all-purpose) flour

450ml/¾ pint/scant 2 cups stock

45ml/3 tbsp port or sherry

1 Tilt the roasting pan slightly and spoon off almost all the fat, leaving the meat juices behind. Sprinkle the flour into the pan and heat gently for 1 minute, stirring constantly. Gradually add the stock, stirring all the time until thickened.

2 Add the port or sherry, season to taste with salt and freshly ground black pepper and simmer gently for 1–2 minutes.

Onion Gravy MAKES ABOUT 450ML/¾ PINT/2 CUPS

30ml/2 tbsp olive oil

25g/1oz/2 tbsp butter

8 onions, sliced

pinch of caster sugar

15ml/1 tbsp plain (all-purpose) flour

300ml/½ pint/1¼ cups brown meat stock

1 Heat the oil and butter in a pan until foaming, then add the onions. Mix well, so the onions are coated in the butter mixture. Cover the pan and cook gently for 30 minutes, stirring frequently. Add the caster sugar and cook for a further 5 minutes; the onions will soften, caramelize and reduce.

2 Turn off the heat and stir in the flour. Gradually add the stock and return the pan to the heat. Bring the onion gravy to the boil, stirring all the time. Simmer for 2–3 minutes or until thickened, then season with salt and freshly ground black pepper to taste.

Basic Savoury Sauces

A good sauce can provide the finishing touch for a dish and is very easy to make yourself. One of the most basic sauces is the classic savoury white sauce, which can be served as a topping for vegetables or flavoured with additional ingredients such as cheese, herbs, onions or mushrooms. A basic fresh tomato sauce is widely used for pasta dishes, pizza toppings and vegetable dishes and it is worth making when ripe tomatoes are available. Bread sauce is a traditional accompaniment to roast chicken and can be made in advance and reheated. Hollandaise sauce is delicious served with steamed or baked fish.

White Sauce MAKES ABOUT 300ML/½ PINT/1¼ CUPS

300ml/¹/₂ pint/1¹/₄ cups milk

15g/¹/₂/1 tbsp butter

15g/¹/₂ plain (all-purpose) flour

freshly grated nutmeg

1 Warm the milk in a small pan. In a separate pan, melt the butter over a gentle heat, then add the flour and cook, stirring, for 1 minute until the mixture forms a thick paste.

2 Remove the pan from the heat and gradually add the warmed milk, whisking continuously until smooth.

3 Return the pan to a gentle heat and cook, whisking, until the sauce boils, is smooth and thick. Season with salt and freshly ground pepper and plenty of nutmeg.

Fresh Tomato Sauce MAKES ABOUT 1 LITRE/1¾ PINTS/4 CUPS

1.3kg/3lb ripe tomatoes

120ml/4fl oz/¹/₂ cup garlic-infused olive oil

1 large onion, finely chopped

handful of basil leaves, torn, or 30ml/2 tbsp chopped fresh oregano

1 Put the tomatoes in a bowl, pour over boiling water to cover and leave to stand for about 1 minute until the skins split.

2 Drain the tomatoes in a sieve (strainer) and peel using your fingers, then roughly chop the flesh.

3 Heat half the garlic-infused olive oil in a large, heavy pan. Add the chopped onion and cook gently for about 3 minutes, or until softened but not browned.

4 Add the peeled chopped tomatoes and the remaining oil to the pan and cook gently over a low heat, stirring, for 5 minutes or until the tomatoes are soft.

5 Add the herbs, cover the pan and cook the sauce gently for 20–25 minutes, stirring frequently, until the sauce is thick and pulpy. Season to taste with salt and freshly ground black pepper.

VARIATION *Try using different herbs, such as flat leaf parsley, marjoram, thyme, rosemary or coriander (cilantro), in place of the basil or oregano. Alternatively, to make a warm, mildly peppery sauce add a little paprika or, to make a spicy sauce, add a little chilli powder or a finely chopped fresh chilli.*

Bread Sauce MAKES ABOUT 450ML/¾ PINT/2 CUPS

1 onion

6 cloves

1 bay leaf

300ml/¹/₂ pint/1¹/₄ cups milk

150ml/¹/₄ pint/²/₃ cup single (light) cream

115g/4oz/2 cups fresh white breadcrumbs

knob (pat) of butter

1 Stud the onion with the cloves. Put the onion, bay leaf and milk in a pan and bring slowly to the boil. Remove from the heat and leave to stand for at least 30 minutes to allow the flavour of the onion to infuse (steep) into the milk.

2 Pour the milk through a sieve (strainer) into a large bowl and discard the clove-studded onion and the bay leaf.

3 Transfer the milk into a clean pan and add the single cream and breadcrumbs. Bring to the boil over a medium low heat, then reduce the heat and simmer gently for 5 minutes. Stir in the butter just before serving.

Hollandaise Sauce MAKES ABOUT 120ML/4FL OZ/¹/₂ CUP

45ml/3 tbsp white wine or herb-infused vinegar

1 bay leaf

2 egg yolks

115g/4oz/¹/₂ cup butter, chilled

COOK'S TIP
The sauce can be kept warm in a covered bowl set over the pan of hot water for up to 20 minutes. If the sauce is very thick, whisk in a few drops of hot water. If the sauce starts to separate, whisk in an ice cube.

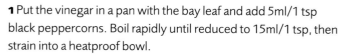

1 Put the vinegar in a pan with the bay leaf and add 5ml/1 tsp black peppercorns. Boil rapidly until reduced to 15ml/1 tsp, then strain into a heatproof bowl.

2 Transfer the vinegar to a clean pan, add the egg yolks and a little salt and whisk lightly until thoroughly combined. Cut the chilled butter into small pieces and add to the pan.

3 Set the pan over a very low heat. Whisk continuously so that as the butter melts it is blended into the egg yolks. When all the butter has melted, continue whisking for about a minute until the sauce is thick and smooth.

4 Season the sauce with salt and ground black pepper to taste, adding a few extra drops of vinegar, if you like, to give a slightly tangy flavour. Serve warm.

Mayonnaise MAKES 150ML/¹/₄ PINT/²/₃ CUP

1 egg yolk, at room temperature

15ml/1 tbsp lemon juice or white wine vinegar

5ml/1 tsp Dijon mustard

150ml/¹/₄ pint/²/₃ cup olive oil

1 Put the egg yolk in a bowl with the lemon juice or vinegar, mustard and a little salt. Whisk together until combined.

2 Gradually add the oil in a thin trickle, whisking continuously until the sauce is thick and smooth. This will take several minutes, so don't lose your nerve after only a minute!

3 Check the seasoning, adding a few drops of lemon juice or vinegar if the mayonnaise is too bland.

4 If the sauce is too thick, stir in a few drops of warm water. Cover the bowl with clear film (plastic wrap) and store in the refrigerator for up to 2 days.

Basic Sweet Sauces

From creamy custard to an elegant fruit coulis, sweet sauces can be used to uplift the simplest desserts to create a truly spectacular dish. They can be served as an accompaniment or make up an intrinsic part of a dish. Simple vanilla ice cream is taken to new levels when served with hot chocolate sauce or a fresh raspberry coulis, while a classic vanilla custard can be used as the base of a sweet soufflé. These sweet sauces rely on just a few basic ingredients and minimal effort, producing irresistible results.

Real Custard MAKES 300ML/½ PINT/1¼ CUPS

300ml/¹/₂ pint/1¹/₄ cups full-fat (whole) milk

3 egg yolks

5ml/1 tsp cornflour (cornstarch)

45ml/3 tbsp caster (superfine) sugar

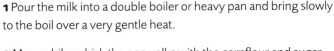

> **COOK'S TIP**
> Adding a little cornflour (cornstarch) to the sauce during cooking helps to prevent it from curdling without affecting the flavour or consistency of the finished custard sauce.

1 Pour the milk into a double boiler or heavy pan and bring slowly to the boil over a very gentle heat.

2 Meanwhile, whisk the egg yolks with the cornflour and sugar until thoroughly mixed. Pour the boiled milk into the yolk mixture, whisking continuously until combined.

3 Pour the mixture back into the cleaned pan and cook over the lowest heat, stirring continuously with a wooden spoon, for 8–10 minutes, or until the mixture coats the back of the spoon.

4 Immediately pour the custard through a sieve (strainer) into a bowl or jug (pitcher) to prevent it from overcooking. Serve warm.

Butterscotch Sauce MAKES ABOUT 475ML/16FL OZ/2 CUPS

200g/7oz/1 cup caster (superfine) sugar

45ml/3 tbsp each cold water and boiling water

75g/3oz/6 tbsp butter

150ml/¹/₄ pint/²/₃ cup double (heavy) cream

> **COOK'S TIP**
> Be very careful when making this sauce, as it involves handling hot sugar, which can give a nasty burn. You should always wear oven gloves.

1 Put the sugar and 45ml/3 tbsp cold water into a pan and heat very gently, without stirring, until all the sugar has dissolved.

2 Bring the mixture to a rolling boil. Boil until the sugar starts to turn golden, then quickly take the pan off the heat and immediately plunge the base into cold water, to prevent the sugar from overbrowning.

3 Standing as far back as possible, and protecting your hand with an oven glove, add the 45ml/3 tbsp boiling water to the caramel mixture, which will splutter and spit.

4 Add the butter and tilt the pan to mix the ingredients together. Leave to cool for 5 minutes.

5 Gradually stir in the cream and mix well until thoroughly combined. Pour into a jug (pitcher) and serve warm or cool.

Rich Chocolate Sauce MAKES ABOUT 250ML/8FL OZ/1 CUP

130g/4¹/₂oz caster (superfine) sugar

175g/6oz plain (semisweet) chocolate, broken into pieces

25g/1oz/2 tbsp unsalted (sweet) butter

30ml/2 tbsp brandy or coffee liqueur (optional)

1 Put the sugar in a small heavy pan with 120ml/4fl oz/¹/₂ cup water and heat gently until the sugar completely dissolves. Bring to the boil and boil for 1 minute.

2 Remove from the heat and stir in the chocolate and butter, stirring until the chocolate has melted and the sauce is smooth.

3 Stir in the brandy or coffee liqueur, if using, and serve warm.

Chocolate Fudge Sauce MAKES ABOUT 250ML/8FL OZ/1 CUP

175ml/6fl oz/³/₄ cup double (heavy) cream

45ml/3 tbsp golden (light corn) syrup

200g/7oz/scant 1 cup light muscovado (brown) sugar

75g/3oz/¹/₂ cup plain (semisweet) chocolate, finely chopped

1 Put the cream, golden syrup, sugar and a pinch of salt in a small pan. Heat gently, stirring, until the sugar has completely dissolved.

2 Add the chopped chocolate and stir until melted. Simmer the sauce for about 20 minutes, stirring occasionally, until thickened.

3 Use the sauce immediately. Alternatively, to keep the sauce warm until you are ready to use it, pour into a heatproof bowl, cover, and place over a pan of simmering water.

Summer Fruit Coulis MAKES ABOUT 250ML/8FL OZ/1 CUP

130g/4¹/₂oz raspberries, washed and hulled

130g/4¹/₂oz strawberries, washed and hulled

10–15ml/2–3 tsp icing (confectioners') sugar, sieved

15ml/1 tbsp orange liqueur or Kirsch (optional)

1 Place the raspberries and strawberries in a food processor and process until smooth. Press the mixture through a fine strainer set over a bowl to remove the tiny seeds.

2 Return the strained fruit purée to the food processor or blender and add 10ml/2 tsp of the icing sugar with the orange liqueur or kirsch, if using, and process briefly until well combined.

3 Check the sweetness of the coulis, then add a little more icing sugar if necessary and process again to mix.

COOK'S TIP
Gently warm this delicious coulis and drizzle over vanilla ice cream for a luxurious dessert. You could also mix some cold coulis into natural (plain) yogurt.

VARIATIONS
• To make raspberry and vanilla sauce: scrape the seeds from a vanilla pod (bean) and add to the food processor with 200g/7oz/1 cup raspberries and 30ml/2tbsp icing (confectioners') sugar. Process to a purée, adding water to thin, if necessary.

• Substitute any soft summer berries, such as redcurrants, white currants or black currants for the raspberries or strawberries. Adjust the amount of sugar to taste.

Basic Pastries

There is a certain satisfaction to be gained from creating pies, tarts and desserts using pastry that you have made yourself, and most types are very easy to make at home. The exceptions to this general rule are puff and filo pastry, which, unless you are an expert with plenty of time to spare, are often better bought from a store. So try making short pastry to top sweet and savoury pies; shortcrust pastry for special desserts; French flan pastry for making flans and tarts, or choux pastry for making éclairs or profiteroles.

Shortcrust Pastry FOR A 23CM/9IN PASTRY CASE

225g/8oz/2 cups plain (all-purpose) flour

1.5ml/$^1/_4$ tsp salt

115g/4oz/8 tbsp white vegetable fat (shortening)

45ml/3 tbsp iced water

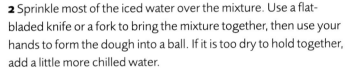

VARIATIONS
- For nut pastry, add 30g/1oz/$^3/_4$ cup chopped walnuts or pecan nuts to the flour mixture.
- For orange pastry, add the finely grated zest of 1 orange.

1 Sift the flour and salt into a large bowl. Add the fat and rub it into the flour with your fingertips until the mixture resembles fine breadcrumbs and all the fat has been incorporated.

2 Sprinkle most of the iced water over the mixture. Use a flat-bladed knife or a fork to bring the mixture together, then use your hands to form the dough into a ball. If it is too dry to hold together, add a little more chilled water.

3 Wrap the pastry in clear film (plastic wrap) and chill in the refrigerator for 30 minutes.

4 Lightly knead the pastry on a floured surface, then roll to the desired shape and thickness using a floured rolling pin.

Rich Sweet Shortcrust Pastry FOR A 23CM/9IN PASTRY CASE

225g/8oz/2 cups plain (all-purpose) flour

15ml/1 tbsp caster (superfine) sugar

175g/6oz/$^3/_4$ cup butter

1 egg yolk

30–45ml/2–3 tbsp iced water

COOK'S TIP
Use cold butter and ice cold water when making pastry. This prevents the fat from softening too much while it is being rubbed in, which would result in an oily pastry.

1 Sift the flour into a large bowl and add the caster sugar. Add the butter and rub it into the dry ingredients with your fingertips until the mixture resembles fine breadcrumbs and all the butter has been incorporated.

2 Add the egg yolk and sprinkle most of the iced water over the mixture. Use a flat-bladed knife or a fork to bring the mixture together, then use your hands to form the dough into a ball. If it is too dry to hold together, add a little more chilled water.

3 Wrap the pastry in clear film (plastic wrap) and chill in the refrigerator for 30 minutes.

4 Lightly knead the pastry on a floured surface, then roll to the desired shape and thickness using a floured rolling pin.

French Flan Pastry FOR A 23CM/9IN PASTRY CASE

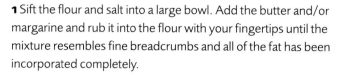

200g/7oz/1³/₄ cups plain (all-purpose) flour

2.5ml/¹/₂ tsp salt

115g/4oz/¹/₂ cup butter or margarine, or half and half of each, chilled

1 egg yolk

1.5ml/¹/₄ tsp lemon juice

30–45ml/2–3 tbsp iced water

COOK'S TIP

It is important to let pastry rest for half an hour before rolling it out, or it may shrink during cooking. Also allow it to rest in the refrigerator once it has been rolled out.

1 Sift the flour and salt into a large bowl. Add the butter and/or margarine and rub it into the flour with your fingertips until the mixture resembles fine breadcrumbs and all of the fat has been incorporated completely.

2 In a small bowl, mix the egg yolk, lemon juice and 30ml/2 tbsp iced water. Add to the flour mixture. Use a fork or flat-bladed knife to mix and moisten.

3 Press the dough into a rough ball. If the mixture is too dry to come together, add 15ml/1 tbsp more water. Turn on to a floured surface.

4 With the heel of your hand, push portions of dough away from you, smearing them on the surface. Continue in this way until the dough feels pliable and can easily be peeled off the surface.

5 Form the dough into a ball, wrap in clear film (plastic wrap) and chill for 30 minutes. Roll out on a floured surface to the desired thickness and shape.

Choux Pastry MAKES EIGHTEEN PROFITEROLES OR TWELVE ÉCLAIRS

115g/4oz/¹/₂ cup butter, cut into small pieces

10ml/2 tsp caster (superfine) sugar (optional)

1.5ml/¹/₄ tsp salt

250ml/8fl oz/1 cup of water

150g/5oz/1¹/₄ cups plain (all-purpose) flour

4 eggs, beaten to mix

1 egg, beaten with 5ml/1 tsp cold water, for glaze

COOK'S TIPS

• To make profiteroles: use two small spoons or a piping bag fitted with a 1cm/¹/₂in nozzle and shape 2.5cm/1in blobs.

• For eclairs: use a piping bag fitted with a 2cm/³/₄in nozzle. Pipe strips 10–13cm/4–5in long on to a baking sheet lined with baking parchment.

1 Preheat the oven to 220°C/425°F/Gas 7. Combine the butter, sugar, if using, salt and water in a large heavy pan. Bring to the boil over moderately high heat, stirring occasionally.

2 As soon as the mixture is boiling, remove the pan from the heat. Add the flour all at once and beat vigorously with a wooden spoon to mix the flour smoothly into the liquid.

3 Return the pan to moderate heat and cook, stirring, until the mixture will form a ball, pulling away from the sides of the pan. This will take about 1 minute. Remove from the heat again and allow to cool for 3–5 minutes.

4 Add a little of the beaten eggs and mix well to incorporate. Add a little more egg and beat in well. Continue beating in the eggs until the mixture becomes a smooth and shiny paste.

5 While still warm, shape choux puffs, éclairs, profiteroles or rings on a baking sheet lined with baking parchment.

6 Glaze with 1 egg beaten with 1 teaspoon of cold water. Put into the preheated oven, then reduce the heat to 200°C/400°F/Gas 6. Bake until puffed and golden brown and fill as desired.

Basic Breads

Nothing beats the enticing aroma of freshly baked home-made bread, which will fill the house with its delectable scent and make your mouth water. By baking your own bread, you will not only be saving money, but you will be able to control exactly how much salt goes into each loaf, and create breads that are exactly to your taste. Try some of the many variations offered below, or experiment with your own ideas by adding combinations of herbs, cheeses, olives, sun-dried tomatoes, grains, nuts and seeds.

Basic Yeast Bread MAKES FOUR LOAVES

25g/1oz fresh yeast

10ml/2 tsp caster (superfine) sugar

900ml/1^1/$_2$ pints/3^3/$_4$ cups tepid water, or milk and water mixed

15ml/1 tbsp salt

1.3kg/3lb/12 cups strong white bread flour, preferably unbleached

50g/2oz/scant ^{1}/$_4$ cup white vegetable fat (shortening) or 50ml/2fl oz/^{1}/$_4$ cup vegetable oil

VARIATIONS

• You can form the dough into loaf shapes or about 36 rolls and bake on greased baking trays. Baking time for rolls will be 15–20 minutes.

• For granary bread, replace the white flour with granary flour, or half and half granary and strong white bread flour.

• For rosemary bread, finely chop 30ml/2 tbsp of fresh rosemary and mix it with 15ml/1 tbsp olive oil. Work through one-third of the dough after it has risen once, then shape and bake 1 loaf as above.

• For walnut bread, follow the recipe for rosemary bread, but substitute the rosemary with 115g/4oz/1 cup finely chopped walnuts.

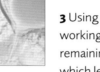

1 Cream the yeast and caster sugar together in a measuring jug (cup), add about 150ml/^{1}/$_4$ pint/^{2}/$_3$ cup of the measured liquid and leave in a warm place for about 10 minutes to froth up.

2 Meanwhile, mix the salt into the flour and rub in the fat (if using oil, add it to the remaining liquid).

3 Using an electric mixer with a dough hook attachment or working by hand with a mixing bowl, add the yeast mixture and remaining liquid to the flour, and work it in to make a firm dough which leaves the bowl clean.

4 Knead well on a floured surface, or in the mixer, until the dough has become firm and elastic.

5 Return to the bowl, cover lightly with a dish towel and leave in a warm place to rise for an hour, or until it has doubled in size. The dough will be springy and full of air. Meanwhile oil four 450g/1lb loaf tins (pans).

6 Turn the dough out on to a floured work surface and knock back (punch down), flattening it out with your knuckles to knock the air out. Knead lightly into shape again, divide into four pieces and form into loaf shapes.

7 Place the dough in the loaf tins, pushing down well to fit into the corners, then leave to rise again for another 20–30 minutes. Meanwhile, preheat the oven to 230°C/450°F/Gas 8.

8 When the dough has risen just above the rims of the tins, bake the loaves in the centre of the oven for 30 minutes, or until browned and shrinking a little from the sides of the tins; when turned out and rapped underneath they should sound hollow. Cool on wire racks then slice and serve.

Focaccia MAKES ONE ROUND 25CM/10IN LOAF

25g/1oz fresh yeast

400g/14oz/3¹/₂ cups unbleached strong white bread flour

10ml/2 tsp sea salt

75ml/5 tbsp olive oil

10ml/2 tsp salt

VARIATIONS

Focaccia is often baked with one or more of a selection of different toppings. Before baking, lightly sprinkle over any or a combination of the following: chopped pitted olives; finely chopped red onion; slices of red, green or yellow (bell) pepper; sprigs of fresh rosemary or diced sun-dried tomatoes.

1 Dissolve the yeast in 120ml/4fl oz/¹/₂ cup warm water. Allow to stand for 10 minutes. Sift the white bread flour into a large bowl, make a well in the centre, and add the yeast, salt and 30ml/2 tbsp oil. Mix in the flour and add more water to make a dough.

2 Turn out on to a floured work surface and knead the dough until smooth and elastic. Return to the bowl, cover with a cloth, and leave to rise in a warm place for 2–2¹/₄ hours until doubled in bulk.

3 Knock back the dough and knead again for a few minutes. Press into an oiled 25cm/10in flan tin (pan), and cover with a damp cloth. Leave the dough to rise again for 30 minutes.

4 Preheat the oven to 200°C/400°F/Gas 6. Poke the dough all over with your fingers, to make little dimples in the surface. Pour the remaining oil over the dough, using a pastry brush to take it to the edges. Sprinkle with the salt.

5 Bake for 20–25 minutes, until the bread is a pale gold. Carefully remove from the tin and leave to cool on a rack. The bread is best eaten on the same day, but it also freezes very well.

Pitta Bread MAKES TWELVE PITTAS

25g/1oz fresh yeast

370ml/12 fl oz/1¹/₂ cups warm water

500g/1¹/₄lb/5 cups unbleached strong white bread flour, or half white and half wholemeal (whole-wheat) flour

15ml/1 tbsp salt

15ml/1 tbsp olive oil

VARIATION

To cook the breads in the oven, preheat the oven to 220°C/ 425°F/Gas 7. Fill an unglazed dish with hot water and place in the bottom of the oven. Heat a non-stick baking sheet. Place two or three pieces of flattened dough on to the baking sheet and place in the hottest part of the oven. Bake for 2–3 minutes in the preheated oven.

1 Dissolve the yeast in 120ml/4fl oz/¹/₂ cup warm water. Allow to stand for 10 minutes. Put the flour and salt in a bowl and stir in the yeast mixture. Mix together the oil and remaining water, and stir enough liquid into the flour mixture to make a stiff dough. Place in a bowl, cover with a clean dish towel and leave in a warm place for at least 30 minutes, and up to 2 hours.

2 Knead the dough for 10 minutes, or until smooth. Lightly oil the bowl, place the dough in it, cover again and leave to rise in a warm place for about 1 hour, or until doubled in size.

3 Divide the dough into 12 equal-size pieces. With lightly floured hands, flatten each piece, then roll out into a round measuring about 20cm/8in and about 5mm–1cm/¹/₄–¹/₂in thick.

4 Heat a large, heavy frying pan over a medium-high heat. When hot, lay one piece of dough in the pan and cook for 15–20 seconds. Turn it over and cook the second side for about 1 minute. When large bubbles start to form, turn it over again. It should puff up.

5 Using a clean dish towel, gently press on the bread where the bubbles have formed. Cook for a total of 3 minutes, then remove from the pan and repeat with the remaining dough. Wrap in a dish towel, stacking them as each one is cooked, and serve hot.

Pickles, Chutneys and Relishes

Making pickles, chutneys and relishes is a fantastic way to preserve seasonal vegetables and fruits for use later on in the year, and home-made versions have an infinitely superior taste to store-bought varieties. Pickled onions, turnips and beetroot make a great addition to any meal of left-over cold meats, while gluts of tomatoes or over-ripe mangoes can be transformed into flavoursome chutneys to accompany bread and cheese, curries or grilled meats. Plums and cherries can be used to make a sweet-and-sour relish that complements rich poultry or game.

Pickled Onions MAKES 4 x 450G/1LB JARS

1kg/2¹/₄lb pickling onions

115g/4oz/¹/₂ cup salt

750ml/1¹/₄ pints/3 cups malt vinegar

15ml/1 tbsp sugar

2–3 dried red chillies

5ml/1 tsp brown mustard seeds

15ml/1 tbsp coriander seeds

5ml/1 tsp allspice berries

5ml/1 tsp black peppercorns

5cm/2in piece fresh root ginger, sliced

2–3 blades mace

2–3 fresh bay leaves

1 Trim off the root ends from the onion, then cut a thin slice off the top (neck) end. Place in a bowl and cover with boiling water. Leave to stand for 4 minutes, then drain and peel off the skin.

2 Place in a bowl and cover with cold water, then drain the water into a large pan. Add the salt and heat slightly to dissolve it, then cool before pouring over the onions. Use a plate to keep the onions submerged in the brine. Leave to stand for 24 hours.

3 Meanwhile, place the vinegar in a large pan. Wrap all the remaining ingredients, except the bay leaves, in a piece of muslin (cheesecloth). Bring to the boil, simmer for 5 minutes, then remove from the heat. Set aside and leave to infuse overnight.

4 The next day, drain the onions, rinse and pat dry. Pack into sterilized 450g/1lb jars. Add the spices, except the ginger. Pour the vinegar over to cover and add the bay leaves.

5 Seal the jars with non-metallic lids and store in a cool, dark place for at least 6 weeks before eating.

Pickled Turnips and Beetroot MAKES ABOUT 1.6KG/3¹/₂LB

1kg/2¹/₄lb young turnips

3–4 raw beetroot (beets)

about 45ml/3 tbsp coarse sea salt

about 1.5 litres/2¹/₂ pints/ 6¹/₄ cups water

juice of 1 lemon

1 Wash the turnips and beetroot, but do not peel them, then cut into slices about 5mm/¹/₄in thick.

2 Put the salt and water in a bowl, stir and leave to stand until the salt has completely dissolved.

3 Sprinkle the beetroot with lemon juice and place in the bottom of four 1.2 litre/2 pint sterilized jars. Top with sliced turnip, packing them in very tightly, then pour over the brine, making sure that the vegetables are covered. Seal the jars and leave in a cool place for 7 days before serving.

Tomato Chutney MAKES ABOUT 1.8KG/4LB

900g/2lb tomatoes, skinned

225g/8oz/1¹/₂ cups raisins

225g/8oz onions, chopped

**225g/8oz/generous 1 cup caster
(superfine) sugar**

**600ml/1 pint/2¹/₂ cups
malt vinegar**

1 Chop the tomatoes roughly and place in a preserving pan. Add the raisins, onions and caster sugar.

2 Pour the vinegar into the pan and bring the mixture to the boil. Simmer for 2 hours, uncovered, until soft and thickened.

3 Transfer the chutney to warmed sterilized jars. Top with waxed discs and lids. Store in a cool, dark place and leave to mature for 1 month. The chutney will keep unopened for up to 1 year. Once the jars have been opened, store them in the refrigerator.

Mango Chutney MAKES ABOUT 1KG/2¹/₄LB

**900g/2lb mangoes, halved, peeled
and stoned (pitted)**

2.5ml/¹/₂ tsp salt

225g/8oz cooking apples, peeled

**300ml/¹/₂ pint/1¹/₄ cups distilled
malt vinegar**

**200g/7oz/scant 1 cup demerara
(raw) sugar**

1 onion, chopped

1 garlic clove, crushed

10ml/2 tsp ground ginger

1 Using a sharp knife, slice the mango flesh into chunks and place in a large, non-metallic bowl. Sprinkle with salt and set aside. Quarter, core and peel the apples, then chop the flesh roughly.

2 Put the vinegar and sugar in a preserving pan and heat gently, stirring occasionally, until the sugar has dissolved completely. Add the mangoes, apple, onion, garlic and ginger to the pan and slowly bring the mixture to the boil, stirring occasionally.

3 Reduce the heat and simmer gently for about 1 hour, stirring frequently towards the end of the cooking time, until the chutney is reduced to a thick consistency and no excess liquid remains.

4 Spoon into sterilized jars, cover and seal. Store in a cool, dark place and allow to mature for at least 2 weeks before eating.

Plum and Cherry Relish MAKES ABOUT 350G/12OZ

350g/12oz dark-skinned red plums

350g/12oz/2 cups cherries

2 shallots, finely chopped

15ml/1 tbsp olive oil

30ml/2 tbsp dry sherry

60ml/4 tbsp red wine vinegar

15ml/1 tbsp balsamic vinegar

1 bay leaf

**90g/3¹/₂oz/scant ¹/₂ cup demerara
(raw) sugar**

1 Halve and stone (pit) the plums, then roughly chop the flesh. Stone all the cherries.

2 Cook the shallots gently in the oil for 5 minutes, or until soft. Add the fruit, sherry, vinegars, bay leaf and sugar.

3 Slowly bring the mixture to the boil, stirring until the sugar has dissolved completely. Increase the heat and cook briskly for about 15 minutes, or until the relish is very thick and the fruit is soft and tender.

4 Remove the bay leaf and spoon the relish into warmed sterilized jars. Cover and seal. Store the relish in the refrigerator and use within 3 months.

Jams and Sweet Preserves

With just a few basic ingredients, a surplus of seasonal fruits can be transformed into delectable home-made jams, jellies, marmalades and curds. These can be spread on toast or served with scones and cream for tea; used to sandwich sponge cakes together; drizzled over ice cream; or used to make tarts and desserts. Here are a few simple recipes to give you some ideas and show you how easy it is to make delicious sweet preserves. A preserving pan and sugar thermometer are useful pieces of equipment, but are not essential.

Raspberry Jam MAKES ABOUT 3.1KG/7LB

1.8kg/4lb/10²/₃ cups firm, ripe raspberries

juice of 1 large lemon

1.8kg/4lb/9 cups sugar, warmed

COOK'S TIP
To test, put a spoonful of jam on to a cold saucer. Allow to cool slightly, and then push the surface of the jam with your finger. Setting point has been reached if a skin has formed.

1 Put 175g/6oz/1 cup of the raspberries into the preserving pan and crush them. Add the rest of the fruit and the lemon juice, and simmer until soft and pulpy.

2 Add the sugar and stir until dissolved, then bring back to the boil and boil hard until setting point is reached, testing after 3–4 minutes (*see* Cook's Tip).

3 Pour into warmed, sterilized jars. When cold, cover, seal and store in a cool, dark place until required. The jam will store well for up to 6 months.

Blackcurrant Jam MAKES ABOUT 1.3KG/3LB

1.3kg/3lb/12 cups blackcurrants

grated rind and juice of 1 orange

475ml/16fl oz/2 cups water

1.3kg/3lb/6¹/₂ cups sugar, warmed

30ml/2 tbsp cassis (optional)

COOK'S TIP
This jam has a rich, fruity flavour and a wonderfully strong dark colour. It is punchy and not as sweet as some other jams. It tastes wonderful with home-baked scones for tea or spread on croissants for a continental-style breakfast.

1 Place the blackcurrants, orange rind and juice and water in a large heavy pan. Bring to the boil, reduce the heat and simmer for 30 minutes.

2 Add the warmed sugar to the pan and stir over a low heat until the sugar has dissolved.

3 Bring the mixture to the boil and cook for about 8 minutes, or until the jam reaches setting point (105°C/220°F).

4 Remove the pan from the heat and skim off any scum from the surface, using a slotted spoon. Leave to cool for 5 minutes, then stir in the cassis, if using.

5 Pour the jam into warmed sterilized jars and seal. Leave the jars to cool completely, then label and store in a cool, dark place for up to 6 months.

Cranberry Jelly MAKES ABOUT 900G/2LB

900g/2lb/8 cups cranberries

450g/1lb sweet eating apples, washed and chopped with skins and cores intact

grated rind and juice of 1 orange

600ml/1 pint/2^1/$_2$ cups water

about 900g/2lb/4^1/$_2$ cups preserving or granulated sugar, warmed

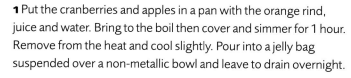

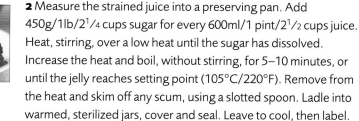

1 Put the cranberries and apples in a pan with the orange rind, juice and water. Bring to the boil then cover and simmer for 1 hour. Remove from the heat and cool slightly. Pour into a jelly bag suspended over a non-metallic bowl and leave to drain overnight.

2 Measure the strained juice into a preserving pan. Add 450g/1lb/2^1/$_4$ cups sugar for every 600ml/1 pint/2^1/$_2$ cups juice. Heat, stirring, over a low heat until the sugar has dissolved. Increase the heat and boil, without stirring, for 5–10 minutes, or until the jelly reaches setting point (105°C/220°F). Remove from the heat and skim off any scum, using a slotted spoon. Ladle into warmed, sterilized jars, cover and seal. Leave to cool, then label.

Oxford Marmalade MAKES ABOUT 2.25KG/5LB

900g/2lb Seville (Temple) oranges, skins scrubbed, then peeled with a vegetable peeler and cut into thick slices

1.75 litres/3 pints/7^1/$_2$ cups water

1.3kg/3lb/6^1/$_2$ cups sugar, warmed

COOK'S TIP

Traditionalists say that only bitter oranges such as Seville should be used to make marmalade. Although this isn't always true of all marmalades, it is most certainly the case when making traditional Oxford marmalade.

1 Put the orange rind in a large pan. Chop the fruit, reserving the pips (seeds), and add to the pan with the water. Tie the pips in a piece of muslin (cheesecloth) and add to the pan. Bring to the boil, then cover and simmer for 2 hours. Add more water during cooking to maintain the same volume. Remove the pan from the heat and leave overnight.

2 The next day, remove the muslin bag from the oranges, squeezing well, and return the pan to the heat. Bring to the boil, then cover and simmer for 1 hour. Add the warmed sugar to the pan, then slowly bring the mixture to the boil, stirring until the sugar has dissolved completely. Increase the heat and boil rapidly for about 15 minutes, or until setting point is reached.

3 Remove from the heat and skim off any scum from the surface. Leave to cool for 5 minutes, stir, then pour into warmed sterilized jars and seal. When cold, label, then store in a cool, dark place.

Lemon Curd MAKES ABOUT 450G/1LB

juice and zest of 3 lemons

200g/7oz/1 cup sugar

115g/4oz/8 tbsp unsalted (sweet) butter, diced

2 large (US extra large) eggs

2 large (US extra large) egg yolks

1 Place the lemon zest and juice in a large heatproof bowl. Set over a pan of gently simmering water and add the sugar and butter. Stir until the sugar has dissolved and the butter melted.

2 Beat the eggs and yolks in a bowl, then add to the lemon mixture, and whisk until combined. Stir constantly over the heat until the lemon curd thickens and coats the back of a spoon.

3 Remove from the heat and pour into sterilized jars. Cover, seal and label. Store in the refrigerator for up to 3 months.

Index

Acknowledgements

The Publishers would like to thank the large team of contributors to the book:

Recipe Writers: Pepita Aris, Catherine Atkinson, Josephine Bacon, Alex Barker, Ghillie Basan, Michelle Berriedale-Johnson, Angela Boggiano, Janet Brinkworth, Georgina Campbell, Carla Capalbo, Lesley Chamberlain, Kit Chan, Jacqueline Clark, Maxine Clark, Frances Cleary, Carole Clements, Andi Clevely, Jan Cutler, Trish Davies, Roz Denny, Patrizia Diemling, Stephanie Donaldson, Matthew Drennan, Sarah Edmonds, Joanna Farrow, Rafi Fernandez, Jenni Fleetwood, Christine France, Silvano Franco, Yasuko Fukuoka, Sarah Gates, Shirley Gill, Brian Glover, Nicola Graimes, Rosamund Grant, Carole Handslip, Juliet Harbutt, Rebekah Hassan, Deh-Ta Hsiung, Shehzad Husain, Jessica Houdret, Christine Ingram, Judy Jackson, Becky Johnson, Bridget Jones, Manisha Kanini, Sheila Kimberley, Soheila Kimberley, Lucy Knox, Masaki Ko, Elizabeth Lambert Ortez, Ruby Le Bois, Clare Lewis, Sara Lewis, Patricia Lousada, Gilly Love, Lesley Mackley, Norma MacMillan, Sue Maggs, Kathy Man, Sally Mansfield, Maggie Mayhew, Norma Miller, Jane Milton, Sallie Morris, Janice Murfitt, Annie Nichols, Maggie Pannell, Katherine Richmond, Rena Salaman, Jennie Shapter, Anne Sheasby, Ysanne Spevack, Marlena Spieler, Jenny Stacey, Liz Trigg, Christopher Trotter, Hilaire Walden, Laura Washburn, Steven Wheeler, Jenny White, Biddy White-Lennon, Kate Whitman, Carolo Wilson, Elizabeth Wolf-Cohen, Jeni Wright

Home Economists: Eliza Baird, Alex Barker, Julie Beresford, Sascha Brodie, Jacqueline Clark, Fergal Connolly, Joanne Craig, Stephanie England, Joanna Farrow, Annabel Ford, Christine France, Tonia George, Carole Handslip, Kate Jay, Jill Jones, Clare Lewis, Sara Lewis, Lucy McKelvie, Emma MacIntosh, Emma Patmore, Bridget Sargeson, Jennie Shapter, Joy Skipper, Carole Tennant, Linda Tubby, Sunil Vijayakar, Jenny White

Photographers: Karl Adamson, Edward Allwright, Peter Anderson, David Armstrong, Tim Auty, Steve Baxter, Martin Brigdale, Nicki Dowey, James Duncan, Gus Filgate, John Freeman, Iain Garlick, Michelle Garrett, Will Heap, Peter Henley, John Heseltine, Amanda Heywood, Ferguson Hill, Janine Hosegood, David Jordan, Andrea Jones, Maris Kelly, Dave King, Don Last, William Lingwood, Patrick McLeary, Michael Michaels, Steve Moss, Thomas Odulate, Debby Patterson, Juliet Piddington, Peter Reilly, Craig Robertson, Simon Smith, Sam Stowell, Polly Wreford

Stylists: Alison Austin, Shannon Beare, Madeleine Brehaut, Frances Cleary, Tessa Evelegh, Marilyn Forbes, Annabel Ford, Nicola Fowler, Michelle Garrett, Carole Handslip, Jo Harris, Cara Hobday, Kate Jay, Maria Kelly, Lucy McKelvie, Marion McLornan, Sarah O'Brien, Marion Price, Jane Stevenson, Helen Trent, Sophie Wheeler, Judy Williams